D1577097

A SHADOWED MAN :

Henry Williamson
1895–1977

by

Lois Lamplugh

Second Edition

THE EXMOOR PRESS

© Lois Lamplugh
First published by Wellspring 1990
Second, revised edition 1991

THE EXMOOR PRESS
Dulverton, Somerset

British Library Cataloguing in Publication Data
Lamplugh, Lois
A Shadowed Man: Henry Williamson, 1895-1977. 2nd ed.
1. English prose. Williamson, Henry, 1895-1977
I. Title
828.91209

ISBN 0 900131 70 5

Printed in Great Britain by G. P. Printers, South Molton, Devon

Contents

Acknowledgements

I would like to offer grateful thanks to the following:

the Trustees of the Henry Williamson Literary Estate for permission to quote from letters written by Henry Williamson to my parents and myself, and to reproduce photographs that appear between pages 42–43 and 130–131;

to Richard Williamson for writing the foreword to this book;

to Stephen Clarke, Clearwater Books, Wimborne, for providing a checklist of Henry Williamson's major works;

to Peter Rothwell for his illustrations;

to Oswald Jones for giving me permission to reproduce photographs that appear between pages 130–131 and 154–155;

to Knights Photographers of Barnstaple for giving me permission to reproduce the photographs of Georgeham in the Twenties;

to all those members of the Henry Williamson Society whose interest and encouragement have sustained me in the publication of the first edition of this book, and especially to Ted Wood for his help in obtaining photographs for this edition.

Foreword

One of the strengths of my father's writing lies in his ability to capture the resonant atmosphere of place and time. In particular, that of north Devon.

In Lois Lamplugh's *A Shadowed Man* another facet of place and time in north Devon is revealed. For the strength of this book is that Lois was there, in the village of Georgeham, in the 1920s and 1930s when my father was actually writing his most famous book *Tarka the Otter,* the *Village* books, and those compelling novels that form *The Flax of Dream,* particularly *The Pathway*. Lois Lamplugh's parents, fortunately for Henry, were willing listeners to his daily writings. He needed to be heard as well as to be read: this seemed to clear his mind for the next day's work.

It took fifty books for Henry to set out his idiosyncratic vision, and I'm sure that many books will be needed to be written about him before we can begin to see this complicated man clearly.

For people who are moved by the lyrical writing of *Tarka* and feel empathy with the man are bewildered by his political leanings. Some find his farming experiences the most satisfying to read. Some only have interest in the reconstruction of suburban London life. Some see him as the first of the Greens; others only want to immerse themselves in those brilliant trench warfare scenes. There are devotees of the magical village life scenes, as there are for those pictures of the sophisticated upper class 'Evelyn Waugh' set. All these are but parts of the total man, for whichever way you turn in the first half of this century, Henry was there with the controversial view, the accurate description, the absorbing detail, the compelling story.

So we are fortunate to have Lois Lamplugh to guide us through a part of the intricate web of reality in this sympathetic but objective work which sets us very surely upon our exploratory journey.

Richard Williamson

Dedication

To
My Husband

CHAPTER ONE

First Years in Georgeham: Skirr Cottage

Henry Williamson, author of *Tarka the Otter*. Identified so often in this way, he may seem to the casual reader a man of one book. In fact, by the time Tarka appeared in 1927, he had already published three novels and three collections of animal stories, and in the next fifty years he was to write more than forty other books, many of which sold well and are still in print.

It is undeniable that his reputation was first made by *Tarka,* when it was awarded the Hawthornden Prize for Literature in 1928 and received much critical acclaim from such writers as Thomas Hardy and John Galsworthy. It has been translated into many languages, and continues to sell steadily. The film based on the book, made in the year of Henry Williamson's death, is widely known, and has been transmitted on television more than once.

Yet as he grew older, and wrote more and more, the author became exasperated by the emphasis on *Tarka,* and at times would be almost dismissive of that remarkable achievement of his young manhood. In a writing life of fifty years, his output was large and varied, and included more than a score of novels of the human world, including the four volumes making up *The Flax of Dream,* written in the Twenties, and the fifteen-volume sequence, *A Chronicle of Ancient Sunlight* written, or at least brought to a conclusion and published, in the Fifties and Sixties.

Who then was this man, author of *Tarka the Otter* and a great deal more? He was born and grew up in a south London suburb, and in boyhood escaped from it whenever he could into the countryside of Kent, where he began the observations of wildlife that were to develop into a deep and instinctive empathy, far removed from the arid disciplines of the academic naturalist. He was educated at a good grammar school, leaving in 1913, at the age of 18, with a hearty dislike of the whole process of being educated. After a year as a clerk in a City office, he spent the next five years as a soldier, seeing service in France for considerable periods, and being wounded. Like thousands of others, he emerged from the war physically sound – his wounds were not serious – but filled with a mental distress that would never be wholly assuaged.

After leaving the army he lived at home in Lewisham and worked on the fringe of the newspaper world. The impulse to write had already taken hold of him; he gradually became convinced that writing could and should earn him a living. Not, however, at home, where he was perpetually at odds with his father and out of sympathy with his younger sisters and his formerly adored mother. Not, above all, in a London suburb in which he had never felt at home. Even the fields and woods of Kent no longer satisfied him. As a youth of eighteen, in the last months of peace, he had discovered a region where he felt he truly belonged: it could be said, quite literally, to have enchanted him. He had visited it twice since then. By 1921 he was drawn back to this one place where he felt confident that he could work and develop as a writer. Here, in a sense, his life – the life of the creative imagination – began, and his gifts were set free.

* * * * * * * * * * * *

In March, 1921, three months after he had celebrated his twenty-fifth birthday, Henry Williamson left his parents' house, 11, Eastern Road, London, SE4, and rode to north Devon on his Norton motorcycle. Already the first of his novels to be published, *The Beautiful Years,* had been accepted by Collins; it was due to come out in the autumn. From now on, he believed – rightly – that he would be able to make his living by writing.

The village in which he was to settle for the next eight years was Georgeham. This was the place that had put its spell on him when he had spent a holiday there in May, 1914, during the year he spent as a clerk in a City branch of the Sun Insurance office – a year he pretended for much of his life had not existed, substituting a fantasy of having gone straight from school to the trenches as a boy of seventeen. His two weeks spent in solitary but not lonely exploration of new landscapes, to which he responded with rapture, may be seen as determining his life-long attachment to this part of Devon, and confirming his bent to make natural history a means of supporting himself through a combination of life out of doors and writing.

In August, 1916, he returned to Georgeham on sick leave after the first battle of the Somme, his life preserved by the chance of receiving comparatively light wounds. Then he had been able to wander about on the deserted shore at Putsborough, at the southern end of Woolacombe Bay, naked, seeing only 'gulls, hawks, jackdaws and, very occasionally, a tiny dark figure moving, almost impercep-tibly, on the skyline of the headland'. This headland, majestic but inelegantly named, was Baggy Point; at that time the only buildings in that part of the bay were an abandoned limekiln and two limeburners' cottages, known as Vention, reputedly because when first introduced, limeburning was regarded as 'the new invention'. They gave their name to that part of the beach, Vention Sands.

In 1919, after being demobilised, Henry had made for Georgeham again, and rented a cottage alongside the stream that ran beside the churchyard wall. There were white owls, or barn owls, in the roof space under its thatch, and the sound they made as they floated back to their roost was 'Skirr-rr-rr', Henry said, and thus his dwelling became Skirr Cottage. He wrote the name on its white door in letters several inches high, and painted beneath it, in yellow, a version of the owl symbol that was to appear on his books.

There is a Skirr Farm in *The Beautiful Years,* and in using the name, Henry was perhaps echoing the title of a book he would almost certainly have read in his youth, R. D. Blackmore's *The Maid of Sker*.

One of his early loves, the young married woman he called Evelyn – or Eveline – Fairfax in *The Dream of Fair Women,* shared the cottage for a while that summer. To avoid scandalising the villagers, he invented for himself a wife who had recently died, and pretended that 'Evelyn' was his sister-in-law – though why it should have been regarded as acceptable that he was living with his sister-in-law is not clear. To one sympathetic listener – the wife of Georgeham's rector – he described his fictitious wife's death so vividly that his voice weakened and his eyes brimmed with tears, as they so easily did: an interesting example of the way his imagination, having projected a fantasy, could instantly transform it, for him, into a substantial reality: it was the mainspring of his talent as a writer.

The affair with 'Evelyn' came to its end; he sublet Skirr Cottage and went back to London, to live at home and exasperate his father by drinking heavily and often staying out until the early hours of the morning. On other nights he would shut himself in his room and write for hours, by candlelight, enjoying 'the soft scratch of my pen moving rapidly, jerkily, over paper; a further five thousand words by midnight, and then out under the stars and their mystic truth'.

By day he worked in Fleet Street. An uncongenial job selling advertising space did not last for very long. Another did at least involve him in writing of a sort: in the summer of 1920 the editor of the 'Weekly Dispatch', Bernard Falk, offered him the chance to write a column about what were called light cars. Henry gave tips on saving oil and petrol, discussed new designs in light cars, motor cycles and vehicles known as cycle cars, and reviewed the motor show at Olympia. This may sound another unsuitable job for a man who was soon to become known, above all, as a nature writer – yet one side of Henry was fascinated by machines and speed; he had been an enthusiastic car driver and motor cyclist when on leave or home service during the war.

He wrote a few articles on other subjects, and also offered Bernard Falk nature notes, most of which the editor declined, evidently with genuine regret, saying that such submissions had to be pushed aside to make way for everyday news items. Ten years later Henry entitled his contribution to *The Book of Fleet Street* 'Confessions of a Fake Merchant'. The title is significant. In part it reflected his poor opinion of journalists; in a letter written in 1941 he assured me that no good writer stays in journalism: 'The good ones go up in money: the poor ones remain low-paid reporters (apart from which no decent artist could remain on a newspaper, with its killing, materialistic idiom)'. Yet there is perhaps an additional shade of meaning. He had told Falk – in the words he would one day put into the mouth of Phillip Maddison in *The Innocent Moon* – that he could write about anything. Underlying this claim was the knowledge that in so doing, he was always as ready to invent, if observation failed, or did not seem colourful enough, as the most unscrupulous journalist. Intermittently, throughout his life, he seems to have had a sense of being a 'fake merchant', perhaps because his wild fantasising, in childhood, had been sternly condemned by his father and by schoolmasters.

The last column of Light Car Notes appeared in the 'Weekly Dispatch' in January, 1921. At about this time, mutual recriminations between Henry and his father came to a head. It was time to leave home and become a full time writer, without distractions. For that, the cottage in Georgeham was the ideal place.

Georgeham lies around the sides of a hollow near the head of a valley which curves westwards to reach the sea at Croyde Bay. In the 1920s its people, like those of many small villages of the time – especially in a county as remote from London as Devon – lived as though the Victorian age had scarcely ended. Almost all had been born and brought up in Georgeham or Croyde; there were as yet few incomers. Very occasionally a car or lorry passed, but the more familiar vehicles were horse-drawn carts, pony traps and a carrier's van. (A bus service to Barnstaple by way of the coast road cut in Edwardian days from Croyde to Saunton and Braunton only began to run in the middle of the decade.) On farms in the area, tractors were unknown; all farm machinery except the steam threshing machines that visited in autumn were horse-drawn. No minor roads were macadamed; they were made up with a reddish local stone, and a stone cracker could often be seen at work by the roadside, splitting big quarry stones to the size needed by the road menders.

There were no mains services. Water was pumped from wells or dipped from the stream; cottages were heated by coal or wood fires; cooking was on coal-fired ranges or oil stoves (a few villagers used the cloam, clay-lined, wood-fired wall ovens); oil lamps or candles were lit after dark. The only street lighting came dimly through curtained cottage windows. Broken glass, china and tins were buried in gardens; other rubbish was burned.

Wages, rents and the price of goods were low. Most men worked on farms, as owners, tenants or labourers. The latter, in 1920, had suddenly found themselves better paid than ever before: a tribunal with compulsory powers fixed their wages (which in 1910 had been thirteen and sixpence a week) at forty-two shillings, although this high level was not to be maintained for long. Nevertheless, it was still possible, in the early 1920s, to pay as little as one and sixpence a week for a cottage. In *The Lone Swallows,* published in 1922, Henry noted, 'My Devon hermitage is rented at four pounds a year'. Elsewhere he wrote that it was five pounds; whichever it was, it meant that he could earn the price of a roof over his head with two newspaper articles a year.

Built of cob, and thatched, Skirr Cottage had two lime-washed bedrooms, a single living room with a kitchen range, and no other amenities whatever. Henry delighted in it. He had been born and

brought up in Brockley, in the borough of Lewisham, then one of
the outer suburbs of London. His parents' house, which stood on
the edge of a recreation ground called Hilly Fields, had been built in
the 1890s. (It still stands, although some houses in the road have
gone, replaced by a block of flats. The remaining houses have been
renumbered: the former No. 11 is now No. 21. On 19th May, 1984,
as a result of sustained efforts by friends and admirers, a maroon-
coloured plaque commemorating Henry's association with the
house was unveiled; among those who attended the ceremony were
the Mayor of Lewisham and the local M.P., Mr Jon Silkin.)[1]

During the early twentieth century, the Williamson household
enjoyed all the conventional suburban comforts of the period, and
Henry clearly did not miss them in the least. Like so many men of
his generation, he had undergone the terrors and hardships of
trench warfare in France; after that, what did the lack of gas-lit,
comfortably furnished rooms and indoor sanitation matter? He was
alive, he was free, he had somewhere to live which was all the better
for being shared by his beloved owls. A very small disability
pension provided just enough to live on, by his frugal standards,
and he was convinced that he would, before long, become not
simply self-supporting as a writer, but famous and successful – a
conviction he confided to almost everyone he met.

For a few months he shared the cottage with the friend he refers
to in *The Sun in the Sands* (and who appears as a minor character in
The Dream of Fair Women and *The Pathway*) as Julian Warbeck, a
devotee of Swinburne, said to be capable of drinking up to 32 pints
of beer a day. Having served in the Royal Flying Corps (which on
the 1st April, 1918, became the Royal Air Force) Julian was living on
a remittance of two pounds a week from his father, posted to Henry
and doled out in daily amounts. At first, Julian pleased Henry by
addressing him half seriously as 'Maitre', conceding that he had
powers as a writer which he himself lacked and that the book Henry
was then writing *(Dandelion Days)* was 'damned good' (though he
reminded Henry of the folk connotations of dandelions by remark-
ing that the French called them *pissenlits*). Later, the two men got on
each other's nerves. With his usual openness, Henry quoted Julian's
unflattering opinion of him as 'a paranoid, a decadent, probably
tubercular, an introvert, in fact, unnatural', and added, 'There is
some truth in that; often I think that I am self-deluded'.

After a few months they had a furious quarrel, during the course
of which Henry fired off both barrels of his twelvebore gun at the

coal-house door. (He enjoyed discharging this gun; on another occasion, irritated by the ticking of death-watch beetles, he fired both barrels at the invisible insects.) Julian moved out to live in another cottage, and later returned to London.

Left alone, Henry gathered animals around him. He acquired a small black and white cat called Pie, and sometimes took in injured birds he found, or which were brought to him by villagers – a crow, a gull, a jackdaw, an owl. He bought two spaniel pups from the blacksmith (partly because Richard Jefferies' Bevis owned a spaniel). One he gave away on impulse not long afterwards, but the other, named Billjohn, Bill or Biell (the last his neighbours' pronunciation of the name) remained a faithful if sometimes neglected companion for nine years. Most importantly, he took care of an otter cub he rescued with another ex-officer.

Georgeham was divided into what were known as Higher Ham and Lower Ham. Each part had its own pub, the Rock Inn and the Kings Arms respectively. It was for this reason, rather than any joking political reference, that they were often known as the Higher House and the Lower House, names Henry used in his books, although in *The Dream of Fair Women* and *The Pathway,* the Rock Inn becomes the Nightcrow Inn. The licensee was Albert Jeffery, an easy-going man whom Henry liked. By this time the compulsive drinking of his London life seems to have come to an end; perhaps it had been largely an expression of rebellion against his father, and the tedium of living in the city and trying to adjust to civilian life after the comradeship of the army. In the village pubs he would usually drink a pint or two of beer while he listened to talk that offered him material for articles on country life that he could sell to newspapers – especially the 'Daily Express' – and magazines. 'In the Higher and Lower Houses I heard many tales of falcons, foxes, badgers, ravens, men, which afterwards I wrote as stories', he recalled in *The Village Book* after he had left Georgeham.

Henry was lucky in choosing to leave London when he did. It so happened that 1921 was one of the finest summers of the twentieth century. Day after day he was able to walk down to the beach at Putsborough, still little frequented, to swim or walk along the tideline, or lie naked in the warmth of the low sandhills stretching towards Woolacombe. At night he might write until midnight or later, as in London, often completing some four or five thousand words at a stretch. When work was going well, he claimed, he could write at the rate of a thousand words an hour, and was almost

certainly not exaggerating; many of his novels – most of them in
excess of a hundred thousand words – were written in a comparatively short time. Not only did he write fiction and his early stories
of the countryside and animals; he kept an extensive diary. Regular
diary writing was a habit he was later to urge on other writers; his
own were an invaluable source to him, from his schooldays
onwards.

Even after writing for several hours, he was capable of going out
to walk far from the village; he walked, he said, 'at sunrise and
sunset, in moonlight and the clear darkness of stars'. He often gives
the impression that he scarcely slept at all, and there is little doubt
that he was capable of making do with only a few hours of sleep a
night. From boyhood he had found that sleep did not come easily;
lying in bed he would endure what he called 'the battle of the brain',
the painful restlessness of an over-active mind.

To food, also, he was usually indifferent. Fifteen years after his
arrival in Georgeham he was to write, 'Food is a nuisance; a pity
one can't be fed through the skin, by the sun's rays'. In a sense he
was; being out of doors in sunlight almost invariably revived him
during periods of depression or fatigue. According to Ruskin, the
last words of the great painter, J. M. W. Turner, were, 'The sun is
God'. For Henry, this was a lifelong truth. He said that to write
effortlessly he needed 'to let the sun absorb me; otherwise the spirit
of the sun, served by the sense of sight, from which my writing was
unconsciously distilled, would not flow into and renew me'.

However, during his years at Skirr Cottage he seems to have
eaten a fairly high protein diet; it included eggs, bacon, cheese,
sardines, bully beef and rabbit or mutton stew, as well as bread and
butter. Later, fruit and vegetables were to be of more importance to
him; for a time, under the influence of a girl he was in love with, he
was a vegetarian, but he reverted to meat eating after the girl had
gone out of his life. He was thin, and people remarked on it. The
comment made by Evelyn Fairfax in *The Dream of Fair Women,* 'You
look as though a good square meal wouldn't be amiss . . . I believe
you must be half-starved' may be typical of many he received. Yet
by his own account thinness was natural to him; in the early sections
of both *The Flax of Dream* and *The Chronicle of Ancient Sunlight* he
portrayed his other selves, the cousins Willie and Phillip Maddison,
as skinny little boys with nervous stomachs that, when they were
tense or excited or afraid, were quick to reject food. As a young
man, alcohol in any quantity made him sick.

It is probable that a light diet suited him; at the same time much of the irascibility that characterised him as he grew older – and which he himself described and deplored in his autobiographical books – may have been the result of frequently allowing his blood sugar level to drop, through a refusal to accept regular meals, and even a strange contrariness that made him abstain from food when he was actually hungry. (Phillip, in *Young Phillip Maddison,* having vehemently rejected his mother's offer of food after fasting all day, reflects smugly and perversely, 'self-imposed suffering made you feel very clear and simple, somehow'.)

In his early Devon years, Henry wondered whether his thinness was a symptom of disease. In London in 1920 he had some kind of collapse or fainting fit in the Adelphi Gardens, and was taken to hospital. The cause was probably lack of sleep and food, but 'in those days, worn with the terrible war and the terrible peace, I did not think I would live much longer', he recorded in the essay 'A London Owl'. He was left with a suspicion that his heart was weak. Absorbed in the writing of the first three novels of *The Flax of Dream,* he looked forward to the fourth and final volume, and exclaimed in his diary, 'Oh, if only I may be able to write it as I conceive it, how great and noble a book it will be. I must live to write it, I must, I **must**, I MUST!'. Again, on summer days, he would often run alone across Putsborough Sands, with a super-stitious feeling that he must not stop before reaching the Black Rock, about a mile away, 'lest bad luck come upon me, and the tetralogy never be finished. For that was my inner fear, to die before I had written my book'. Talking to friends, he echoed Keats', 'When I have fears that I may cease to be, Before my pen has glean'd my teeming brain . . .'.

One morning he frightened himself when doing shadow boxing; he imagined that his breath was 'wheezy and harsh' in his throat. At once he thought of a young ex-officer who had come to the village after a spell in a sanatorium. He had had a tubercular throat, and Henry pictured his own bronchial tubes 'eaten away with consumption. That was the cause of my melancholy, my depression'.

A local doctor reassured him, saying that he led far too healthy a life to be tubercular. At the same time he advised him to find someone to cook his food for him. Henry duly arranged to have his meals in the cottage of John Clibbert Thomas, known as Clibby, the village postman-sexton, who appears as Mules in *The Pathway.* He did not enjoy them. Every Sunday he was given overdone beef

with Bisto gravy, every Monday cold beef, and every Tuesday
Shepherd's pie or beef rissoles. Clibby had a tall, good-looking,
auburn-haired daughter whose rich contralto voice graced the
Georgeham church choir, but she does not seem to have been
among the girls attracted to Henry. She received his plainest state-
ments, he said, with bantering incredulity, 'It's a dirty lie, mister
Wisson. Tidden true, you know! Is it, Mister Wisson?'

The doctor made the conventional comment that it was not good
for a man to live alone. Henry half agreed. He enjoyed the freedom
to write as and when he wished, to follow what he called 'the mind's
falcon-flash', a feeling 'not to be explained, or analysed'. Nevertheless he was convinced that 'he who was visited by this feeling would
always be lonely'; when it was gone it left an emptiness 'in which
doubt lay heavy; it was then that one longed intensely, not for a
woman, but for Love'. Walking on the sands, he imagined the
perfect companion, a 'sun-maiden, who would share with me all the
loveliness of my new world'. More disconcertingly, he longed for 'a
mother-maiden, whose arms would fold round me, and by whose
cherishing I would lose the fatigue of past and present'. What girl
of flesh and blood was ever likely to be able to fulfil for long this
unreal role?

The record of his friendship with a woman called Irene, in *The Sun
in the Sands,* is evidently much fictionalised. He meets her on
Woolacombe beach, apparently in 1921 or 1922. She is separated
from her husband, a judge in India, and is trying to shake off a recent
lover, a heavy-drinking Swede. She has a daughter, a fourteen-
year-old with 'a mass of hair the colour of ripe barley, almost white',
who is therefore called Barley (sometimes Barleybright). The girl
becomes devoted to Henry; at the end of the book, when he has
visited Irene in a Pyrenean village where she is now staying, Barley
loses her life while trying to reach Henry to prevent him from
crossing a dangerous mountain pass to join other friends.

With this episode the book, written in 1934 but recording the
years 1921 to 1924, moves far from its autobiographical beginnings; this was perhaps the main reason for its being announced,
when it was eventually published in 1945, by Faber, as a 'novel-
autobiography'. As will be explained later, the real 'Barleybright'
does not belong to the Twenties but to the early Thirties, which is
why the story 'Migration', written in 1933 and added to the enlarged
edition of *The Lone Swallows,* was dedicated to Barleybright. It was a
name that stayed with Henry; in *It Was the Nightingale,* the ninth

volume of *A Chronicle of Ancient Sunlight,* Phillip Maddison's first wife, who dies in childbirth, is once again Barley.

The friends Henry was supposed to be crossing the mountain pass to see had a very real existence in Devon. They were a family called Stokes, a widowed mother with two daughters and a son, who took a cottage in Georgeham in 1922. Henry called the daughters Queenie and Annabelle in *The Sun in the Sands;* the son appears as 'the boy Marcus', their young cousin. When his second collection of animal stories, *The Peregrine's Saga,* was published in 1924, it was dedicated to 'Esther Frances Stokes for many deeds in amity'. It seems that both the sisters teased him, and did not take him seriously (Queenie especially being prone to exclaim, 'Don't be an ass, Henry,') but for a time he convinced himself that he was hopelessly in love with Annabelle, the sixteen-year-old schoolgirl.

He claimed that he acquired a reputation for 'immorality and bad behaviour'; the rector's wife soon discovered that his story about a young wife who died in childbirth was untrue. Mothers warned their daughters against him, and he was asked to resign from a local tennis club. With men, or with securely married couples of which the wife had no inclination to give him encouragement for amorous imaginings, his relationships were happier. One friendship he particularly valued, because it helped him in his nature writing, was with Dr Frederick Elliston Wright. Dr Wright had joined a Braunton practice in Edwardian days as a junior partner. By now he was the senior partner in the same practice. He was a renowned local character. Like Henry, he enjoyed riding a motorcycle. He used this for most journeys, medical and otherwise, though sometimes he rode a pony, his feet dangling because he disdained stirrups. At one time he was the owner of a west country sailing ketch, the *Agnes,* which traded round the coasts; occasionally the fancy took him to go for a voyage in her, with her captain, Will Mitchell.

Henry spent many days in the countryside with Dr Wright, talking of birds, moths and flowers. 'He was an expert, a scientific naturalist; he knew all the wild flowers, the rare rushes and ferns, of the Saunton Burrows . . . we had often roamed there together, he the master, I the mere sensuous writer'. Despite that 'mere', there is no question that Henry set the work of the 'sensuous writer' high above any deriving from an academic approach. Nevertheless, when Dr Wright's book *Braunton: A Few Nature Notes* first appeared in 1926, Henry reviewed it in a west country newspaper and reproduced the review in the 'Books and Authors' section of *The Linhay on the Downs*. Whenever he could, he recommended the book to anyone likely to be interested.

More incomers were arriving as residents in the villages of Georgeham and Croyde; among them, in 1923, were my parents. They had been living, since their marriage three years earlier, in a house called Hollacombe, standing alone on the south bank of the river Taw, near the then small village of Bickington. It would seem that Henry met them at some time in the summer or autumn of 1921, though how I do not know, and occasionally rode his Norton to Hollacombe for a meal, or to stay the night.

My grandparents lived in Barnstaple, where my grandfather was vicar of the parish of St Mary Magdalene (its church, built in the 1850s, was demolished in 1980; flats for the elderly have been built on the site). Henry's enthusiastic recommendation of Georgeham may have played a part in deciding my grandmother to buy a house there called, somewhat pretentiously, Vale House. There was a Vale Cottage nearby, which still preserves its old name, but later owners called Vale House Crowberry Cottage.

My grandmother let Vale House to two elderly spinsters, whom she may have visited from time to time, with my father driving her the nine miles from Barnstaple. Possibly on such a visit my parents heard of a cottage to let opposite the lych gate of the church. It belonged to the post-mistress – though not apparently the same one who had been Henry's landlady when he stayed in the village in 1914 – and was called Chertsey Cottage.

It would be surprising if Henry had not begun to read his work aloud to my parents on visits to Hollacombe; certainly he frequently visited Chertsey Cottage, usually late at night, to read the latest chapters of his work in progress. Thus they listened to several nature essays, passages from his diary, and an early version of his mystical fantasy *The Starborn*, which was not to be published until 1933. Above all, they listened to *The Dream of Fair Women*.

CHAPTER TWO

Spinning the Flax of Dream

By the end of 1923, Henry was the author of four published books – two novels, *The Beautiful Years* and *Dandelion Days,* and two collections of nature and animal stories, *The Lone Swallows* and *The Peregrine's Saga*. On December 1st, 1923, he celebrated his twenty-eighth birthday, although for many years he misled his readers as to his true age. In chapter 15 of *The Sun in the Sands* appears the flat mis-statement, 'I had been born half an hour before midnight on 1st December, 1896'. The correct year was 1895.

It is a remarkable idiosyncrasy. In a series of autobiographical books, he maintained it to accord with his claim to have been a boy of seventeen when he enlisted in the army in August, 1914, whereas of course he was then within a few months of his nineteenth birthday.

When he wrote a prefatory note for the one-volume, much-revised edition of his tetralogy, *The Flax of Dream,* which Faber brought out in 1936, he claimed that 'the humour of Book 1 *(The Beautiful Years)* was not refined from its twenty-two-year-old crudity and inexperience; nor was the romanticism of Book 3 *(The Dream of Fair Women)* changed to a more mature aspect of the hectic "peace" period . . . *The Flax of Dream* was completed, with the finishing of Book 4 *(The Pathway)* when the author was thirty years old'. He finished *The Pathway* in 1928, when he was thirty-two.

In *The Flax of Dream,* Willie Maddison pretends that he is older than he is in order to join up, but why his creator should have found the fantasy of early enlistment a necessity to him is a puzzle. Was it because he told it to a man he admired, or a woman he loved, and for many years afterwards could not bear to abandon it? As late as

1941, when *The Story of a Norfolk Farm* appeared, he was referring to his service in the infantry as a volunteer *two* years under age, whereas in previous books he had been content to claim to have spent his eighteenth birthday, in December, 1914, in the trenches.

However, it remains undeniable that, like huge numbers of others, he was only a youth when, having joined the Territorial Army a few months earlier, he was plunged into the mass atrocity that was trench warfare. He emerged from the experience with strong, almost obsessional ideas concerning the origins of the conflict, and the need to refashion society – especially the educational system – to avoid a recurrence.

Coming on a copy of Richard Jefferies' *The Story of My Heart* soon after the end of the war, he was momentarily transfixed, standing in a second-hand bookshop – sometimes said to be in Dover, sometimes in Folkestone – reading for an hour before buying the book to read and re-read. In chapter ten of *The Pathway*, Maddison describes the incident to Diana Shelley: Jefferies, he says, seemed to be 'with me, and of me. I grew and grew in spiritual strength; and I realised that all the world was built up of thought . . . Change thought, and you change the world'. Nearly forty years later he repeated the passage almost word for word, as straightforward autobiography in *A Clear Water Stream,* adding that 'If ever the dead befriended the living, Jefferies was my friend in youth'.

Feeling that his own self, which had been smothered during the hectic days of war, had been revealed to him, he began to write with a messianic sense that it was his destiny to 'change thought' and by doing so, in some mysterious and almost magical way, bring about the happiness of humanity. 'If I could reveal the past of one human being truly, clearly and objectively, then the causes of personal unrest, which were the causes of strife in the world between individual masses, nations, would be made plain for the first time in human history. A novel of pure cause and effect was needed in the world'.

Many years later he was to say in a letter that he had written 'three long novels before *The Beautiful Years,* which in itself was immature . . . Any one of those earlier three books would have damped down my start'. These earlier novels still exist, preserved in the Henry Williamson Archive in Exeter University Library. Written in longhand in seven large notebooks (some of them Army issue; one containing twenty pages of notes on gas warfare, evidently made when Henry, like his Phillip Maddison in *A*

Chronicle of Ancient Sunlight, was on a course) they show the beginning author's attempts to shape and control narratives of personal experience.

Some are dated, and offer information about the later stages of his army career. One bears on its cover 'Lieut. H. W. Williamson 1st Battn Bedfordshire Regt., 5 Division B.E.F.' Others show him at No. 1 Dispersal Unit, Shorncliffe and No. 3 Rest Camp, Folkestone in the spring of 1919, and at Brocton Camp, Staffordshire, in September, 1919. There are also two folders containing a typescript, lacking the first three chapters, of one of his novels, which was to have been given the title he eventually used for his tetralogy, *The Flax of Dream.* Another title he thought of using in the early months of 1919, during the period of his love affair with 'Evelyn Fairfax' (here referred to as Mignon) was *Three Phases,* 'the story of his heart, maybe, being what he really believes in this world of sometimes pathos and disappointment but now exquisite beauty'. The manuscripts have a particular interest in that they contain not only foreshadowings of the happenings which would be recreated with greater force and authority in the four novels making up the published *Flax of Dream,* but also many incidents that would wait more than thirty years to form the basis of chapters in novels in the sequence *A Chronicle of Ancient Sunlight,* when it would be Phillip Maddison, not Willie, as in these manuscripts, who would enjoy days as a leader of the Bloodhound Patrol, and later experience the fears and excitements of life in France during the First World War.

During his two years in London after leaving the army, Henry was grateful for the help and encouragement he received, first from his agent, Andrew Dakers – to whom he dedicated *Dandelion Days,* and who was to appear in his last long novel sequence, *A Chronicle of Ancient Sunlight,* as Anders Norse – and later from his publisher's reader, the novelist J. D. Beresford, to whom he dedicated *The Dream of Fair Women.* He was invited to literary parties at Beresford's house, where he met poets, including Walter de la Mare and the Devon-born J. C. Squire (later Sir John Squire) and novelists such as Storm Jameson, St John Ervine, Violet Hunt and May Sinclair. He also met Mrs Dawson Scott, who was to found the P.E.N., and said that she was a dear, who had always been kind to him, despite the fact that she considered his early attempts at writing 'wishy-washy stuff', and reproved his fantasising with, 'You say things which are not, my dear boy'. She had, he noted, 'a small and silent husband, who never appeared during the afternoon parties, but remained in the basement, typing his wife's latest novel with two fingers. "Do you like literature?" Henry asked him. "I hate literature", he replied, and went on typing with two fingers.'

The Beautiful Years was published by Collins in October, 1921. Henry received the then standard advance, for a first novel, of twenty-five pounds. It had the sub-title, 'A Tale of Childhood'; this Henry later removed, because when he 'enquired anonymously of its merits at a certain large library in Oxford Street . . . a lady librarian . . . regretted that she could not recommend it. "It's only about a child," she said, "and will only bore you".' This must have been a considerable blow, as must the book's small initial sale, despite some encouraging reviews. Visiting my parents in the mid-Thirties, Henry said, self-mockingly, as so often, that he had imagined that its influence would be great and immediate; as he put it, 'everyone would suddenly be ten feet tall with green hair'. In 1921, there was certainly little sign that his first 'novel of pure cause and effect' was likely to change the world.

It seems an interesting instance of his idealistic yet unrealistic ways of thought that he had supposed it could. Rather than the past of one human being revealed 'truly, clearly, objectively', it is indeed 'A Tale of Childhood' – the childhood of a sensitive, wayward, often timorous and tearful boy who is fascinated by the country world about him, and its creatures.

The setting is Rookhurst, a village, or hamlet, not far from a town called Colham. These places have no precise geographical location, either in *The Flax of Dream* or when they necessarily reappear in *A Chronicle of Ancient Sunlight,* Rookhurst being the birthplace of Phillip Maddison's father, Richard, and Richard's many brothers and sisters. It is said to be in the West Country; reading *The Beautiful Years* as a child, I supposed Rookhurst to be in Devon, as the speech of its country people and of Biddy, the kindly and indulgent housekeeper who looks after the motherless Willie Maddison and his father, sounded much like that of the people of Georgeham. At one point the village is described as being near Richard Jefferies' home, which would of course put it in Wiltshire. However, although the Maddison family house is named Fawley, which would suggest Hampshire, the locality is eventually identified, in *The Phoenix Generation,* as mid-Dorset.

Yet Rookhurst does not belong exclusively to any county: it is a place of the imagination, a compound of all Henry Williamson's joyful boyhood countrysides: those of Kent and Surrey, to which he cycled at weekends and during school holidays, and those of the Bedfordshire-Buckinghamshire border which he came to know when staying with cousins. Nearly forty years later, he was to write that the book 'had all the freshness of an early morning of the summers of my boyhood'.

The child, Willie Maddison, is seven when the book begins, and just ten when it ends. If it is clear that his character derives much from that of his author, his circumstances are very different. Henry Williamson was born and grew up in Brockley, between Lambeth and Lewisham; both his parents were alive – and indeed were to live until he was a man in his forties – and he had two younger sisters. Willie is an only child, his mother having died giving birth to him. His father is a lonely man; embittered by the loss of his wife, he has withdrawn from the world. The consoling adult figures in Willie's life, apart from Biddy the housekeeper, are the eighteen-year-old Dolly, a servant on a neighbouring farm which Henry took pleasure in naming Skirr, after his cottage, and Jim Holloman, with whom Dolly is in love. Jim is an outcast figure of mysterious origin (it seems that, Chatterley-wise, he is the illegitimate son of a local colonel's young wife and a gamekeeper's son). Willie's best friend is Jack Temperley, of Skirr Farm.

Willie and Jack have read Richard Jefferies' *Bevis,* as Henry had done just before beginning to write his book. In the original, 1921 version, their activities owe a great deal to Jefferies: they sail a catamaran on the Longpond, organise and fight a battle and so on. In the revised version published in 1929, much of this was cut. There are two grotesque deaths: a shepherd is frozen in a snow-drift and his eyes pecked out by crows, and Jim Holloman falls into a burning limekiln, having slept too near its edge.

When writing his foreword to the one-volume edition of *The Flax of Dream,* Henry observed, 'This long novel . . . has for its theme the unhappiness of the child: the thwarting of the social instinct which can only be developed by imagination freed from mental fear'. Certainly Willie Maddison is afraid of his father who, anxious lest he has inherited the weaknesses of his grandfather, the heavy-drinking, womanising spendthrift, beats him for lying, disobedience and truanting; he hates the learning process demanded of him at Colham Grammar School, to which he is sent as a day boy at the early age of nine. Nevertheless he repeatedly provokes the impatience of both his father and his schoolmasters – and sometimes of his schoolfellows – by his behaviour; although the prospect of

beatings terrifies him, he knowingly courts them by the things he
does. At the same time he can be indifferent to proffered kindness:
the book ends with his rejection of his father's attempts, on his
tenth birthday, at a reconciliation. In this scene, as elsewhere in the
book, Henry is careful to show the father as an unhappy man rather
than a harsh one.

Even if Henry was disappointed by the reception of *The Beautiful
Years,* by the time it appeared he had not only finished its successor,
Dandelion Days, but was full of plans for the remaining two novels
of the sequence. *Dandelion Days* continues the story of Willie
Maddison's schooling at Colham Grammar School. Henry's own
schooldays began at Brockley Primary School, from which he
obtained a scholarship to Colfe's Grammar School, less than two
miles north east of his home. (It may be assumed that he derived the
name Colham from a telescoping of Colfe and Lewisham.) In an
essay written in the 1960s he said that he had been 'an idiot at
Euclid, etc. etc.' and also poor at games. However, he passed the
Senior Cambridge Local with third class honours in December,
1912, just after his seventeenth birthday, and was at least in the
school cricket team and the football second eleven; he was also
Captain of Harriers. In his last year he won a school prize (as
Willie wins the Bullnote Prize in *Dandelion Days);* it is somewhat
surprising to learn that this was awarded for divinity.[1]

In later life he looked back to certain members of the staff with
respect, even affection, especially the headmaster, F. W. Lucas, and
said that all the masters save one were amiable and kind. Yet in
books written during the 1930s he referred to the educational
system he had experienced as 'mental sawdust' and 'mental barbed
wire'. He claimed that European educational policies deriving from
'the internecine financial system' had broken and enslaved the
natural intelligences of the children of Europe 'and the Great War
was the result'. He was aware that many readers would not accept
this particular chain of cause and effect. In an 'Epistle Apological'
(sic) to his literary agent, Andrew Dakers, included in the first
edition of *Dandelion Days,* he said that it might be thought that he
had failed to show 'that there was any basic wrong in the present
system of cramming the immature mind; on the contrary, that I
have merely shown its unsuitability for one small boy'.

Like *The Beautiful Years, Dandelion Days* in its original version
owes much to *Bevis.* However, the humour of the school scenes was
entirely Henry's; it was energetic and youthful, with a strong

element of caricature in his portrayal of the masters. Henry greatly enjoyed writing it, and in the mornings, sitting in his living-room-kitchen in Skirr Cottage, would laugh aloud at passages written the night before. Later in life he was to dismiss it as a farrago. Even by the late 1920s he was deeply dissatisfied with it, and when Faber took over the tetralogy for reissue, rewrote it more thoroughly than any of the other three (*The Pathway,* completed when he was, he said, more sure of himself, was hardly revised at all.)

En route to stay with a friend in Essex, he took the manuscript of *Dandelion Days* to J. D. Beresford in Collins' editorial office, and characteristically offered to read it aloud. Beresford, himself so prolific as a novelist and short story writer that it is astonishing that he had time to read for a publisher, replied 'with patient weariness' that he would get a better idea if he read it himself. When in due course he wrote his opinion of it, he warned Henry that he would 'rather spoil the prospects of your market by this book'. It was too like *The Beautiful Years;* it spent too long on Willie's adolescence, though the school was well done 'but just a little overdone – a little too realistic. For your realism is infinitely more drastic than that of Wells or Bennett. Yours is the spirit of fact and theirs is so often (always in Bennett) the comparatively unconvincing letter'. There were other warnings: against the use of such words as 'recrudescence', 'gracile', 'umbral' and 'spilth', against the 'too too purple patch', against becoming too deep in 'the contemplation of Henry Williamson down there in Devon'.

However, Collins took the book, and Henry again received a modest advance. Meanwhile, on his return from Essex in the early spring of 1922, he learned that Andrew Dakers had sold his long five-part story, 'The Peregrine's Saga' to the 'Pictorial Review' in America for five hundred dollars, and a number of other animal stories to English magazines of good quality for good fees. More-over, Henry had been encouraged by the literary editor of the 'Daily Express', Beverley Baxter, to submit country stories, and a number of these had appeared in the paper. Dakers managed to interest Collins in publishing selections from these early pieces, and so *The Lone Swallows* appeared, with a dedication to Richard Jefferies, in 1922, and *The Peregrine's Saga* in 1923. (The latter was published in the U.S.A. as *Sun Brothers.*) Henry was beginning to prove that he had been right to believe that he could make a living by writing.

Henry was so much under the influence of Jefferies in 1920 and 1921, when many of the stories of *The Lone Swallows* were written, that some – for instance 'Meadow Grasses', 'The Incoming of Summer' and 'The Passing of the Blossom' (the latter dedicated to Walter de la Mare, Henry having asked the poet's permission at a literary party in London) are almost Jefferies pastiche.

The title story is a simple and poignant account of something Henry observed soon after his arrival in Devon in the spring of 1921: a single pair of swallows appeared on the coast exceptionally early, and for a week or two were seen on the headland of Baggy, or inland over the millpond which then existed in Croyde. The villagers took pleasure in the sight of them – but before any other migrants joined them, they were killed by peregrine falcons. In stories such as this, Henry recorded dispassionately the operation of natural laws; in others he portrayed human cruelty to animals, arising sometimes from stupidity, sometimes from viciousness, sometimes from fixed ideas about sport. He described the effect of gin traps; he watched badger digging in order to write about it; not for many years would either be illegal. He wrote a short book, *The Wild Red Deer of Exmoor,* in which he offered both sides of the controversy on hunting. As a young man he went fox hunting, and he repeatedly followed otter hounds, though without enthusiasm – he needed the knowledge gained in order to write *Tarka.*

When Putnam brought out a uniform edition of *The Lone Swallows, The Peregrine's Saga, The Old Stag* and *Tarka the Otter* in 1933, with line drawings by C. F. Tunnicliffe, Henry as usual took the opportunity to make changes. In the case of *The Lone Swallows* these were mostly additions, among them 'A Boy's Nature Diary', written, Henry said, in 1913, when he was sixteen, although he would have been seventeen in that year. They show that when, in *Dandelion Days,* he introduces some entries from the 'Official Diary of Observations . . . signed Will Maddison the Bird-Man of Rookhurst', he was evidently making use of a genuine diary kept during his schooldays. *The Lone Swallows* entries cover the months from February to April. They show Henry and his friends cycling into Kent to watch birds and search for nests on the estates of several landed gentry.

Henry had permission to visit several of these estates. In an article written many years later he explained that he had written 'formal letters, as instructed in a book of etiquette studies in the public library' to a number of landowners, and in each case had received a gracious reply. (*In Young Phillip Maddison* he showed Phillip noting down the names of villages within a dozen miles of his home, obtaining from a directory the names of landowners and copying out the correct style to be used in writing a letter 'to a peer or peeress of the realm'.) The Dowager Countess of Derby, called Mersea in the novel, was one of those who granted him permission to visit her property. This was Holwood Park, Keston, about a mile west of Farnborough. Among others were Dunstall Priory, near Sevenoaks, and High Elms, the property of Lord Avebury which, like Holwood Park, is not far from the village of Down and Downe House where Charles Darwin spent the last forty years of his life.

The whole valley of the Darent, flowing north from Westerham to Dartford, was within twelve miles of Brockley. Henry and his friend Terence Tetley, who may be the original of Jack Temperley in *The Beautiful Years* and *Dandelion Days*, and to whom the short piece 'Winter's Eve' in *The Lone Swallows* is dedicated 'In Memory', sometimes cycled to Squerryes Court, near Westerham; the Darent rises in its park. They followed the course of the river, seeing old ruined mills, and must have visited Shoreham, where from 1826 to 1833 Samuel Palmer painted his paradisal pastorals. Sometimes they talked to gamekeepers, and examined the melancholy displays of shot or trapped creatures on their vermin poles – a common country sight in those days, as Richard Jefferies had pointed out a few decades earlier.

Henry had cousins in Bedfordshire, in the village of Aspley Guise. Ancestors of his, bearing the name Turney, had lived in the Aspley Guise-Husborne Crawley area for generations. In novels in The *Chronicle of Ancient Sunlight* sequence he was to make use of this surname for the family of Phillip Maddison's mother; he would call his cousins' house Beau Brickhill, after the village of Bow Brickhill a few miles to the west in Buckinghamshire, and give the name Husborne Abbey to Woburn Abbey – which was in fact used as a convalescent home for officers in the First World War – when Phillip recovers there from mustard gas burns in 1918.

Staying with his cousins in Aspley Guise, Henry shot sparrows, chaffinches and cole tits without compunction, in order to stuff them. He explored the grounds of Woburn Abbey, and on one of the Duke of Bedford's farms came across a crow starver, a twelve-year-old boy employed, like Hardy's Jude the Obscure, to drive away rooks, crows and jackdaws from the growing corn. From this encounter came not only the short piece 'Boy' in *The Lone Swallows*, but the character of Bill Nye, the illegitimate child in *Dandelion Days* who earns a few shillings a week as a crow-starver.

The diary shows that the reality of life for the seventeen-year-old Henry Williamson was not, mercifully, the miseries of trench warfare in France, as he was so often to claim, but the freedom at week-ends and in school holidays – and even in term-time when he truanted – to enjoy with friends who shared his interests the open-air life that was, and remained, his greatest happiness.

During Henry's boyhood, 'The black county of London was steadily invading the green county of Kent', as he was to put it many years later, and several of the stories in these early books, such as 'The Change' and 'The Old Pond' in *The Lone Swallows* and 'Aliens' in *The Peregrine's Saga,* chronicle the effects of this invasion. 'Aliens' is a requiem for the Ravensbourne, which appears in *A Chronicle of Ancient Sunlight* as the Randisbourne; flowing through Lewisham to join the Thames at Deptford, it had been a clean country stream in the 1890s, but by 1920 was polluted and lifeless.

In 1933 Henry removed several stories that had appeared in the first edition of *The Old Stag* and substituted a somewhat strained and unconvincing piece, 'Zoe', which might well have been omitted. It describes the shooting of a bitch otter by someone called Sir Godfrey Crawdelhook, and the rescue of one of her cubs by an ex-officer, badly wounded in the war, who cares for the cub and calls it Zoe – which, it transpires later, is the name of his wife who ran away with Sir Godfrey during the war. As the local otter hounds kill Zoe, the ex-officer shoots himself. The origin of this fabrication is less melodramatic. In 1921, when Henry was living alone in Skirr Cottage after the departure of his friend the Swinburne-loving classicist, an invalid ex-officer called to tell him that he believed he knew where there was an orphaned otter cub. Together they found the cub, and Henry's little black and white cat became its foster mother. Later, on one of his nocturnal walks, he found the cub held by one paw in a gin trap. When he released it, it ran away, and he never saw it again, although at intervals over the years he searched for it. The cub appears in *The Dream of Fair Women* as Izaak, one of the many animals and birds which share Willie Maddison's tumble-down cottage, and swims in the sea with him. In *Goodbye West Country* Henry was to recall that he wrote about a dozen short stories about otters, linked together. When he sent them to magazines, two were taken and printed; the others he withdrew, as later knowledge told him that they were not faithful to fact.

Evidently *Tarka* was waiting to be written from that time onwards, but it remained at the back of his mind while he was engrossed in the third volume of his tetralogy. He dated the original edition of this novel 'London – Devon. November, 1919 – November, 1923', which would imply that he was unusually slow in completing it. However, its beginnings in London in 1919 were written in one of the notebooks already referred to as forming part of Exeter University's Henry Williamson Archive. In one of these notebooks he recorded that the novel had been 'mentally composed' during 1919, and that he had begun to write it down on 14th November of that year. The version that was to be published by Collins in 1924 was written after the completion of *Dandelion Days*.

He gave my parents a copy of *Dandelion Days,* and I think read much or all of it to them. He certainly read *The Dream of Fair Women* to them while still in the process of writing it. The title he adapted from Tennyson, in whose poem, 'A Dream of Good Women', the poet falls asleep after reading Chaucer's 'The Legend of Good Women', and dreams of such fatal beauties as Helen of Troy, Cleopatra and Fair Rosamond.

Henry inscribed my parents' copy, 'Aubrey and Ruth Lamplugh with Henry Williamson's love. October 1924. Oh, the pains and miseries caused by this book, and my words so patiently listened to by you!' He signed it with his owl symbol and initials.

If they listened patiently, they also sometimes listened sleepily, as the readings were always late at night, and they were less enthralled by the hours around midnight than was Henry. Yet they were impressed by what they heard, and willing to believe their friend's insistence that in time he would become famous.

The 1922 edition of *Dandelion Days* ended where Willie says a reluctant farewell to the fields and woods and wild creatures of Rookhurst before leaving for London to begin a job in the Moon Fire Office. The 1930 edition added a letter from the headmaster of Colham Grammar School to Private W. P. Maddison 'serving in a territorial infantry battalion in the Ypres Salient (whither a lie about his age had prematurely taken him)'. It might therefore have been expected that the next volume would be concerned with Willie's war experiences, but although, as has been said, he had written of the war in early notebooks, Henry had evidently decided to postpone a full treatment of this part of his life until later – a decision for which he was to be thankful. So *The Dream of Fair Women* begins in the summer of 1919, with Willie Maddison demobilised and living in a village called Brakspear St Flammea. (St

Flammea is not to be found in the calendar: the former, Linnaean, name for the barn owl is Strix Flammea.)

Willie's cottage, known locally as Rats' Castle, is set in a combe, or goyal, which runs down to the sea in what is called Shelley Cove, so spelled to suggest some connection with one of Henry's most venerated poets, although there is in fact a Shelly (sic) Cove at the far end of Saunton Down. Nearby are shafts of derelict iron mines; in one lives Jack o' Rags, 'a poor mazed miner', brain damaged by a premature explosion during blasting. In creating Rat's Castle, Henry had the pleasure of transferring Skirr Cottage, in his imagination, to a combe above the stretch of sands – not a cove – already described, the three miles of Woolacombe Bay; the iron mines were those of Spreacombe, some two miles north-east of Georgeham, which the eighteen-year-old Henry had explored in May, 1914, finding 'a ruinous cottage, with a forge, washing trough, and other buildings . . . a place of magpies, vipers and solitude'.

In comparing the two versions of *The Dream of Fair Women* (which for ease of reference may be called **1924** and **1931**) it is seen that **1924**'s three parts are headed 'The Web and the Flax', 'The Scarlet Thread' and 'The Broken Web' respectively. This natural sequence is not followed in **1931**, where, although Parts 2 and 3 have their original titles, Part 1 becomes, clumsily enough, 'The Policy of Reconstruction, or, True Resurrection' – the title of the book on which Willie is working (and also a title which Henry at one time thought of using).

Both versions move from Devon to Folkestone (called Findlestone in **1924**) in telling the story of Willie's infatuation with Evelyn Fairfax, but whereas **1924** begins with a rapturous evocation of his free, half-wild life in the tumbledown cottage – a whole-hearted *Et in Arcadia ego* – and a chance meeting with Evelyn on the headland nearby, **1931** begins with Evelyn and her escort of the moment, the supposed Old Etonian, Captain Colyer, D.S.O. and bar, calling at Rat's Castle to look for Willie, having heard where he is living from his cousin Phillip. The opening chapters provide hints that Colyer is an impostor; his arrest by the Military Police is described near the end of the book. It may have been Henry's intention to underline the perfidiousness of Evelyn by showing her, from the outset, as associated with a man like Colyer. However, the early chapters hardly gain from the change; those of **1924**, for all their immaturity, have a greater naturalness and vigour.

In the social climate of 1919, the lightly promiscuous Evelyn appears as a femme fatale; having introduced Julian Warbeck as one of the circle of men attracted to her, Henry is able to give him appropriate lines from Swinburne's 'Dolores' to quote: 'Ah, beautiful passionate body, That never has ached with a heart', and so on. However, by the time he was reading *The Dream of Fair Women* aloud to my parents, he was well aware that in rejecting him for another man (or other men) Evelyn had done him a kindness. From then on, he seems to have fought shy of mature and experienced women, and to have been repeatedly attracted to very young girls, such as those to whom, in *The Sun in the Sands,* he gave the names Annabelle and Barleybright – or girls who, if a year or two older, were sexually inexperienced. In London in 1920 there had already been a girl of about seventeen; he called her Spica, after the star Spica Virginis. She had an unromantic job, working with white mice in a VD clinic; she had told Henry that she could not love anyone and, evidently a practical girl, had added, 'What would you do with a wife, you poor man, you can't even look after yourself, how then could you look after a wife and family?'

Yet even in 1924, it was not perhaps a wife and family he was seeking, but the shadowy ideal companion, that impossible mother-maiden. In the summer of that year, when he had turned away temporarily from beginning *The Pathway,* the last volume of *The Flax of Dream,* to concentrate on his otter book, he believed that he had found her.

CHAPTER THREE

First Marriage: Vale House

A few months after the publication of *Dandelion Days,* Henry, spending Christmas in London with his parents, was invited to a party at Walter de la Mare's house. There he met the poet's son, Richard, who was just down from Oxford and beginning to work in publishing as a reader for Selwyn and Blount. Later he would become a director of Faber and Faber, and Henry's kindly and diplomatic literary adviser over the long period during which Faber published his books. Henry showed him the first few chapters of *The Starborn,* saying 'half-honestly' that it might be very bad. When Richard de la Mare said that he would like to see the rest of the book, Henry became 'shy, or perverse', and showed him instead the beginning of what he was then calling *The Otter's Saga.* When interest was expressed in this also, he protested that it must be entirely re-written, and took it back with him to Devon.

For much of 1923 he was occupied with both *The Starborn* and the final draft of *The Dream of Fair Women.* Although he was to write later that he lost the manuscript of *The Starborn* in the autumn of that year, some of it must have survived, or been re-written, as he quotes from it in *The Pathway.* He completed *The Dream of Fair Women* and delivered it to Collins, who accepted it for publication the following year. After this he was able to turn back to the otter book. It was in search of accurate information about otter hunting that, in the summer of 1924, he went to a meet of the Cheriton Otter Hounds. This hunt, founded in 1846, pursued the otters of several north Devon rivers – the Taw, the Torridge, the Bray and the Mole; they met at places as far apart as Eggesford on the road from Barnstaple to Exeter, and Meeth, only some nine miles north of

Okehampton. Its oldest member at this time was Charles Calvert Hibbert, who lived at Southclose, Landcross, near Bideford. He was a widower, with three sons and a daughter. His daughter and youngest son were also followers of the otter hounds, but the two older sons may by 1924 have been too busy with the engineering business they had set up to go hunting.

It is possible that Henry was introduced to Mr Hibbert; it is equally possible that he quickly noticed Mr Hibbert's charming daughter, Ida Loetitia, who was to be referred to as Loetitia in Henry's autobiographical books, but was always Gypsy to him and his friends, including my parents. (It was not until the mid-Thirties, when *Goodbye West Country* appeared, that I learned that her name was Loetitia.) She was called Gypsy, not because of anything wild and impulsive in her nature – she was in fact calm and gentle – but because of her beauty of colouring and features.

Although the Hibberts do not seem to have been a particularly bookish family (Mr Hibbert's favourite reading, like that of Uncle Sufford Chychester in *The Pathway,* was Sexton Blake stories) they had some of Richard Jefferies' works in their house. Loetitia had read and re-read *Bevis,* as Henry soon discovered. This, added to her other attractions, drew him to her irresistibly. Now he had found the embodiment of Mary Ogilvie, and he began to write *The Pathway* rapidly and with happy ease.

Having planned the tetralogy carefully from the beginning, he had prepared the way for Mary's main role in *The Pathway* long before he met Loetitia Hibbert, by introducing her in each of the first three books. At first she appears as a friend of Elsie Norman, the girl with whom the schoolboy Willie Maddison believes himself in love. Pining for Elsie in *The Beautiful Years* and *Dandelion Days,* he ignores the patient and sympathetic Mary. In the first chapter of *The Pathway* he arrives at the Ogilvies' manor house, Wildernesse, on Santon (Saunton) Burrows on a bitter winter night; he has been invited by Mary's somewhat farouche sister Jean. Jean has met him at Instow and recognised him from a meeting on the sands at 'Cryde Bay' four years earlier. (For some reason Henry referred to Instow, Appledore and Bideford by their actual names, but here and in other books preferred to use the names of some villages – Saunton, Braunton, Croyde and Georgeham – as they appear in Saxton's map of Devon of 1575: Santon, Branton, Cryde and Ham. For Ilfracombe and Barnstaple he usually used Combe and Barum, as local people often did.)

At last Willie appreciates Mary. He becomes a frequent visitor to Wildernesse. Henry sited this imaginary house more or less where Marstage Farm stands, behind Saunton Burrows and near the edge of Braunton Great Field. His description of the house may owe a little to Southclose, but it is perhaps more a Jefferies house, bearing a resemblance to Coombe Oaks in *Amaryllis at the Fair,* or the farm in *Bevis*. His knowledge and love of the Burrows – then remote and little visited, now roared over daily by aircraft taking off and landing on the R.A.F. station at Chivenor – irradiate the book.

Writing about the book many years later, Henry recalled that Part One of *The Pathway* had been written in London, in an empty house in which his uncle, who he said was the original of Hugh Turney in *A Chronicle of Ancient Sunlight,* had recently died 'in pain and torment'. This would have been 12, Eastern Road, S.E.4; Henry's grandfather Thomas William Leaver had lived there, next to his daughter and son-in-law, as grandfather Turney lives next door to Hetty and Richard Maddison in the *Chronicle*. Happily he showed Willie being assimilated into the warm kindliness of the Ogilvies' family life, as he himself had been assimilated into that of the Hibberts. Yet since he was writing a novel, and not autobiography, he depicted a household that differed considerably from that of Southclose, Landcross. At its head is Sufford Calmady Chychester ('Uncle Suff'), a character who may be seen as a half-affectionate, half-exasperated portrait of Mr Hibbert, with whom, Henry recorded, he never felt at ease. Uncle Suff was formerly the owner of Heanton Court (an actual house beside the river Taw between Braunton and Barnstaple; it was the original of Narnton Court in Blackmore's *Maid of Sker*). He has become impoverished by the failure of investments, and therefore lives with his niece Connie. Connie has lost not only her 'irresponsible and intemperate husband Charles', who drowned while trying to save a stranger's life, but a son in the war. Her surviving children are Mary and Jean and the schoolchildren Ronnie and Pam. Finally there are Miss Edith Chychester, Uncle Suff's profoundly deaf sister, and a boy called Benjamin, the illegitimate son of one of Uncle Suff's sons who also died in the war.

The real family Henry began to visit so often, riding from Georgeham to Landcross on his much-loved Norton motorcycle, was neither so large nor so complicated. It consisted of Mr Hibbert, Loetitia and her three brothers, referred to as the Boys. Mrs Hibbert had died a few years earlier, and so Loetitia was housekeeper to the four men, her life a constant round of cooking, shopping, cleaning and washing clothes. According to Henry, when he first knew the family, they were poor but happy; he used to carry them sacks of rabbits, putting his little cat Pie in with the dead rabbits and letting his dog Billjohn ride on the petrol tank of the motorbike. At other times their supper would consist of shrimp paste sandwiches and Camp coffee. Henry was enchanted with their unworldliness, and told himself of his good fortune 'to be among such simple and sweet people; and as for Loetitia, she was beautiful as Desdemona, she was a Shakespearian heroine in the flesh. O fortunate author! to have found among the post-war bitterness, disillusion and hatred, a family whose modesty and simple kindness was entirely natural'.

Unfortunately their unworldliness extended to their engineering business: Henry spent some time trying to extricate the brothers from its temporary collapse. He caused them, and himself, considerable strain – only to find that the eldest brother had received news of what was then a fairly large bequest from an aunt but had not thought to mention it because the money was not yet in his hands. Henry lodged proof of the inheritance with the bank, obtained an overdraft, and the crisis was over. Yet neither Henry nor, perhaps, the Boys, were able to forget that he had indulged in furious denunciation of their carelessness. He felt remorse for that, and for interfering at all in their affairs.

My parents were by this time among his confidants. When he had been deeply troubled by gossip concerning himself uttered by a lady member of the tennis club he had joined, my father had spoken to him of the possibility of his bringing a case for defamation of character, and had recommended a Barnstaple solicitor, George Lefroy, who was one of the churchwardens of my grandfather's parish. In *The Sun in the Sands,* Henry gives the solicitor the name Lamprey, enjoying the joke of using a name resembling my father's. Mr Lefroy obtained on Henry's behalf a somewhat lame apology, which did little to abate his sense of being persecuted by the conventional-minded.

During his weeks in London at the end of 1924, Henry enjoyed a certain amount of social life, sometimes visiting the Cafe Royal, where he met some of the writers and artists who frequented the place. Among these were Jacob Epstein and his wife. At Christmas Henry sent my parents a card containing a printed verse:

> 'No stately wish I send
> But just the good old phrase

A Merry Christmas, friend,
And many happy days'.

The words 'the good old phrase' were underlined. On the opposite page he wrote:

'Yoss, I knows de poet Davies. Yoss, I 'ave doon ees 'ead. (It cost 'im dree undert Guinesses – nunno, I mean guineas.) Yoss, I will 'ave anoder dooble, and my wife, she will have a boddle of Burgundy. Thonk you. Yoss, I 'ave done Shaw. Yoss, I think him a goot, yoss, a goot wrider! Anozzer dooble, I think. Yoss, and my wife, she will have another Burgundy – a boddle, eef you please.

Yoss, I 'ave done many 'eads. Well, as you are so pressing, I will haf anoder dooble!" (Extract from 'My Memoirs' by Lord Skirr of Skirr)'

The speaker, Henry explained when he next saw my parents, was Epstein. He signed the card 'from the one and only Dooble-Omblepoomp at Skirr Cottage.'

He spent Christmas with the Hibberts, but he and Loetitia were not altogether happy, partly because of Henry's inability to feel at ease with Mr Hibbert. My parents, who had heard – and of course read in his novels – various accounts of his earlier loves, wondered at first if this one would last, but it soon became clear that Henry, at twenty-nine, was earnestly set on marrying 'the beautiful, modest and tender girl' (as he called her many years later) to whom Tarka had, as it were, given him the introduction.

They were to begin their married life in the sparse comforts of Skirr Cottage. It seems that Henry planned improvements of some sort and discussed them with my father. It must have been in the early months of 1925 that he began to come to Chertsey Cottage quite often in daytime, whereas previously his visits had been mostly at night, long after I was in bed. My first memories of him therefore date from this year. Once, in the dusk of a spring afternoon, he brought a young owl to show me. On another day, noticing that I had discovered the delights of scrawling on paper with pencil or crayon, he handed me a notebook to use. My parents saw that it contained notes of characters and scenes that appear in *The Beautiful Years* and *Dandelion Days,* and protested against its destruction. Although Henry dismissed the little book as of no further interest, my parent's admiration for his work luckily ensured that they substituted other scribbling material, and kept the notebook, so that I still have it (see end of chapter).

In April Henry went to London to see his parents before the wedding. He wrote to my father to ask him to send some revised measurements to a firm of builders in Barnstaple for the work he wanted done. At the end of the letter he wrote, 'By the way, I've smashed up the Norton, wrecked lamps, bars, forks, etc., crashed in mud coming back from London. Unhurt otherwise'. This sounds like the crash that he attributed, in the third chapter of *The Sun in the Sands,* to his journey to Devon in March, 1921.

Another letter, also dated from 11 Eastern Road, S.E.4., shows that Henry was trying to act as a representative of Hibbert Brothers in the sale of motorcycles; he offered to get a reduction of $7\frac{1}{2}$ per cent on a new Matchless for my father. However, my father was planning to buy a car. He chose a remarkable vehicle called an Arrol Johnston which was luxuriously upholstered, had curtains looped back with silk-tasselled cords and even a little silver-plated flower vase in a bracket, but was mechanically a disaster. Not long afterwards it was exchanged for a Trojan, about which Henry was later to write as though he had conflated it with the Arrol Johnston.

Henry was buying a new Norton – with a sidecar to carry his wife-to-be. At the end of the letter about motorcycles he added, 'I must now type some of the otter book, how I hate it'. *The Pathway* having been temporarily set aside, he was now at work on one of the drafts of *Tarka*.

On 5th May, 1925, Henry married Loetitia Hibbert at Landcross Church. It seems to have been a quiet wedding. Neither of the leading North Devon weekly newspapers, the 'North Devon Journal' or the 'North Devon Herald', reported it. It was left to the even more local 'Bideford Gazette' to include a short account. This began by observing that an escort of Girl Guides lined the aisle and also formed a guard of honour; it pointed out that the bride was a cousin of Lady Ashcombe, and that Mr Henry Williamson was 'an author of note' who had written *The Lone Swallows;* it did not mention his novels. There were two bridesmaids, Miss Hibbert and Miss L. Hibbert, cousins of the bride; as has been said, Loetitia had no sister. Henry's future publisher, Richard de la Mare, was best man. The report concluded by saying that Mr and Mrs Williamson were spending their honeymoon in France.

So they were, but not immediately, as the following postcard sent to my parents shows:

'I forgot to put the table into the cottage, and if you would do it, I should be grateful. May return for flying visit on Friday, to straighten up before going to France. The little sidecar was ready on the 6th inst., but I couldn't drive! And it was a good thing too, seeing the weather on Exmoor.

Have been doing a lot of walking, and feel very fit, did ten hours yesterday. Very interesting place this, have learned much since coming here, about snakes, birds, etc. – probably got two stories. Did you see some of the photos in Daily Sketch and other London papers? Pretty ugly things, but true to me. I shall be here probably till Thursday morning. Love to all from both of us'.

The signature takes the form of two owl symbols. It is an interesting message to have been written by a man on his honeymoon. Until the final 'us' and the second owl symbol, Loetitia's existence is not acknowledged – and Henry is shown as first and foremost a writer in search of material.

The card was dated 10th May, 1925, and the address was given as 'Higher House, Wheddon Cross, Taunton'. Wheddon Cross is a cross-roads hamlet on the eastern edge of Exmoor, only some three miles south-east of Dunkery, but more than twenty miles from Taunton.

The part of France that Henry had chosen for the remainder of his honeymoon was the area of the battlefields he had visited during the spring of the previous year, on his much-fictionalised walking tour, described in *The Sun in the Sands*. He also went to Flanders; at

Wyteschaete, he said, some oafish young men made suggestive remarks to Loetitia, and he set about them with a chair.

Home again in Skirr Cottage, he went on with his otter book. Before summer ended, Loetitia knew that she was pregnant, and at last Henry acknowledged that it was time to find somewhere slightly less primitive to live. The two elderly ladies who had been my grandmother's tenants at Vale House had recently died within a month or two of one another; the place stood empty. It was arranged that Henry and Loetitia should move in.

They were not poor, Henry was to record many years later, though all their worldly goods, sold at auction, would probably not have made more than forty pounds in all. 'I cared nothing for money, so long as I owed none and could pay my way', he observed. He worked to brighten the walls of Vale House with limewash, and replaced damp patches of plaster with concrete, which he mixed with sand brought from Putsborough beach on his motorcycle. 'Once I carried dog and stones in front, with Loetitia on the carrier behind, but we fell off at a muddy patch, so we didn't try again'. Any danger to Loetitia, or even the dog, was evidently discounted; one may wonder, too, why he did not use the sidecar.

The former tenants had left quantities of rubbish in the old wash-house at the back of the house; this he burned or buried in the raised garden, in the absence,in those days, of any organised refuse collection.

He and Loetitia spent much of that summer and autumn on the sands, or walking on the headland of Baggy, which he loved (in his books it is sometimes Bag Leap, sometimes the Corpsnout) and over the fields around Georgeham, Croyde and Woolacombe. Often my parents met them on the beach, but by this time my father had the Trojan, and drove my mother and myself down the narrow road to the sea. Henry scorned to use his motorbike and sidecar; he and Loetitia always walked. To the end of his life he was a tireless walker.

We spent Christmas, 1925, with my grandparents in Barnstaple, and Henry sent a card inscribed 'To all at St Mary's Vicarage, from the Owl and his Mate'.

Loetitia was to go to a midwife's house in Braunton for the birth of her baby, but by the beginning of February, 1926, it was clear that to be taken there in the sidecar, when the time came, would be uncomfortable, and my father's offer of the Trojan as an alternative was accepted.

In the original version of *The Children of Shallowford*, published in 1939, the first six chapters described the early years of Henry's marriage. Later, when a proposed new edition gave him the chance to make changes, he cut out these chapters. (W. B. Yeats, an enthusiastic reviser of his own poems, once remarked that a poem was never finished, only abandoned; Henry seems to have had much the same opinion of his books.) Chapter One of the 1939 edition is headed 'February 17-18, 1926'. Henry describes his anxiety over Loetitia, who is evidently in labour. It is an exceptionally dark night; despite his years spent 'in night wanderings in the fields and lanes' he has to grope his way cautiously up the village street. In the Lower House (the King's Arms) a skittles match is going on, Georgeham versus Crosstree (Braunton). Dr Shardeloes-Lane (one of Henry's name jokes: Shardeloes Road is a turning off Lewisham Way, then called Lewisham High Road) is playing for Braunton. The doctor, who is of course Henry's naturalist friend Dr Wright, waits to finish the match before coming to examine Loetitia. He advises Henry to take her to the midwife. Henry goes out and makes his way to 'Valentine's square of yellow blind opposite the churchyard'. (For some reason he chose to rechristen my father Valentine, although he referred to my mother by her true name, Ruth.)

In the next few pages Henry indulges in the sort of extravagant, mocking hilarity of which he was sometimes capable, both in his writing and in daily life. His entry into Chertsey Cottage is greeted by the dull boom of a bottle of home-made beer exploding. According to Henry, my father made this beer in the tin bath in which, as he arrives, my parents are bathing me in front of the fire. (I was in fact bathed in an enamelled hip bath.) Having extracted considerable fun from the beer-brewing, he enjoys some more with my father's sturdy Trojan.

This car, like most examples of that remarkable model, with their unmistakable, quiet, putt-putting engine note and their solid tyres, was very reliable. During the past summer it had carried five adults and a child, without mishap, on an extended tour of France, reaching the foothills of the Pyrenees and the Alps. Henry's description of the repeated stalling of the smoking engine which, when going, made a noise like a coffee-grinding machine, might have been appropriate to the unlamented Arrol Johnston; it hardly fits a fairly new Trojan.

Once Loetitia had been safely delivered to the care of the midwife,

Henry returned with my parents to Chertsey Cottage, after fetching a celebratory bottle of port from Vale House. The drinking of the port was accompanied by one of the long, inconclusive arguments that were a feature of their friendship. Henry claimed to dread these arguments, usually about 'social reform, war, unemployment and the general impracticability of my theories'. They gave him the feeling of being torn internally. 'I was as obstinate and tenacious as he was, but whereas he enjoyed argument and contradictions, I felt it a spoliation of life itself. Yet I was not firm enough to resist arguing about what was, in truth, unreasonable: for one cannot truly argue about one's emotional beliefs . . . I was foolish to maintain (these arguments) for Valentine was a friendly cheerful fellow, without a thought of harm to anyone in his head. Most evenings I left his cottage vowing to myself that I would never return; but always that friendly cheerfulness drew me back'.

My mother, too, dreaded these arguments; her peaceable nature urged her to try to divert the minds of the disputants to less provocative subjects. Yet on one winter evening she herself offended Henry, though unintentionally. As a thrifty form of fuel, a sackful of sea-worn pieces of bark of the sort then washed ashore in quantities had been brought back from the beach. While Henry was reading aloud she threw a shovelful on the fire, forgetting that, though dry, they would be impregnated with salt. They cracked and spat and hissed and shot great sparks across the room. Henry got up and stalked out of the house, slamming the door; he did not return for some days.

On the night of his first child's birth he went home to Vale House about midnight, and lay awake for a time, thinking of past and future, especially the future of the child; '. . . my eyes started tears of remorse for past unkindnesses, rough words, to my mother, to Loetitia, to my sisters, to Valentine, and others'.

In the morning, characteristically, he walked the three miles over the hills to Braunton, to find Loetitia safely delivered of a son. Christened Henry, he was always known as Windles, deriving from the repeated query 'Windees, dear, Windees?' when he cried with wind pains. One of Henry's first reactions on seeing the baby was that of the ever-observant writer: he noted 'with sudden eagerness of a new authentic detail for the book of the London cousins to be written in future years, that the nails of the baby's hand were perfectly formed, and his palm was already fully lined and creased'. Here is an indication that, even before he had finished the last volume of *The Flax of Dream*, he was already planning a book that would grow into the much longer sequence, *A Chronicle of Ancient Sunlight*.

A page from Henry Williamson's early notebook: see page 31.

CHAPTER FOUR

Tarka the Otter and the Hawthornden Prize

On moving from Skirr Cottage to Vale House, Henry took over as his writing place a room above the garage that had been built between the house and the containing wall of the raised garden. It was a light room with windows on two sides, a door into the garden and another, with glass panels, leading by way of a tiny balcony to one of the bedrooms. From this balcony, Henry claimed, he would sometimes fire his double-barrelled shotgun at the weathercock on the church tower, fortunately just out of range.

On wet days, the rain drummed noisily on the corrugated iron roof. There, usually at night, Henry went on with *Tarka;* the twelfth version, he was to record later. He had a crystal set on which he could listen to music. Since boyhood he had been drawn to music, especially that of the nineteenth and early twentieth century romantic composers – Wagner above all, but also Schumann, Chopin, Dvorak, Grieg, César Franck, Delius and Elgar. In London, after the war, he had been able to go to concerts and to Covent Garden; now he had to make do with whatever broadcasts of classical music he could tune in to, although he also bought records to play on an old Decca portable gramophone.

On his shelves were the books he valued – Jefferies above all, not only *The Story of my Heart* and *Bevis,* but *The Amateur Poacher, Life in the* Fields and others. In poetry, as in music, his taste was for the Romantics – Shelley and Francis Thompson's essay on Shelley, Keats, Blake and Francis Thompson's own poems. The classical temper in art seems never to have had any appeal for him; he was himself by temperament supremely and, one might say, superbly a Romantic, almost a throw-back to the heyday of the Romantic

Movement. Not for nothing did he give the hero of his novel *The Gold Falcon* the Byronic name Manfred.

During 1926 Henry went on with the writing and re-writing of *Tarka*. A note at the end of the published book records that it was begun in June, 1923, and finished in February, 1927, but he had, of course, written much else during those four years. He was still verifying facts about the life and habits of otters; in *Devon Holiday* he describes a visit he made to Dartmoor in January, 1926, with Robin Hibbert, the youngest of Loetitia's brothers; on the night after Windles' birth, he says, he and Robin got drunk on port and the next day, after breakfast at the house of Clibby Thomas, walked off their hangovers on Halsinger Down, some five miles east of Georgeham. They rode to Dartmoor on the Norton; afterwards, Henry claimed, he wrote thirty-seven versions of the Cranmere chapter of *Tarka*. Unusually, Henry did not include a dedication, but the 1933 edition, with C. F. Tunnicliffe's fine illustrations, is dedicated to Loetitia – not by name, but as 'Windles' Mother'.

In 1926 it was not his books that were profitable; none of his novels had as yet earned its advance, and the collections of stories 'of the wild birds and animals observed in the fervours of boyhood and youth' had done little better. With freelance journalism he was more successful. Since the day when he had been excited at the news that 'The Peregrine's Saga' had earned five hundred dollars, a number of such stories had been sold on both sides of the Atlantic. They provided a moderate income for a couple who, like so many in those days, were quite content with a standard of living which by today's mercenary and materialistic standards would be disdained as poverty.

Within a few months of his marriage, Henry was lamenting that his life with Loetitia was not altogether happy 'in part for causes which probably go back to my childhood; and also for differences of mind and nature. Loetitia was serene, because not too quickly imaginative; I was often agitated, because vividly imaginative . . . though in my own way I was tenacious'.

With the birth of Windles things did not improve. When he had longed for his 'mother-maiden', Henry had not considered that when maiden became mother, her maternal feelings would be directed primarily towards her child. When he came to write *The Pathway,* he would show Willie Maddison, on Saunton beach with Mary Ogilvie, drawing a circle on the sand to enclose them and saying that he was exorcising unhappiness. 'Creating a new world, with you and me in it only. And the circle is made up of two halves'. But by the time he wrote that, there was a third in the circle, and to his dismay Henry soon found that he was, in effect, jealous of the newcomer. 'The mother and son in the house with me were living in their own shared world . . .'

The first few weeks of Windles' life were in any case unhappy ones: Loetitia developed cystitis, and lay in bed feverish and unable to feed the baby. Henry was to describe a number of times, in interviews and in his autobiographical books, how he wrote the seventeenth and final version of *Tarka,* late at night, with the baby cradled in the crook of his left arm, so that Loetitia might sleep. (In *The Dark Lantern* he was to show Richard Maddison cradling Phillip in a similar way while he copied the journal he had found after his father's death.) That Henry re-wrote *Tarka* seventeen time was not, for him, exceptional. All his manuscripts and galley proofs preserved in Exeter University Library show that every one of his books went through numerous re-writings and revisions. Astonishingly, it may be seen that there are twenty versions of *Lucifer Before Sunrise.* Nevertheless, it can hardly have been the final version of *Tarka* he was writing in February, 1926, if he did not finish the book for nearly another twelvemonth.

Henry claimed that he did all the cooking, housework and washing during Loetitia's illness, but he had regular help from a village girl, and friends lent a hand. My mother made a contribution by doing some washing and ironing; in the rather dark kitchen of Vale House a primus stove hissed, heating one flat iron while another was in use. While a pile of warm, clean linen grew on the table I played with an assortment of toys, or wandered out into the wintry garden to look down into the village street some six or seven feet below. I have no recollection of seeing Henry on these occasions. Perhaps he was in his writing room, or out somewhere with his spaniel.

When Loetitia was well again and the baby, fed on Savory and Moore's patent food, was beginning to thrive, Henry regretted that her household preoccupations kept her from being the companion he had dreamed of. For the most part, he went for walks alone, but felt that it was not the same as in the old days before his marriage. 'I had been solitary then, and on my walks had felt myself one with the spirit of the sky, the sea, and the green earth dear; the coming of Loetitia had seemed the consummation of their spirit. But now I was lonely, and somehow the evening fields had lost their serenity'.

In that summer of 1926, and the next, we sometimes met Henry and Loetitia on Putsborough beach, with Windles, and shared a picnic fire of driftwood. We took a kettle and tea things in the car, while Henry as usual insisted on walking. From a hole in the rocks at the back of the beach a tiny spring of fresh water flowed; someone – perhaps Henry – had fixed a short length of pipe in the hole to make kettle-filling easier. On dry sand a fire would burn brightly in a little hearth of stones, the kettle propped over it. In September, reassured because there was an R in the month, we might collect mussels from the rocks at the foot of the cliffs running out towards Baggy Point and, after the kettle had been boiled for tea, refill it to boil mussels, which we ate with vinegar and bread and butter.

The beach seemed to become Henry's personal domain when he was with us. He had, after all, laid claim to it as his Eden in 1914 and 1916 when, a wandering Adam, he had had it to himself. On top of a pyramidal rock he had cemented a diving platform, usable only when the tide was high; the wet cement had been carried down in a bucket on the Norton. Under another, much larger group of rocks, the sea often scooped out a deep tunnel, some four yards long; each receding tide left it full of water. Halfway along, a shaft through the rock gave a dim light. I often contemplated this tunnel with awe, having been told that Henry, for a bet, had once swum along it.

He loved to swim and leap through the breakers that curled and burst into brilliant, hissing foam and ran whispering up the beach. Afterwards he enjoyed what he called 'seaweed-slinging and pool-splashing fun' with my father, behaviour which surprised me: here were grown-ups playing like children. As an isolated only child, I had hardly encountered such delights.

At home, Henry still deplored his realisation that he was becoming 'almost chronically irritable with Loetitia' and that he had brought her from her former 'gentle life' to 'a completely strange environment of ideas, with almost perpetual girding against the present human world.' She can have had little suspicion, before her marriage, of what life with Henry would be like, although he may have warned her, as Willie Maddison warns Mary Ogilvie in *The Pathway,* that he would make her unhappy.

Henry saw that a split had developed in him in childhood: between his fretful and resentful attitude to his life at school and at home, and his joyful absorption in every aspect of the country places in which he spent all the time he could; between his love for his mother – which he saw as being comparable to that of D. H. Lawrence for his mother – and his lack of affection for his father. Then, ironically, '. . . when about the age of thirty I found the traits which as a boy and youth I had hated in my father, developing in myself, I found my sympathy, or understanding – for sympathy not based on understanding is spurious – turning towards my father. I saw all the reasons why he had been so vexed, so upset, so irritable, so lonely; and thereafter I had little patience with my mother. This grieved me, but I could not help it'.

He was writing this in the late Thirties. Nearly a quarter of a century later he was to give to Richard Maddison, grown dissatisfied with his young wife, 'a sympathy denied to him during his father's life. He realised now, through his own experience of being married, that his father had had a lot to put up with from a wife who had not really been able to share his life, but had thought only of the children'.

As Henry stated in a television interview that Phillip Maddison in *A Chronicle of Ancient Sunlight* was himself, it follows that Richard Maddison is Henry's perception of his father, William Williamson; in which case Richard's father, the spendthrift, bibulous and womanising Captain Maddison, who is said to be deliberately cruel to his wife and children and is feared and hated by Richard (in one striking episode in *The Dark Lantern* Richard, visiting the neighbourhood of Rookhurst, in which he grew up, jumps over a hedge and hides behind it to avoid his father, seen approaching in the distance – and he is at this time a man of twenty-five or so) is based on William Williamson's father, Henry William Williamson. If this is the case, it offers a tragic example of the way in which, not the sins, but the neuroses of the fathers may be visited upon the children, quite literally unto the third and fourth generation. As Windles grew up, he would in his turn develop a resentment, and sometimes, as Henry recorded in *The Children of Shallowford,* a fear, of his father.

In October, 1927, Putnam published *Tarka the Otter* in an edition of eleven hundred copies, only one thousand of which were for public sale. The remaining hundred had been printed on handmade paper, bound in vellum and numbered and signed by the author, for sale to subscribers. The diplomatic dedication was to W. R. Rogers, Master of the Cheriton Otter Hounds, who had given Henry much helpful advice.

To Henry's great pleasure, Sir John Fortescue agreed to write an introduction. Sir John, born at Castle Hill, Filleigh, was the fifth

Henry Williamson with Arthur and Phyllis Brown in about 1920 (sitting on the mounting block outside Sunnyside Cottage, Georgeham, where he was temporarily staying).

Looking downhill from the Kings Arms, Georgeham, past the churchyard in the 1920s. Chertsey Cottage is opposite the lychgate.

Skirr Cottage, Georgeham, in the 1920s.

Vale House (later Crowberry Cottage), Georgeham, in the 1920s.

The Williamson and Lamplugh families on Putsborough beach in 1927. Henry Williamson, in the foreground, characteristically ignores the camera; his spaniel Billjohn lies beside him. The wearer of the toque is Mrs Richard Lamplugh.

Loetitia Williamson and Windles, 1927.

Henry Williamson on a Canadian river in 1930.

son of the third Earl Fortescue (and ninth child of a family of fourteen). Deprived of a hoped-for military career by poor eyesight, he had become a scholar; he was librarian of Windsor Castle. In 1927 he was approaching the end of his great thirteen-volume *History of the British Army,* begun in 1899. Yet it was a quite different book, *The Story of a Red Deer,* written at the request of a nephew two years before he began his *History,* that Henry admired. (His eager recommendation of it to my grandmother resulted in her giving me, for my birthday in 1928, a copy of the handsome edition Macmillan brought out in 1925, with illustrations by G. D. Armour.)

In his introduction, Sir John remarked that the biographers of animals were apt to 'endow their heroes and heroines with human attributes, and to make them think as human beings. I am myself a sinner in this respect, and it is in consequence of this sin that I am asked to introduce to the public Mr Williamson's far sounder and deeper biography of Tarka the Otter. If I have any claim to take by the hand the one whose excellent work enables him very well to walk by himself, it is rather because I am an historian of one phase of human nature and in that capacity have been driven to exercise observation and imagination'.

The element of anthropomorphism in *The Story of a Red Deer* is certainly greater than in *Tarka.* Sir John's animals talk among themselves, and there are class distinctions, the patrician deer, salmon and pheasant speaking standard English, while foxes, rabbits and other creatures speak the broad Devon of western Exmoor. Nevertheless, Henry was inevitably accused by some of attributing thoughts, and above all human feelings, to his animals. He did it because he wanted to, and defied purists who complained; his sense of empathy with wild creatures made it impossible for him to write in any other way. As a young man, at least, he had little patience with scientific naturalists, despite his friendship with Dr Wright. The theory that bird song was exclusively territorial jarred on him. In *The Pathway* he allows Willie Maddison to dismiss the idea, saying that it is 'an empty snail shell, and probably came from some young writer trying to be original'. To him, bird song expressed joy and love; in the stories in his early nature books he may be accused of sentimentality in such passages as: 'A long-tailed tit was gathering the down from the hazel catkins, calling, or rather, murmuring, in shy ecstatic love to her mate as she did so . . . I watched the two birds, so happy with each other, and heedless of anything but the immediate joyful moment . . . The ecstatic little titmice were not alarmed by my presence; I stood within two yards of their nest, but they flew into the hedge and out again without fear or distress'.

In *Tarka* he speaks of swallows as 'joyous and pure in spirit, and alien to the ways of man'; he was convinced of this joyfulness in the life of all animals other than man; this is the reason for the subtitle of *Tarka:* 'His joyful water-life and death in the country of the Two Rivers'. His cast of mind being what it was, his view of nature remained that of the Romantic. At the same time his knowledge of plants, birds, animals and the weathers and seasons which governed their lives steadily grew, and his confidence with it.

Tarka is an extraordinary feat of sustained imaginative visualis-ation. During the last thirty years or so we have grown used to the marvellous results of patient camera work showing minute details of all kinds of natural life on the television screen – yet Henry's intensely perceptive eyes and his transforming mind filmed his otter's life, as it were, long before modern techniques were developed. At the end of his life Tarka was at last made into a film by David Cobham, with a script which Cobham wrote in collaboration with Gerald Durrell. It is a sensitive production, faithfully, lovingly and beautifully presented – yet in a sense it was an impossible under-taking; nothing could wholly replace the precise and evocative images of every page of the book.

Once it was complete Henry did not immediately turn to anything else; no doubt he felt a combination of relief and weariness. Then, suddenly, he took up *The Pathway* again. The immediate stimulus, he said, was a film, 'The Somme'. This was shown at the Theatre Royal, Barnstaple, on the 2nd, 3rd and 4th of February, 1928; billed as 'The finest War Film ever made', it was shown by permission of the Army Council. Henry took Loetitia to see it, but emerged indignant; he considered that it had been 'wickedly, that is ignorantly, made'. It sent him at once 'to the world of my inner self, which had been deserted since my marriage'.

It would seem that during the period of dormancy the story of *The Pathway* had become fully developed in his subconscious mind. Certainly its resumption produced one of those remarkable bursts of creativity of which he was often capable; he recalled writing all night, all the following day and into the second night. When at last he paused to rest, 'My being was filled with deep content'. He finished the book, he said, after a month of hard, continuous writing.

He called Willie Maddison his *doppelgänger*, and made a distinction between the Maddison of Part One and of the remainder of the book; the latter, he said many years later, had become 'irritable and haggard, a ranter at times, immediately remorseful, but doomed by his own nature'. It is however difficult to discern much difference; even in Part One, in his first days at Wildernesse Manor, Maddison excitedly declaims his ideas on war and religion, and is in a nervous, unhappy state of mind. Henry had second thoughts about the ending. In *The Sun in the Sands,* he says that on a walk with 'Julian Warbeck' above 'a tract of wide and far-lying sandhills' (Saunton Burrows), he looked towards the distant estuary and exclaimed that that was where Maddison was to die. A few weeks later he was writing in his diary that he had decided to give the tetralogy a happy ending: 'A new Europe shall arise out of the ruins of the old; and Maddison's triumph shall be the formula for the new way of thought . . . Maddison . . . refuses to die, to be drowned, to be crucified . . . By power of his personality, his genius, he is going to pull through, he is going to give a new idea to others!'

By 1928 he had returned to his original intention: Maddison, a Christ-figure (significantly the book's epigraph is 'I am the way . . .') has to become a sacrifice. Although the Christ parallel might suggest that Henry was indulging in delusions of divinity, he always made it clear that Jesus was, to him, simply an inspired visionary, to be numbered among those who acted as 'light-bringers' to humanity. In Henry's individualistic creed, these light-bringers were mostly creative artists, and in the years after the war he began to believe that he was one of them, which is why he make Willie Maddison tell Mary Ogilvie that he used to think he was a Christ, and explains to the local vicar that 'If Jesus was human, and of course he was . . . there is hope for us who are human, for we can become Christs while we are on earth'.

On a merely practical level, the stage-managing of Willie's death is not altogether satisfactory; the ebb tide in the Taw-Torridge estuary can sweep a swimmer out into Barnstaple Bay to his death very quickly, but Willie necessarily goes out at dead low water to stand on the Sharshook (Middle Ridge) to wait for the salmon boats to come in. Even at night he would have been able to see that, although the boats were not coming, the rising tide was and, as it has been shown that he can swim, he would have made rapidly for the shore. Even if he had left it very late he would have stood a reasonable chance of being carried upriver to some point where he could land.

However, it suited Henry's purpose that Willie should die; the period of his life which the character represented was over. There is irony in the fact that the sorrowing Mary – for whom Loetitia was the avowed model – is made to cry out, 'He was too good for us, and so he was taken away'. His cousin Phillip caps this with, 'If we had understood him better, he would not have needed to go away at all' – suggesting that Willie's death was suicide.

Julian Warbeck, who happens to be present, quotes Swinburne's 'Itylus', somewhat irrelevantly. He wants to cremate the body, Shelley-fashion, in a huge fire made by smashing up a beach hut but – a bathetic touch – only Willie's dog, drowned with his master, is incinerated.

The book ends with Mary 'thinking of the darkness of men's minds, pierced in vain by the shining light of Kristos, and of the agony of Christ, at the end of the Pathway'.

In adolescence I found this ending moving; re-read in later years, it seemed merely mawkish. A reader can hardly avoid a feeling of discomfort when a character in a novel who is admittedly based on the author is fulsomely praised or reverenced by other characters.

The novel has no dedication. Originally it was to have had what Henry called 'a dedication on two planes . . . . 1. To the son, and the Mother, in the hope that the pathway to the Light lies in the sun. 2. To Zoroaster, Jesus, Paul, Shelley, Blake, Hardy, Jefferies, Lenin, Shaw (T. E. and G. B.)'. Fortunately, 'prudence, and the experience of literary critics' caused this to be struck out in proof. The list offers interesting evidence of the 'lightbringers' of that stage of his life.

The overall title of the complete tetralogy, *The Flax of Dream*, puzzled many readers. In a foreword to the one-volume edition brought out by Faber in 1936, Henry explained that it was taken from a book, *The Incalculable Hour*, written by an aunt in 1910.[1] The passage quoted from this book is interesting, both for its content – a yearning for some kind of vague spiritual regeneration in the world – and its style, which here and there resembles that of the young Henry Williamson. The essential paragraph runs: 'Our Land of Heart's desire is woven of our own thoughts and longings and emotions, and no two weave alike. And it is well if, returning thence, we bring with us gifts worthy of acceptance. For many, to whom the Weaver gives the flax of Dream, weave hurriedly, and the web is spoilt. It needs time to gather the joy and sorrow, the love and suffering, the wisdom that go to make the perfect design; and through all the weft of it must run the thread of self-sacrifice like a scarlet flame, touching it to inconceivable beauty.'

The original headings of the three parts of *The Dream of Fair Women* were evidently taken from this passage.

The aunt's name – or the name under which she had her forty-page book produced by the printers, Hazel, Watson and Viney – was J. Quiddington West. One may suspect that Henry drew her portrait as Theodora Maddison, Phillip's aunt, in *A Chronicle of Ancient Sunlight*. A graduate of Girton with a degree in Classics, Aunt Dora is an admirer of Pestalozzi, a Suffragette who suffers under the Cat and Mouse Act, and a self-sacrificing worker for unpopular causes, who eventually withdraws to live in a cottage in Lynmouth. She introduces Phillip to the works of Shelley and Francis Thompson. (Henry said in a broadcast in 1961, in the series 'World of Books', that he first read Thompson's poems in Flanders in 1917, in a volume sent him by an aunt.) Whatever her real life story, it would be interesting to know how much the author of *The Incalculable Hour* (who, like Aunt Dora, spent some years in Greece) and her ideas influenced Henry in his boyhood and youth.

When he spoke to Collins about *The Pathway,* he met with a rebuff: they did not want it. The poor sales of the first three novels told against it; they would not even read and consider it. Henry had no need to worry. His faithful agent, Andrew Dakers, had no difficulty in placing the novel. Jonathan Cape's reader, Edward Garnett, the most eminent, perceptive and revered of publishers' readers, was already interested. George Jefferson, in his biography of Garnett, recalls that as early as 1926, after the publication of *The Old Stag,* Galsworthy had written to Garnett recommending Henry as a 'strange and sensitive nature lover . . . he can see and he can write'. As a result, Garnett had written to Henry enquiring – too late – about *Tarka*. It is therefore surprising that, in the eleventh volume of *A Chronicle of Ancient Sunlight, The Power of the Dead,* Henry portrayed both Garnett and Galsworthy – but especially Garnett – in far from flattering terms, as Edward Cornelian and Thomas Morland. Never one to welcome advice, it is probable that he resented Garnett's suggestions for revising *The Pathway,* and resented also Garnett's opinion that when he eventually began his 'novels of the London cousins', he should do so in 1914, not the 1890s. More importantly, he advised Jonathan Cape against taking over the three earlier novels making up *The Flax of Dream.*

By the time *The Pathway* appeared in the autumn of 1928, Henry's

status as an author had changed: in June, it was announced that
Tarka the Otter had been awarded the Hawthornden Prize for
Literature for 1927. He wanted to broadcast the news to everyone
he met, both those who had doubted him and those who, like my
parents, had believed in him. We had moved from Georgeham
during the previous year – only a mile down the valley, but it meant
that Henry could no longer hurry across from Vale House to
Chertsey Cottage on the spur of the moment with confidences,
anecdotes of village life, or a few newly-written chapters to be read
aloud. However, he rushed down to our long bungalow on the road
to Croyde (it had once been a miniature rifle range) in ebullient
spirits to pass on his news soon after he had received it. The
presentation, he said, was to be at the Aeolian Hall; he was
delighted that it was to be by John Galsworthy. He recalled reading
the *Forsyte Saga* in Shorncliffe Camp, Folkestone, in the last months
of 1918, and feeling that he had been aware of everything the author
had felt while writing the novels. Moreover, Galsworthy was a
Devonian, a man whose ancestors had lived for centuries in the
parish of Buckland Brewer, a village in north-west Devon lying
between Clovelly and Great Torrington (he is said to have based
many of the characters in the *Saga* on members of his family) and
who had himself lived for a number of years at Manaton, on the
eastern border of Dartmoor.

The ceremony received a fair amount of notice in the press, partly,
perhaps, because Galsworthy was then regarded as one of Britain's
greatest living writers (he was to receive the Order of Merit in 1929
and the Nobel Prize for Literature in 1933, the year of his death.). In
his speech Galsworthy called *Tarka* 'a truly remarkable creation . . .
the result of stupendous imaginative concentration, fortified by
endlessly patient and loving observation of nature'. The 'Daily
Telegraph', under the heading 'A Romance of Literature', gave the
event more than half a column, and printed one of Henry's nature
sketches, 'With a Boy on the Headland', from *The Lone Swallows*.
Reporters sought interviews, and Henry happily told them about the
seventeen versions, Loetitia's illness and his care of Windles while he
wrote at night.

For ten years, since the last months of his army service, Henry
had been striving towards this moment: the recognition he had
craved was now his, and with it came increased sales of his books
and thus a greater financial security. He knew at once what he
wanted to buy with his hundred pounds prize money. He had long

been drawn to a field and copse by the crossroads called Oxford Cross, at the top of the hill leading northwards out of Georgeham. The name Oxford Cross appears on nineteenth century maps, but Henry would have none of it; he insisted that it was the result of an Ordnance surveyor's mis-hearing, in Edwardian days, of a stone-cracker's pronunciation of Ox's Cross, because it had been where drovers rested their oxen. Ox's Cross remained his name for it. The field that attracted him, once apparently part of the Pickwell Manor estate, was called Down Close; Henry was to give this name to the house in Dorset in which Lucy Copleston lives with her father and brothers in *It Was the Nightingale*.

During his unforgotten holiday in 1914, Henry had often climbed the hill on his way to explore the abandoned iron mines in the Spreacombe Valley. More recently, he and Loetitia had visited the field again and again; they talked of owning it, camping in it, perhaps building a hut there . . .

Now this dream was one he could fulfil. He went to the owner and made an offer; it was accepted, and Henry wrote the cheque. The field on his 'hill of winds', as he liked to call it, was his. From there, five hundred feet above sea level, he could look west to his beloved headland, Baggy, and south across a range of hills to the Taw-Torridge estuary, and out to the great promontory of Hartland.

The field was to be his hold-fast for the rest of his life. Even when he moved away, first from Georgeham, later from Devon, he would come back again and again. After the Second World War he would return to live in it. He built the hut he wanted, and other huts, and brought to them wives, children, friends, lovers. It became his refuge from the self-made storms of his personal saga, his sanctuary from the daemon that drove him, and above all his preferred writing place in which book after book was drafted or revised or brought to completion.

CHAPTER FIVE

The Move to Shallowford, Filleigh

Henry claimed to know exactly when and where his second son, John, had been conceived: during an early spring-time walk 'in a little plantation of salt-ruined firs and lichened ash and chestnut trees' on Pickwell Down. For the birth of this baby, Loetitia chose a nursing home in Barnstaple, to which Henry was able to drive her himself; he had bought a six horse-power Peugeot out of *Tarka* royalties. John was born on 29th October, 1928, and this date is the title of chapter six of the original version of *The Children of Shallowford*.

According to Henry's account of events, he met my parents in Barnstaple on that day, and they invited him to visit them in the evening. Henry arrived with a copy of *The Pathway,* which he said had been published that very day. He proceeded to read it aloud to an audience of four – two cousins of my father's were staying with us. (I had been despatched to bed, as too young for late night readings.) Needing little encouragement, he read on and on. Pots of tea were made and drunk, batches of sandwiches cut and eaten, he said, 'and still the story flowed on, through the small hours of the new day and only when the dawn was rising in the clear eastern sky above the hills was it finished'. On that night, Henry claimed, he and my father won each other's respect. 'In the history of Maddison, the unknown soldier, we both saw an image of our hopes and dreams, we who once were young soldiers, but now were commonplace fathers of families'.

At that time, however, as the author of eight published books, one of which had been awarded a prestigious prize, Henry was more than ever aware that he at least was not commonplace. Already readers were beginning to be drawn to Georgeham in the hope of seeing the author of *Tarka the Otter*. Some called at Vale House and, according to Henry, drank beer with him and stayed to lunch, to supper, and overnight, returning later for weekends and bringing friends with them. Loetitia, he said, 'cheerfully cooked and served the extra food'. Nevertheless, Henry jibbed when village children began to conduct holiday visitors to his door to ask for autographs. Improved roads were bringing more and more people to the area every summer. At Putsborough, above the once-deserted Vention Sands, a hotel of sorts was being built, largely of asbestos sheeting; nearby a small bungalow called Dolce far Niente arose. Cars drove down the steep lane to the beach; Henry reported gleefully that one or two could not drive up again, and had to be hauled up by horses. He lamented that the places he had known and written about were all changing. The attitude of the villagers towards him was changing too. Once he had been a sort of local jester, an enjoyable subject for laughter and gossip, an oddity: as he himself expressed it, 'an author of sorts who was always talking about fame and success and yet remained steadily unfamous and unsuccessful'. Now a measure of success and fame had arrived. and some of his less worldly-wise Devonshire neighbours resented it – especially as they exaggerated the amount of money his books were bringing him. By a strange process of reasoning they concluded that some of the money was owed to them: had they not given him material for animal stories – as he had publicly acknowledged – and had they not appeared as characters in his sketches of village life?

It was Henry's nature to be restless; after eight years in Georgeham he might in any case have begun to fret for new surroundings. On visits to my parents, he began to speak of needing new stimulus for his work; Georgeham was 'written out'. It was time to move; but where?

He already knew Castle Hill, Filleigh, on the road from Barnstaple to South Molton; the birthplace of Sir John Fortescue who had written the introduction to *Tarka*. One day in 1929 Henry heard that a cottage on the Fortescue estate was to let. According to one account, he was told of this by his dentist while having a tooth filled; according to another, he simply saw an advertisement in the local weekly paper. Whichever it was, his attention was caught by one detail: two miles of trout fishing in the Bray went with the cottage. He had not fished since his adolescence, when he had cycled from Brockley to Kentish lakes and rivers; the idea of taking up the sport again excited him. With Loetitia he visited the cottage, which was of a fair size, with four bedrooms and four downstairs rooms. It had been built as three adjoining cottages, and converted into one by the clerk of works of the estate.

They walked into the deer park of Castle Hill. Henry stood on the little hump-backed ornamental bridge, which still exists; seeing trout in the water below him, he 'experienced a feeling that the day was fixed immortally, for ever, in blue space. For a moment I was back in the summer of boyhood. Water, mysterious water, was speaking to me again'.

After looking over the cottage, they went to the agent's office and declared themselves eager to take the house and the fishing. The total rent, exclusive of rates, was £60 a year.

In due course Henry had an appointment to meet the 'shy old nobleman', the fourth Earl Fortescue, and was told that his application for the tenancy was approved. At Michaelmas, 1929, he was free to begin redecorating the cottage, with the help of an apparently reformed alcoholic, an old soldier who had often been given shelter by the rector of Georgeham between drinking bouts. In the original version of *The Children of Shallowford,* Henry portrayed him as Coneybeare, and called him his butler-handyman; in *A Clear Water Stream* he referred to him more grandly as 'my manservant'. Corney, Manfred's devoted ex-batman in *The Gold Falcon* and Rippingall in *The Phoenix Generation* are other portrayals of this servant, who proved himself unsatisfactory and slovenly. One morning, soon after a party at Shallowford, Coneybeare and, by his own account, Henry, got very drunk in the small hours of the morning. Coneybeare departed before daybreak and did not return to the Williamson household.

He was replaced by the former housekeeper of an eccentric sportsman, Arthur Heinemann, who had at one time been Master of the Cheriton Otterhounds, and was a cousin of the publisher, William Heinemann. This lady, Anne Rawle, was known as Galloping Annie; she had been whipper-in to hounds during the First World War. She too did not stay for very long. In her stead came a 'plump little local cottage woman' to whom Henry gave the name Mrs. Ridd; she was cheerful, kindly and efficient, which must have been an immense relief to Loetitia: when her daughter Margaret was born – again at a Barnstaple nursing home – on April 15th, 1930, Windles was just four and John eighteen months old.

For the third time, the birth of one of Henry's children more or less coincided with the publication of one of his books: his remarkable evocation of the experiences of a private soldier on the Somme, *Patriot's Progress,* was brought out by Geoffrey Bles in April, 1930.

The genesis of this book was unusual. At about the time he was finishing *The Pathway,* Henry had been in touch with the Australian-born artist, William Kermode. Kermode is most widely known for his illustrations to that quirky, short, perennial seller, *The Specialist,* by Charles Sale, the celebration of a privy builder, which was published by Putnam in New York in 1930. In the 1920s Kermode, an ex-soldier, produced more than a hundred woodcuts – or more precisely linocuts – of scenes of the First World War. It was his hope that they should be published with captions by Henry. Henry, once he had seen the woodcuts, decided that the collaboration should take a different form. He would write a story around the ideas aroused by Kermode's work, which could then be used as illustrations.

To accord with the wishes of the demanding author, Kermode found himself having to re-draw a number of his scenes of war. His style has been described as deliberately crude and archaic, possibly influenced by the German 'Die Brücke' group of 1905-1915. The ten dozen or so linocuts that appear in *Patriot's Progress* are certainly crude, wooden and sparse in detail, yet in their starkness, they convey the barbarism of the war with economy and force.

The story they accompany is simple in outline and, for Henry, very short; it runs to some 35,000 words, or a quarter of the average length of his other novels. It is divided into five sections headed 'First Phase', Second Phase' and so on. The choice of a name for the central character, John Bullock, indicates that he is intended as a representative figure.

John Bullock is a youth of eighteen or nineteen in 1914; he has had a Council School Education and works as a junior clerk in an office in the City. He joins the Army at the outbreak of war and, after undergoing the usual training of an infantryman, is posted to what seems to be a reserve battalion encamped somewhere on Salisbury Plain. Incredibly enough, as he and his companions are all young and fit, they are not drafted to a regiment in France until September, 1916. They serve for a short time in a northern sector of the Front and then see action on the Somme. In the autumn of 1917 John Bullock, transferred to a hutted camp near Poperinghe, experiences German air raids and earns fourteen days' field punish-

ment for being drunk and missing parade, before his battalion is
sent in to the attack in the third battle of Ypres. John's leg is shot
off and he survives two days in No Man's Land, followed by rough
and ready first aid treatment and a jolting ambulance journey to the
base hospital. In England he slowly recovers. 'The stump healed
clean. He grew fat and happy, and lost all interest in the war. Never
wanted to hear of it again. It hadn't been such a bad time, taken all
round: he wouldn't have missed it, really. They said you could do a
lot on an artificial leg'. On November 11th, 1918, he is out in the
streets on crutches, to be told by an old man that he is a hero.
Assured that England won't forget 'you fellows', he smiles and
answers 'We are England'.

Henry's style in this book is very unlike that of anything he had
previously written; it bears no resemblance to the lyrical and
dithyrhambic language of, for instance, *The Flax of Dream* and his
early nature essays. 'First Phase' is written as a plain, relaxed
narrative; in Second, Third and Fourth Phases the tone sharpens,
the tempo in the battlefield scenes grows staccato and urgent. There
are moments of harsh beauty in the front line scenes by night, and
of gross horror in those of the death-sown morass of the repeatedly
fought-over battlefields. Arnold Bennett called the book a prose
work which of its kind had never been surpassed. In *Genius of
Friendship,* Henry was to refer to it as tedious hackwork, written
reluctantly and with curses that it had been undertaken; he had
'forced one bare word after another'. Halfway through he left it
aside for a year, disheartened by the enormous success of *All Quiet
on the Western Front.* When he was persuaded to finish it, he was
relieved to find that it sold 5,000 copies before publication.

Even before he had seen Kermode's illustrations, Henry had been
reliving the war by yet another visit to northern France and
Flanders. If the final paragraph of *The Sun in the Sands* is to be relied
on (and, as has been said, much of the later part of the book seems
to belong to the world of fiction) he ended his walking tour of the
Pyrenees in 1924 by travelling north to Albert and walking over the
battlefields he had known on the Somme 'with aching heart for all
things remembered in ancient sunlight but with hope for the
future'. His return on his honeymoon has been mentioned. In the
spring of 1927, perhaps soon after *Tarka* was finished, he travelled
to London to join one of the somewhat ghoulish organised parties
of sightseers who were escorted by couriers on tours of the
battlefields.

It is possible that the trip was the suggestion of the friend who went with him, an ex-Tank Corps officer whom Henry called, somewhat unamiably, Four Toes, because he had lost a toe from each foot through frostbite. However, in his introductory chapter, 'Apologia pro Vita Mea' in *The Wet Flanders Plain,* his account of this journey, Henry described standing in Georgeham church tower during bell ringing practice and being transported by the 'great sound' of the bells to 'the wide and shattered country of the Somme'. He decided he must return 'to my old comrades of the Great War – to the brown, the treeless, the flat and grave-set plain of Flanders, to the rolling, heat-miraged downlands of the Somme – for I am dead with them, and they live in me again'.

Waiting for a train on Calais station he remembered de-training at St. Omer in November, 1914, and regarding survivors of Mons with awe. '. . . the old soldier sees many things by which he may recall, with a sort of quiet glamorous melancholy, those days of the war which are almost romantic, because of their comradeship, activities, immense fears, turmoils, miseries, light-thralling barrages – dwelt on in the dimness of memory, now that he is safe, free and happy. Romantic! Yes, sometimes, late at night, the war is recalled with an indescribable feeling of immense haunting regret'. Elsewhere he referred to the years of the war as not so much terrible as 'full of such movement and excitation and comradeship that when they had passed the world seemed poor and dispirited'.

This tendency, in certain moods, to romanticise the war was to remain with Henry, though he would usually check it impatiently, as he makes Willie Maddison do in *The Pathway,* when, after remembering the frozen winter of 1916-17 on the Somme, he thinks '. . . they were great days – no, great only in memory, when only the glamour of stupendous and terrible scenes was recalled, and the spirit of friendship, and love, between men who were banded together . . . Great days! Christ! How easy to fall into false thought! . . . Ghastly days!'

He and his friend were invited by some other ex-officers to join them on charabanc rides around the Salient, and to Wytschaerte and Messines. They attended a service for the unveiling of a divisional memorial at Langemarck; they admired the Canadian memorial, to Henry the most beautiful thing in the Salient; they visited Hill 60. Left alone by his friend, who returned to England because his feet were painful, Henry visited St Leger, where German and English dead were disinterred by Flemish labourers for reburial in national cemeteries.

On his last day, in an estaminet in Miraumont, Henry told the patron and his wife, in his 'weak French', that he was meditating a novel, or novels, of the War, 'the story of an insignificant and obscure family which had helped, in its small way, to prepare and make the Great War'. Here, as in his account of his first sight of Windles, is an indication that he planned the novel sequence that would become *A Chronicle of Ancient Sunlight* while still at work on *The Flax of Dream*. He told the French couple that he would draw on his own experiences, as Henri Barbusse had done in *Le Feu*, and their faces lit up at the name of that author.

Le Feu, which was published in English as *Under Fire*, was a book that Henry admired greatly, and often recommended to anyone interested in knowing what it had been like to see active service in France.

When he walked near Thiepval Wood and saw the trenches 'like old mole runs', he was filled with 'indescribable emotion – the haunting of ancient sunlight'. After spending the night at an estaminet in the valley of the Ancre, he woke full of longing for his home, wife and child, and thankfully set off on his return journey. It may be noted that the phrase 'ancient sunlight', which recurs again and again in his books, and in the title of his last great novel sequence, was simply Henry's way of referring to the past. Jefferies, in *The Story of my Heart*, speaks of 'Sesostris on the most ancient sands of the south, in ancient, ancient days, was conscious of himself and of the sun. This sunlight linked me through the ages to that past consciousness'. Henry found in this an affirmation of something sensed, perhaps vaguely, since boyhood. The love of the sun shared by most of temperate-zone humanity acquired in him a mystical element; the feeling of regret for time present, measured by the sun, continually slipping into time past, had for him a more than ordinary keenness; and awareness of the sun as the chief source of life on earth was in him more constant and conscious than it is for most of us. Yet although he travelled occasionally to the Mediterranean, these were only holiday visits; nothing seems to have tempted him to spend his time in countries where he could have expected the sun to pour down on him daily: it was the *English* sun he loved. Nevertheless, when he came to write *The Gold Falcon*, although he said that the sun was 'the symbol for all things true and fair in human life', and used the phrase he repeated so often in conversation and in other books, 'the sun sees no shadows', he also revealed a temporary impatience with his solar obsession; he put into the mouth of the central character, Manfred Cloudesley, the self-criticism that he was dirty, indolent, and wrote of sunlight because he lived unnaturally.

His feeling for the recent past – he apparently had little liking for the history of academics – was intense. In *The Sun in the Sands* he remembered the May month before the war, when he discovered the derelict iron mines near Georgeham; he felt that 'my heart, or stomach nerves, ached; my eyes brimmed with tears. This was not crying; I had not cried since the time of being frozen in No Man's Land in December, 1914. No one else appeared to have these feelings for the past, although Delius the composer must know the haunting of what to myself I call ancient sunlight'.

Henry dedicated *The Wet Flanders Plain* to the war artist, C.R.W. Nevinson, whom he had met at the Cafe Royal, but he might well have paid tribute to his friend Christopher à Becket Williams, from whom he borrowed the title. Williams, a son of the Reverend Charles Williams, who was for many years Rector of Ashford, near Barnstaple, was both a composer and an author. Himself an ex-soldier, he wrote an elegy for piano in memory of a friend killed at the battle of Loos, and called it 'The Wet Flanders Plain'. He appears as Becket Scrimgeour in *The Phoenix Generation* and *Lucifer Before Sunrise*.

With the completion of these books Henry turned away, for more than twenty years, from the Great War as the major subject of a novel. As has been said, he was later thankful that he had not presented any view of it through the eyes of Willie Maddison, except as haunting memories briefly referred to.

In his first summer in Georgeham, Henry had enjoyed month after month of sunlit days. By contrast the winter of 1929-30 was one of the wettest for years. Beginning in November, 1929, Henry wrote six short pieces for the monthly 'London Magazine'; when he added them to the illustrated edition of *The Lone Swallows* in 1933, he grouped them under the title 'The Country of the Rain'. They show him going back to visit the places he had loved during the previous ten years: Saunton Burrows and Braunton Great Field and Putsborough.

He was not at work on a new book, despite his vague resolve that one day he would write his novel or novels about 'the London cousins'. He spoke of 'emptying interest in the country, of summer joys in the old village remembered with regret'. It rained, and it rained, and it rained, and he would go out to walk in the rain to the fringes of Exmoor – a distance of five or six miles from Filleigh, even as the buzzard might fly. He could not endure the house and 'the petty cares of one's own making'. He was now discovering one of the drawbacks of the house; although it faced south, for six or seven weeks in the depth of winter, its rooms were very dark; the wooded hill opposite cut off the light, and even on the occasional sunny day, no brightness reached them.

Even a good fire was lacking when, in wet clothes, he would come back to try to warm himself by the iron grate of the sitting room. This, he said, was an early Victorian and dreadful thing that drew all the heat of the fire up its chimney. He asked permission to put in a new hearth, and, when this was granted, gave a local mason detailed instructions. While the work was being done he went away. He seemed to have some kind of compulsion to absent himself at such times, instead of staying to see that his very precise wishes were fulfilled, thus inviting disappointments and occasions for rage. On his return to Shallowford he saw, with fury, that the worn blue slate slab, the only part of the old hearth he had wanted to preserve, was gone; in its place was a concrete surface. As this had not quite set hard, Henry scratched his owl symbol into it by way of consolation. (A somewhat self-consciously posed photograph of him warming his hands at this hearth provides a frontispiece to *The Linhay on the Downs*.)

In the person of Manfred Cloudesley, in *The Gold Falcon*, Henry was to give expression to his extreme sense of the importance of the domestic fireplace: 'Manfred's hearths were to him sacred; fire was a Power and a Mercy, arising as a spirit in its own authentic body'. Lighting a fire in Barbara Faithfull's apartment, Manfred vehemently refuses to use a kerosene lighter, calling it a foul thing; he even says that paper is abominable. In his essay 'Wood Fires' in The *Linhay on the Downs* he castigates the habit of burning green wood, saying that wood-stacks should be put down to mature like wine. Using this seasoned wood, the good fire is made 'only with love and forethought'. Even to see anyone using a pair of bellows in what he considered the wrong way infuriated him.

Unhappily the new hearth at Shallowford did not become a focus for family life: Henry was soon lamenting that he was sitting alone in his writing room upstairs, by a tiny hearth that tended to smoke, while Loetitia sat by the nursery fire. However, descriptions such as this of his dissatisfaction with the way his life was going appear only in the original version of *The Children of Shallowford;* he cut them from the considerably re-written second edition, and substituted other material.

The books he had written during the Georgeham years were providing an income, and Jonathan Cape had accepted a collection of the pieces describing Georgeham and Croyde and their people, *The Village Book*. This appeared in 1930 with a photograph of Henry in the doorway of Skirr Cottage, taken in 'the brilliant sun of drought, 1921'. He holds the spaniel puppies, Billjohn and his brother; the caption says that the former 'lived until February, 1930, when he was "done away with" for 2/6d, being full of misery, canker and suffering at the decline of walks and his master's care'.

The book, which Henry called 'pages of Field-air and Sea-light', was dedicated in gratitude for much help and encouragement and with 'love and respect' to Loetitia's grandmother, Mrs Hibbert. The village pages were dedicated to 'our old striding friend of the Sussex Downs, Petre Mais'. The 'Contents' pages are somewhat confusing, as some of the pieces are grouped under the heading, 'The Spirit of the Village', and others under 'Air and Light of the Fields and Sea', whereas in the body of the book the two groups are interspersed.

Petre Mais was the industrious journalist, novelist, broadcaster and lecturer, S. P. B. Mais – born, according to reference books, in Birmingham, but claiming links with north Devon through his father and other relations. Ten years older than Henry, he had a master's degree from Oxford and had spent some years as a schoolmaster before beginning to earn a living as a writer. He seems an unlikely friend for Henry, who had a distrust of academics coupled with a sense of deprivation, even inferiority, over his own lack of a university education.

They first met, according to Mais, on the 'Daily Express', and later when otter hunting in the Torridge Valley. In his book, *See England First,* published in 1927, he paid tribute to Henry as a stimulating companion who made him lament a wasted childhood, oblivious of the natural world. 'The very little that I now know of birds and flowers I owe entirely to Williamson's tuition'. He even remarked that he had never discovered the beauties of Georgeham until Williamson revealed them to him, and claimed to be drawn back there by his personality. For all that, Mais's *Orange Street,* published the year before *See England First,* contained a character, Brian Stucley, which Henry recognised as a portrait of himself and, not surprisingly, in view of its nature, resented. Mais gave Stucley a physical appearance and background unlike Henry's own: he is a 'red-headed, red-bearded giant' whose family have been landowners in Chagford for 800 years and who now lives in a large stone-built house in a north Devon village called Stokesay, recognisable as Georgeham. A self- proclaimed genius, he is a poet who also writes short stories, one of which has just been accepted by an American magazine for 500 dollars. He is engaged to Lydia Menhinnit, a tall dark girl whose eyes are 'pools of gentleness, sadness, and passion'. Much of the first half of the book is taken up with the discomforts and discomfitures endured by the central character, Nigel Baring, while staying with Stucley, who takes him on long walks – usually in the rain, as it is January – sets fire to large areas of gorse and heather, taunts a boy to whom he is supposed to be acting as tutor, insults almost everyone he meets, and derides any expression of compassion or concern for the feelings of others. Self-absorbed, noisy, defiant of convention, he plays tricks on his companions – especially the unfortunate Lydia – with malicious glee.

Having led Baring on a twenty-four hour sleepless and foodless walk to Dartmoor, Stucley breaks a leg in a fall and is carried to a farm where a servant girl, Rose, is pregnant by him. Later chapters move the story to Sussex and London, where Baring sorts out the matrimonial troubles that led him to seek Stucley's company in the first place. The adoring but rejected Rose pines and dies, and Stucley marries Lydia, who is no longer as wholly submissive and uncritical of him as when Baring first met her, but has become aware of his 'little calculated cruelties, his amazing self-esteem, his irresponsibility and his utter and complete selfishness', and his habit of telling lies 'just for the sake of creating discomfort . . . to see how far his power over words lasted'.

It might be supposed that this harshly-etched caricature was drawn in a spirit of enmity and revenge, but seemingly it was not. It caused a temporary break between the two very dissimilar authors, but it says much for Henry's ability, at times, to make fun of himself (in *The Phoenix Generation,* Phillip Maddison reads a novel by a friend and laughs at the uncomplimentary picture of himself it contains) that after a while he forgave Mais and resumed their friendship; he was ready to admit that he too had made free in his books with the personalities of those he knew. The character of Thomas Volstead-Wrink in *The Gold Falcon* was to owe something to Mais – the 'Volstead' being a typical name-joke: it was the Volstead Act that introduced Prohibition to the United States.

In *The Village Book* and its companion, *The Labouring Life,* published two years later, Henry showed his amused and sometimes exasperated reactions to the narrow views and limited outlook of Devon villagers at a time when their contact with the outside world had only just started to expand. Not all were literate, and the reading of those who were was usually restricted to one of the two local weekly newspapers, the Bible, and, in the case of women, to paper-backed novelettes. To them, Henry's status as a writer was all of a piece with his general oddity: writing was not work, and no sensible man would sit for hours setting down words on paper when he did not have to. He was mazed, but they tolerated him, and his extraordinary schoolboy pranks, such as pasting newspapers all over the new signboard of the village hall. When he brought to the village a charming wife, and became the father of a small son, a 'little tacker', he gained a degree of respectability in their eyes.

The Village Book was prefaced with a disclaimer, calling it 'an imaginative work which should not be read as the history of any particular village, and certainly not of any man or woman. Even the "I" and the "zur" and the "Mr Williamson" of certain pages, such as those describing the quarrel between the fictitious Zeale brothers, are but devices of story-telling'.

However, in the preface to the American edition of *The Labouring Life,* Henry admitted that the characters were based on living people, although he accused himself of manipulating them, transforming them into Williamson- characters for the purposes of fiction.

A dozen years later, when Faber took over the two books from Jonathan Cape, Henry re-cast and rearranged their contents under new titles – *Life in a Devon Village* and *Tales of a Devon Village* – and asked himself whether he had exaggerated in these earlier writings; he looked for 'errors in the letter, or detail, of truth, as well as for distortions in the spirit of truth; and found there was little to correct or alter'.

Certainly to anyone who remembers Georgeham and Croyde as they were in the late Twenties and the Thirties, the books offer a vivid recreation of their inhabitants, their ways of speech and thought, as well as of the surrounding fields and lanes, the beaches and dunes and headlands, as they were before popularity engulfed them.

The fishing rights in the Bray that went with the Shallowford house – one of Henry's main reasons for becoming its tenant – were not forgotten during the first long, wet winter. In the spring of 1930, Henry once again watched shadowy trout dashing away as he walked along the river banks, and determined to try to recapture his boyhood pleasure in fishing.

With his usual impatient enthusiasm he bought tackle and trout flies, waders, canvas brogues, a waterproof jacket with many pockets and a Harris tweed hat. He discovered from other fishermen that the Bray had been over-fished, and determined to restock it. His landlord – who, he discovered appreciatively, was known to the other tenants on his estate as the Lord of All, while the heir was the Young Lord – agreed to pay a third of the cost of the restocking, provided that the total did not exceed thirty pounds.

In the Morris Minor which had succeeded the second-hand Peugeot, Henry drove with Loetitia to a fish hatchery near Dulverton, on the Devon-Somerset border, and ordered several hundred fish of various ages; these were decanted, the next day, into two or three different stretches of the Bray. Some were soon caught by other fishermen, but most flourished in Henry's stretch of the river, fed regularly with special food bought for them. Later Henry introduced young salmon, and even made a small hatchery of his own, in which he was able to watch the development of 'eyed ova' from the Tay into fish large enough to be transferred to a pond he had dug in his garden. When these developed into smolts, ready to be released into the Bray, he tagged a few with fine silver wire on their pennant fins, and so eventually proved to his own satisfaction that some salmon would return, not to the ancestral river in which, as eggs, they had first known life, but to the river in which they had hatched. Some of the information gained in this way he used in a sentimental story, 'The Maiden Salmon', which he included in *Devon Holiday*.

The Bray had long been a salmon river. Only a month or two after his move to Shallowford, Henry watched one thrusting its way against surging flood water. He began to see these fish as 'noble and tragic creatures, like soldiers in battle . . . upheld only by tenuous dream, which was honour'. It was not long before the idea of a book on the life of a salmon began to grow in his mind – but, as with *Tarka,* the accumulation of the detailed knowledge he needed was to take several years.

CHAPTER SIX

A Stay in New York: *The Gold Falcon*

During the wet early months of 1930, Henry seems to have begun to see himself as trapped in domesticity, with two small children and a third to be born in the spring. He decided that the time had come to build the hut he had planned in the field above Georgeham. He went to stay in the village, at the King's Arms. During his first years in Devon he had regarded Charlie Ovey, the licensee, as a callous, badger-digging old ruffian, but had later come to like him. A builder who had promised to arrive on the 1st May eventually turned up on the 22nd. Foundations were levelled and a concrete base laid down. The village carpenter made 'an oak frame in the shape of a small Saxon church'. Bolted to the base, this was filled in with two-inch thick panels imported from France; Henry had seen such panels on display at the Ideal Home Exhibition. They were made of chemically treated straw within wire mesh, and were supposed to be rot-proof. Wavy-edged planks of elm formed the hut's outer skin. An open hearth, that important feature, was built in brick across the south-east corner of the single room. A wooden platform on which Henry planned to sleep was constructed a few feet above head level. The chimney was of local stone, and the roof of Cornish slates.

In the original version of *The Children of Shallowford,* chapter nine is headed '15th April 1930', the date of birth of Henry's daughter Margaret. In the revised edition of 1959, Henry speaks of going daily to Barnstaple to visit Loetitia in the nursing home, 'sitting up in bed with her baby daughter Margaret in a cot beside her', but if the hut was not begun until five or six weeks after April 15th, it seems unlikely that Loetitia would not have returned home.

Possibly Henry went to stay at the King's Arms as soon as the baby was born, leaving the two boys at Shallowford with a nurse.

It was at about this time that Henry's vegetarian phase began. In Georgeham there had been living, for a number of years, an earnest lady named Miss Johnson, who extolled not only vegetarianism but nudism. One room of her house, The Barn, on the north side of the village, was given over to what would now be called a health food shop, stocked with a variety of vegetarian products. My mother, though not a vegetarian, was an occasional customer; my bed-time meal, as a small child, was a bowl of a porridge-like substance called Cream of Wheat, which Miss Johnson recommended. Henry had known her since his early days in the village, but had remained proof against any attempts to persuade him to abandon the eating of what she called 'bloody corpses'. It may have been a guest at The Barn, rather than Miss Johnson herself, who converted him.

As there was only a limited demand for the products she sold, Miss Johnson supplemented her income by taking in paying guests. Many were young – children whose parents were abroad, or young students from European countries who wanted to improve their English. Miss Johnson was something of a tartar; at least two of her German students fled from her and sought refuge in another household.

It is possible that during the time he was building his hut, or waiting for the building to begin, Henry met and was attracted to a girl staying at The Barn: certainly the early chapters of *The Gold Falcon* – a largely autobiographical novel, like *The Flax of Dream* – shows the central character, Manfred, as enthralled by a very young blonde German girl, Marlene, aged seventeen, with 'a face like the rising sun, broad and strong, always smiling'. She is staying with her brother 'in the boarding house of the queer woman who ate only vegetables, and was always talking so seriously about one thing or another'. Manfred, whose wife is pregnant with her third child, takes Marlene sailing, and reads Wilfred Owen – the war poet Henry admired above all others – to her. He invites her to his home, but she goes away to London. After this Manfred refuses to eat meat, lives on fruit and vegetables, curses whenever he sees joints of beef or mutton on the dining table, and quarrels with his wife, Ann. He drives into the nearest town and buys quantities of oranges, bananas, figs, dates, and a fifty-pound barrel of green grapes. Marlene comes to stay for Christmas, and Manfred tries several times to seduce her – once on a journey by car to London – but she remains virginal. In London he extracts from her a promise that she will go with him to the Pyrenees. A letter from Ann about the drunkenness of the butler, Corney, causes Manfred to drive home. Marlene does not answer his letters. He has his black greyhound, Demon, put down, as the unfortunate Billjohn had been put down early in 1930. ('Either Demon or myself had to go; I could not bear the dog whining to go for walks, scratching, shaking his cankered ears. He and I were one, and part of me had to be destroyed'.) Marlene writes to say that she has gone back to Germany.

Whether or not there was a Marlene in his life at this time (and Henry was not in the habit of giving his central characters loves he had not shared) he described in chapter ten of the original version of *The Children of Shallowford* his sudden decision to eat only vegetables and fruit; in an 'anti-carnivorous rage' he dashed off to Barnstaple and bought oranges, apples and a barrel of grapes. The oranges, he said, were bitter, for marmalade-making, but as the time is apparently summer, not long after the birth of Margaret, this sounds unlikely. He had the barrel of grapes carried to his upstairs writing room, 'and ate all the grapes and rewrote all of *Dandelion Days* in a fortnight, averaging fourteen hours a day writing' – an astonishing feat, since this was so thorough a reconstruction of a long novel. It was after the party given to celebrate finishing the book that 'Coneybeare' departed.

Henry had evidently been writing enthusiastic letters to his American publisher, John Macrea, about his renewed love of fishing and the restocking of the Bray. In August, 1930, he received an invitation to join Macrea and his son on a fishing trip; they were members of the Mastigouche Fish and Game Club in Quebec Province. Henry left the feeding of his semi-tame fish in the Bray to Loetitia and Windles and sailed to Quebec. From there he travelled by train to Montreal, where he was met by his host's son. The Fish and Game Club had a territory of several hundred square miles. Anticipating a 'wild camp life', Henry was surprised, and not altogether pleased, to find wooden buildings with comfortable bunk beds, wash basins with running water, and food cooked by a chef.

He called himself a poor guest who, after the first week, 'showed no desire for portage to distant lakes'. He lay about in the log cabin, lolling in a hammock and *reading* about fishing. He soon began to feel homesick for Devon, as he almost always did when out of England for any length of time. Letters from Loetitia telling him that all was well with her and the children and the trout in the Bray restored him. When the fishing trip was ended, he travelled to New York with his host, rented himself a downtown apartment overlooking Sheridan Square and plunged into an exploration of metropolitan life. At first he found it exhilarating.

In October, he sent my father a coloured postcard of the Boardwalk of Coney Island by night. The message, for some reason – possibly to baffle the Georgeham postmistress – was in a somewhat elementary schoolboy French.

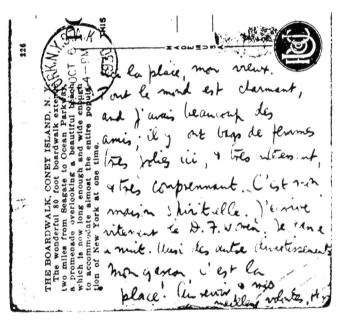

'Ici la place, mon vieux. Tout le mond est charmant, and j'avais beaucoup des amis; il y ont bags des femmes tres jolies ici, and tres interessant, and tres comprennant. C'est mon maison spirituelle. J'ecrive vitement le D. F. Women. Je dance a nuit. Aussi des autres divertissements. Mon Garcon, c'est la place! A revoirs and mes meilleurs volontes. H'.

The reference to the rapid writing of *The Dream of Fair Women* was, of course, to its rewriting for the new Faber edition. Henry recorded later that he had completed it in three weeks.

He had arrived in a United States beset by the twin miseries of the Depression and Prohibition's gangsterism. He sent my father a letter, now sadly lost; for some reason the envelope survives, clearly postmarked December 9th, 1930, Madison Square Station, N.Y.; on it Henry has drawn a muzzy-looking version of his owl symbol with the words 'Kaput! Gone speakeasy!!' written alongside. (In *The Gold Falcon* he was to describe a visit made by Manfred to a speakeasy, where thuggish bouncers give him a fright.)

By way of a Christmas card he sent a photograph of himself standing on a log in what is presumably a Canadian river. He is wearing breeches, boots, a long jacket – perhaps the waterproof jacket with many pockets 'cut in the Norfolk style' which he had bought in St James' Street in the spring – and a strange hat which is neither his Harris tweed nor the cap he often wore in England when fishing, but something which looks like a cross between a solar topi and a sou' wester. He grasps a stout thumbstick. The greeting, in his favourite red ink, reads, 'Best wishes for Christmas and 1931 from this well-known half-wit'. There is indeed something slightly Goonish about the figure: it might almost be of Spike Milligan in one of his antic guises.

Henry was later to remark that six months living alone in an apartment unfurnished except for bed, chair and table had taught him that life in a great city could be more lonely than a moorland valley. Evidently the 'beaucoup des amis' and 'bags des femmes' were not always in evidence. Yet he was certainly not always alone. If there had been a Marlene in north Devon, her image was dimmed by another attraction; he met a girl called Barbara Sincere, to whom he dedicated the sequence of short essays, 'The Country of the Rain', when he added them to the 1933 edition of *The Lone Swallows*. Barbara Faithfull, in *The Gold Falcon,* would seem to owe a certain amount to her.

Apart from the rewriting of *The Dream of Fair Women,* he would have recorded in his diary his impressions of the noisy city and the people he met; he also began a draft of the first chapters of *The Gold Falcon.*

It is unlikely that when he left England he was planning to stay away until the spring of 1931 when, as he put it in *A Clear Water Stream,* 'my wife came to fetch me home'. Elsewhere he wrote of sending an S.O.S. to Loetitia. There is a suggestion that he needed to do this because he had encouraged some impressionable girl to think that he was more in love with her than he was, and could not disentangle himself without the presence of his wife, with her beauty and gentle dignity. In any case, whatever he may have told friends such as my father in the first exuberance of arriving in the city, the idea that New York could be, for long, the spiritual home of that quintessential English countryman, Henry Williamson, is incongruous.

He returned to Shallowford to the realisation of the speed with which 'Time was flowing away with life. And it has really hardly begun!' It seemed to him astonishing to see Windles walking about by himself under the lime trees of the park, wearing a new satchel because he was soon to go to the Filleigh village school. Windles had celebrated his fifth birthday at the end of February, during Henry's absence; John was now two and a half and Margaret had passed her first birthday. Henry was very much a family man.

Even though he longed for – and sought out – the seclusion he needed as a creative artist, he had a natural concern for the welfare of his children. At some time during the year, John became very ill with pneumonia. In the era before antibiotics, there was little to be done but keep the patient warm and quiet, and hope. Loetitia nursed the fretful two-year-old, hardly sleeping for a week, until one evening he reached what was known as the crisis, and lay motionless. She called for Henry's help, and he took the child's hands and willed him to live. John, evidently blessed with his father's strong constitution, gradually recovered, and Henry was left with a sense of having been an instrument of healing. He had a particular affection for this second son (a preference which, as he later admitted, bore hard on Windles). John had been an easy baby. A number of passages of the original *Children of Shallowford* hinted at the strains which Henry's moods of depression and frustration, breaking out sometimes in almost hysterical irritability, imposed on his family. Some of these were cut in the revised version, which laid more stress on the happy hours. In one of the deleted paragraphs he wrote, 'I was glad that my second son was serene, with an equal mind and tranquil temper, like his mother's. I did not want to see the nervous instability of my blood passed on to the children'. To speak of the 'nervous instability of his blood' suggests that he considered it inherent, yet he goes on, 'I believed that my moods of irritability and bad temper were due to a hypersensitive nature being subjected to much paternal fear and unhappiness in childhood'.

Apart from the revised *Dream of Fair Women* (dedicated to J. D. Beresford 'who helped the young writer much; coupled with the name of Walter de la Mare – friends seldom seen, but much beloved'), the only book Henry published in 1931 was *The Red Deer of Exmoor*. This was very short, in fact a booklet, setting out the pros and cons of stag hunting. Towards the end of the year he received a letter, forwarded to him by his publishers, from an old schoolfellow, Victor Yeates, who asked for advice on a novel he had written, adding, 'You can hardly refuse it to one of your own characters in *Dandelion Days*'.

The letter recalled to Henry 'a dreamy, wild-eyed boy at school who used to read Keats under the desk during Maths', a fellow member of the class known as the Special Slackers – though as Yeates died, at the age of 37, a fortnight after Henry's 39th birthday, it is surprising that they should have been in the same form.

Henry found Yeates' novel formless, but real, and told him that the scenes of flying in it were so good that this was what he should write about; he suggested a theme for a book. Yeates was in hospital, suffering from tuberculosis, but he decided that he could not write there, and discharged himself. At a time when complete rest and relaxation – preferably in a warm, dry climate – were virtually the only aids to prolonging the lives of tuberculous patients, this represented a slow suicide.

Yeates set to work steadily on his new novel, and had more or less completed it by the end of 1933. Henry, generous of his time, as always when he believed in the talent of another writer, rewrote the final chapters and recommended the book to Jonathan Cape. It was brought out quickly, so that Yeates was able to see it in print before he died; his dedication read, 'To Henry Williamson, at whose suggestion this book was begun, with whose encouragement and help it was written and ended'.

It is a long and remarkable book, a vividly detailed account, almost day by day, of the experiences of Tom Cundall, a young pilot flying Sopwith Camels in France in the spring and summer of 1918. These unstable aircraft were known as scout planes, but they had a multiple use as fighters, bombers and ground-strafers as well as observers. Yeates wrote, with an illusionless, calm anger, often relieved by sardonic humour, of the nerve-wearying life of the pilots, flying two or three sorties – always known as 'jobs' – a day. He tended to put his older head on the shoulders of Tom Cundall and his friends, seeing the war as simply 'an obscure quarrel between rival gangs of merchants, imperialists, usurers, megalomaniacs' which by mid-1918 had an air of total futility. 'Once (it) might have had a purpose, heaven knew what, but some sort of purpose; now it was just damn silly'.

In honour of Henry, Yeates gave Tom's best friend the name

Williamson, although the character is only thinly realised and is in no way a portrait of Henry. The title originally proposed for the book, *A Test to Destruction* – surely an excellent one – was not approved, but Henry did not forget it, and more than twenty years later used it for the eighth volume of *A Chronicle of Ancient Sunlight*. (In some of the war novels of that sequence Henry introduced a pilot named Tom Cundall, explaining obscurely in his introduction to a new edition of *Winged Victory* in 1961 that 'by this device he hoped that Yeates and his novel would be rediscovered should it happen that it remained unpublished during my lifetime'.)

When his book was already long but still unfinished, Yeates wrote to Henry that the writing of it was 'all hard slogging and chipping words out of my breastbone'. This phrase appealed to Henry; he adopted and would sometimes quote it; he used it on a visit to my parents in 1936, speaking of the exhaustion of writing *Salar the Salmon*. There are indications that reading *Winged Victory* had an influence on *The Gold Falcon,* on which he would have been at work when he began to correspond with Yeates. (Fortunately he discarded the title which appears on an early draft MS, *Auriferous Bird.)*

This novel is an odd-one-out among Henry's works of fiction. To begin with it was originally published anonymously, although its authorship was very quickly revealed when John Brophy reviewed it and, recognising the style, challenged Henry to sue him if he was mistaken. It is not part of a sequence, like the volumes making up *The Flax of Dream* and *A Chronicle of Ancient Sunlight*. Its central character, the sub-Byronic Manfred, is not an ex-soldier but an ex-airman – and echoes of *Winged Victory* may be heard in Manfred's memories of flying. He is not middle-class, like Willie and Phillip Maddison, but belongs to the minor aristocracy: by the end of the book he has inherited his grandfather's title (his father is dead) and become the 27th Baron Cloudesley of Treclew.

He is 33 years old, an Old Etonian war poet who has written a celebrated autobiography. During the war he flew Sopwith Camels, shot down 37 enemy aircraft and received eleven wounds and nine decorations, including the V.C., D.S.O., M.C. and Croix de Guerre (he is said to have returned his decorations to the War Office with the request that his name should be 'removed from the records and lists of award'.) His full name is Major Manfred Fiennes-Carew-Manfred; his family crest is 'a falcon *or* with wings expanded *argent*a sun gold' (sic). Ann, his wife, is the daughter of a West Country parson. After a disastrous wedding night, their marriage has not been happy. They have a son, Hugh; their second son, Peter, has died, after an illness which corresponds closely to that of John in *The Children of Shallowford*. Although Ann is pregnant again, Manfred has come to America – feeling 'sick of all things, while knowing that the sickness was . . . of his own inactivity' – as 'a modern Columbus of the mind'. He is planning to write a half-million word novel beginning in the late nineteenth century with the life of his great-grandfather Cloudesley, whose habit was to spend three months of every year in Bavaria, where he begot seven children.

Manfred's kindly elderly publisher, Homer, the head of a publishing firm called World Books, makes him welcome, plies him with bootleggers' whisky, and listens to the story of his love for Marlene. Homer and his son, Charles, take him to the home of Charles' fiancée, Barbara Faithfull, in New England. Manfred, having rented an apartment on Seventh Avenue, forgets Marlene (who happens to be in New York) in the pursuit of Barbara, who is sufficiently attracted to him to break off her engagement. Their affair apparently remains platonic, as does another intermittent relationship with a girl called Pinky, who is in perpetual mourning for a dead friend, Louise, and drinks heavily. Manfred urges Barbara to come back to his home in Cornwall, saying that this would make it 'such a place of light and gaiety . . . You'd be my handmaid, my mistress, my darling friend, with whom I'd laugh and laugh and laugh'. She is not receptive to this self-indulgent prescription. A cable arrives to say that Ann is very ill. If she dies, Manfred tells himself, he will marry Barbara. Nevertheless he buys a monoplane, fitted with floats, from Charles, and declares his intention of flying to England, though he sees himself as 'a charlatan of heroics'. A widely publicised send-off, with radio interview, is hurriedly arranged, and Manfred takes off from Newark with a full load of fuel. (The Lindbergh parallel is underlined when Manfred jokingly refers to the aircraft as the Spirit of World Books.)

The three chapters that follow offer an example of the sort of sustained, poetic imaginative writing in which Henry excelled. The engine fails when Manfred is about a thousand mile from Land's End. The sea is calm, and for a time the floats maintain buoyancy, but gradually the aircraft begins to sink. Manfred sees a light and, supposing it to be that of a ship, throws a burning flare into the sea. It drifts back and sets the plane alight. Jumping into the water, Manfred realises that the light he saw was not a ship, but the morning star – Henry's beloved Eosphorus or Lucifer, the Light Bringer. Manfred does not drown but, horribly enough, is burned to death by petrol flames on the water. That he should die by fire was necessary for Henry's purpose: an intimation of the phoenix concept that, like the Morning Star, recurred in his personal imagery. At the moment of death Manfred sees a white bird with a golden head, and holds out his arms to 'his falcon which came to him and was of him'.

Henry claimed that *The Gold Falcon* had 'an Old Testament theme of the search for God in a modern setting'. It was 'an entirely objective and deliberated work, as was *Hamlet, Jude the Obscure,* and *Lady Chatterley's Lover;* the falcon was honour, or the soul, or God . . .'

To regard honour, the soul, and God as synonymous is almost as strange as linking *Hamlet* (on whom Manfred lectures to literary ladies, equating him with Everyman but also with the generation that survived the Great War – and equating his father's ghost with the ghosts of those who died), *Jude the Obscure* and *Lady Chatterley's Lover.*

In Manfred's frenetic pursuit of Marlene, Pinky and Barbara, the reader is shown a man who can hardly be taken seriously as a spiritual pilgrim. He is said to dream of 'a Sybil, a Persephone, a Cleopatra, a courtesan of the senses and an Emily Bronte of the mind'; this demanding specification makes his more obvious objective look difficult to obtain. Manfred, endowed to an almost laughable degree with advantages of birth, education and a much-honoured war record that Henry would have liked so much to possess, comes dangerously close to resembling a hero of a woman's magazine story. Nevertheless in some ways he is close kin to Willie Maddison, and hardly more mature.

In *Goodbye West Country,* Henry said that he used only about a third of himself in the character of the 'hero-villain' of *The Gold Falcon,* and did not foresee that readers would confuse fiction and reality in the book. He protested repeatedly that Manfred was not a subjective creation. 'The theme of salvation through suffering moved me deeply; I hoped it would move the reader similarly. It was anonymous because it was completely objective to me, a thing on its own, an affirmation of what in other ages used to be called God'. The logic of this is unconvincing: it was anonymous, one may suspect, because Henry had doubts about the book itself and its probable reception; Edward Garnett had advised Jonathan Cape against accepting it for the sake both of the author and the author's wife.

When Faber published it in 1933 the novel aroused both admiration and disapproval; one critic called it 'a great oozing slab of self-pity, bearing the wet trade mark of Henry Williamson'. Characteristically enough it was Henry himself who quoted this opinion, in *The Linhay on the Downs*. His faithful American publisher, John Macrae, was hurt by the book, and his son was 'deeply mortified'.

Some years later Henry consoled himself with the thought that if he had finished the novel in New York 'it might have had celestial life, instead of the failure it became' (sic).

It had a good initial sale, three impressions being called for in the year of publication. In 1949, Faber decided to bring out a new edition, and Henry was able to do some of the rewriting he could seldom resist. One or two passages have an odd ring in a story set in the early Thirties: for instance a reference to the possibility of 'the complete ruin of planetary life by atomic energy released by man at war with himself' in chapter 61 belongs to the post-Hiroshima era.

In *Devon Holiday*, Henry remarked that 'the detachable psychic part of himself' had been drowned twice – as Willie Maddison and as Manfred Cloudesley. Yet in *The Gold Falcon* he went farther than in *The Pathway:* it is a chilling aspect of the book that not merely Manfred, but his whole family, which bears so close a resemblance to Henry's, is written out of existence, with one exception: his elder son is allowed to survive.

CHAPTER SEVEN

The Healing Sun of Georgia

Writing in the late Fifties, Henry remembered his return from America to Shallowford as a time of elation, when he recognised his good fortune in being able 'to live freely, my own master, beside this moorland stream'. Yet in his autobiographical books of the Thirties he speaks of feeling 'a slow entombment of self', of regretting that there were few days in any year when life seemed full and positive; 'the rest was mooning about alone by the river, or in the writing room, losing one's life away in strings of words, and dreaming of escape into some distant solar companionship of life'.

Yet there were pleasures and compensations; among them was driving along the still uncluttered roads of southern England in a fast, powerful car. In 1930, the Alvis Company brought out its first Silver Eagle sports-tourer, following it with an improved model the next year. Just as in the Twenties Henry had felt proud and happy riding his 'beautiful long-stroke, single cylinder Brooklands Road Special Norton' motorcycle, now in the Thirties he felt perhaps even more pride and happiness in driving a Silver Eagle. And just as his younger self had 'scorned overcoats and lamps as unsporting, even in winter midnights on long journeys', so his Shallowford self scorned to put up the hood of the Silver Eagle, even in rain, and exulted in driving with the windscreen flat, wearing goggles, flying helmet, flying coat and gauntlets. He frequently boasted of doing 70 or 80 miles an hour on suitable roads. As he had in him rather more of the Walter Mitty than the average man, it would be surprising if sometimes, on such drives, sitting in his cockpit-like driving seat, he did not picture himself as a pilot on Yeates' model, patrolling the skies above the Western Front.

More importantly, he began an emotional involvement in the early Thirties that, with several intermissions, was to last a good deal longer than most of his pre-marital or extra-marital infatuations with 'sun-maidens'. She is referred to variously in his books: as 'my devoted scribe', as Ann, as A' Bess (for some reason Henry's children called her Auntie Bess). She was a girl some fifteen years his junior, who acted as his secretary and was willing to walk for miles with him, go with him on long journeys in the Silver Eagle, or build dams in the Bray.

Once or twice he brought Ann to visit us. His attitude to her was bantering: on one chilly summer's day he teased her — rather unfairly, as it seemed to me — because they had been to the beach at Putsborough, and Ann's legs had become blue with cold. To Henry, cold was a matter of indifference. Ann gave the impression that she was used to this rather heavy-handed chaffing.

Despite his moods of dissatisfaction, Henry was steadily absorbing the knowledge he would need to write *Salar the Salmon:* watching the Bray and all its creatures — fish, insects, birds, plants — reading about trout and salmon, talking to anglers in pubs, and to salmon fishermen in the Taw-Torridge estuary, going fishing himself. During his first period of dam-building he virtually stopped writing, enjoying the hard manual work that resulted in physical tiredness, as a rest from the mental tiredness of which he so often complained.

With Loetitia he enjoyed an autumn journey to Scotland. In Coventry they paused so that the Silver Eagle might be given an overhaul. They broke their journey at Blackpool, spent an evening watching the crowds and the illuminations, sampling fairground chutes and sideshows before going back to a boarding house for bed and breakfast. The next night they camped out near Inverary, and then crossed to the Hebridean island of Islay to stay with friends. There Henry fished, meditated on the life of salmon, and walked on the moors.

He drove the full 550 miles home from Tarbert to Filleigh in one day. Lying in bed, sleepless from over-exhaustion, Henry wondered if the salmon felt as he did, after its long odyssey through all hazards to its spawning grounds. Yet the salmon endured for a purpose; he had merely forced himself on a wearying drive to test his powers of endurance. 'Merely that? Was I not, like the salmon, coming to where my heart lay?' After absence, north Devon always renewed its spell.

(In *A Clear Water Stream*, published in 1948, he claimed to have discovered that ancestors on his mother's side, named Shapcote, had lived at Knowstone, a very small village some eleven miles east of South Molton, for at least ten generations before the heraldic visitations of 1610. However, the place was later sold; the family moved to Exeter, and a Sarah Shapcote, having married an Irish naval post-captain called Thomas William Leaver, became his great-great-grandmother.)

The revised version of *The Labouring Life* came out as *Tales of a Devon Village* in 1932; in September of that year *The Gold Falcon* was finished. It was to be published only five months later, just after Henry had begun a frank pot-boiler, *On Foot in Devon*. This was a commission from the publishers, Alexander Maclehose, who, Henry said, 'had an ambition to guide everyone to everywhere in England'. He sub-titled it 'Guidance and Gossip, being a Monologue in Two Reels', and dedicated it to 'Miss A.T., who did all the work'.

With Ann, his 'Scribe', he set off one January morning from Barnstaple Town Station. The little narrow-gauge railway to Lynton was then still flourishing, and they travelled in it the length of the winding, steadily climbing line. (Two years later, not long before the line closed, Henry, again with Ann, took his children on the little train 'for their first and last time' as a treat for Margaret's fifth birthday.) From Lynton they made their way westwards along the coast to Mortehoe before turning south, by way of Georgeham, Croyde and Braunton, to the Taw-Torridge estuary, where they were ferried across to Appledore. This first part of the book ends a few miles from Hartland, at Welcombe on the Devon-Cornwall border; the second describes a walk Henry made alone two months later from Sidmouth to Dartmouth and, after a break of several weeks, to Salcombe. (The break at Dartmouth was made because he hoped to meet T.E. Lawrence at the R.A.F. base at Mount Batten, but he was disappointed: the elusive Lawrence had slipped away, as he so often did.)

The tone of weary facetiousness in which much of *On Foot in Devon* was written indicated that Henry resented having to write it at all. He called it 'a farce and parody of conventional guidebooks' (a *genre* he disliked) and consoled himself by writing about fish and fishing whenever this was at all relevant. Near Beesands he watched men netting a salmon and leaving it to die on the shingle – instead of killing it quickly as Taw-Torridge fishermen would have done – 'a lovely graceful thing seeking in vain the resumption of its god-like life'. He was to remember the death of this fish in a story written some eighteen months later.

The South Devon walk may have been significant to Henry for another reason: it was almost certainly during the course of it that he met the girl who was to become the model of Barleybright in *The Sun on the Sands*. To her he dedicated the story 'Migration' which he added to the 1933 edition of *The Lone Swallows,* with its illustrations by C.F. Tunnicliffe. That she remained an important, idealised being in the life of his imagination is shown by the fact that in the ninth volume of *A Chronicle of Ancient Sunlight, The Innocent Moon,* Phillip Maddison's first wife, who dies in childbirth, is called Barleybright or Barley.

At this time he was writing weekly nature notes for the 'Sunday Referee'. He was to complain, in *Devon Holiday,* that his total earnings from writing in 1933 were only some three hundred pounds, but this sounds an underestimate; even if the fees for his short articles were modest, he would have received part of the advances on three books published that year: *On Foot in Devon* and *The Starborn,* as well as *The Gold Falcon;* on the latter there would also have been royalties on its three swiftly sold impressions. (*The Starborn,* with illustrations by C.F. Tunnicliffe, was published in a mock-anonymous form: it had an introduction by Henry, but its authorship was attributed to Willie Maddison. It will be considered in chapter thirteen, in the revised form which appeared in 1948.) It might be supposed that some royalties were due on earlier books; certainly there must have been some on the illustrated edition of *Tarka* which Putnam brought out in 1932. The black and white illustrations, delicately complementing the text, represent the first of the work with which C.F. Tunnicliffe was to embellish several of Henry's books. According to Ian Niall, in *Portrait of a Country Artist,* Tunnicliffe, having read and admired *Tarka,* approached Putnam at his wife's suggestion with a set of aquatints depicting scenes from the book. The publishers took up the idea of producing, not only an illustrated *Tarka,* but a uniform edition – though with woodcuts and line drawings rather than aquatints – of *The Lone Swallows, The Peregrine's Saga* and *The Old Stag.*

In the beginning, author and artist expressed great admiration for one another's work, but as time went on their relationship soured. Tunnicliffe, a steady, sturdy, happily-married countryman, grew weary of aspects of Henry's excitable temperament, found his behaviour jarring, and resented the older man's didacticism. He did not want to be lectured on either country matters – of which he had profound personal knowledge – or artistic ones; he did not want to be compelled to listen to gramophone records of Wagner; he did not want to be bombarded with letters half about his work as illustrator and half about Henry's amorous entanglements (which at this time would presumably have included the obsession with Barleybright). After criticism of one of his drawings of a salmon, for *Salar,* Tunnicliffe lost patience; this was to be his last set of illustrations for a Williamson work, although he did agree to draw a map of Old Hall Farm to be used in the first edition of *The Story of a Norfolk Farm.*

Whatever Henry's income from writing may have been in 1933, he certainly felt a constant pressure to earn money to support his growing family; his sense of responsibility for those dependent on him was always strong; he wrote of dreading 'the self-stain of debt'. He never subscribed to the convention of the feckless, spendthrift artist.

His son Robert was born in the autumn of 1933, and in the same week, as is recorded in *The Children of Shallowford,* a daughter was born to A' Bess, so that the children were known in the family as The Twins. Evidently in flight from overmuch domesticity, Henry withdrew to his writing hut above Georgeham. He was planning to write the book that was to become *The Sun in the Sands,* but the weeks went by and nothing was written 'except of plaint and repining'. (In *The Linhay on the Downs* Henry included a section headed 'From *The Sun in the Sands',* but this did not appear in the book when it was eventually published.)

Part of the trouble was that he was pining for the unobtainable 'Barleybright'. One evening he called to visit my parents. Ostensibly he had come to offer his sympathy to my mother; she had been hurt in a car accident a few weeks earlier. Her injuries had not been serious, but they caused her considerable pain, not helped by ham-handed medical treatment. The next day he sent a letter – headed simply 'Ox's Cross' – which indicates that his own sorrows had been uppermost in his mind the previous evening.

'Thank you for your friendliness last night; as it happened I was mentally in despair, and I felt less solitary afterwards.

Everything you said about Gypsy was true; and I feel about her qualities as you do, believe me: but the fact remains that we tend to jag each other's life-blood, or nervous energy, and we can't get on together. She is a perfect mother: all her talents are set for that purpose.

In the dilemma and perplexity and mixture of pain and longing and the everlasting wish for death and its release (as Tristan wished in the opera) which has been upon one for some time now, Gypsy has been my confidante, friend and adviser. She advises me to do a certain thing for my sake: and while all my remaining life cries out for that thing, compassion forbids. So you see the impasse! She says "Do!" acting on common sense and fairness and humanity, while regretting the spoliation which has already become an established and inevitable fact; and I advise myself not to do it, because I can't bear the thought of hurting her. So the only end is dissolution in the sunset; for I can bear no more my poignant and loveless state'.

Along one edge of this letter, which is written in pencil on a lined page from a notebook, is added, 'Remember, I am not a philander (sic): it's a question of life or death'. In another margin appears, 'I am just off to London now. I do hope your wrist gets better soon and the effects of that horrid smash will leave you altogether'.

My mother, who had a lasting admiration for Henry's talent as a writer, was inclined to regard the more *outré* aspects of his behavior as regrettable but, at times, slightly comic. 'Very Henryesque,' she would remark. No doubt she found this letter, with its extravagant, Werther-ish self-pity, amounting almost to self-parody, particularly Henryesque. Looking objectively at his situation at this time, she could not take his agonisings at their face value: she recognised that to refer to himself as loveless was unrealistic, when two attractive and remarkably forbearing women were devoted to him.

However, Henry continued to behave as though he were an impressionable youth of the Romantic era who had just been reading the early works of Goethe. Interestingly, he may be seen to have possessed a temperament which in many respects resembled that of the young Goethe of the *Sturm und Drang* period. Both left it on record that they regarded themselves as having chameleonic natures; both often thought of suicide (though both, as it happened, lived to be over eighty). According to Barker Fairley, in his *A Study of Goethe,* the poet, as a young man, was 'changeable, lacking in steadiness of mood or thought'; he was mercurial, volatile, unsure of himself; he had a 'restless, ever-changing, irrational mental life'. He showed, Fairley says, 'a disconcertingly rapid and irregular tempo, as if his mind were set at too fast and too uncertain a pace for others to keep up with. A friend recorded that in the middle of a heated conversation he might take it into his head to jump up, run away and not come back'. He fell in love with one girl after another. All these characteristics and traits, down to the running away in the middle of a conversation he disliked, applied to Henry.

At the end of 1933, American generosity again offered Henry a chance to cross the Atlantic. His benefactor this time was Mrs Robert de l'Aigle Reese, known as Miss Louise, an elderly rich woman with a large house in Georgia. She had read Henry's story about peregrine falcons in the 'Atlantic Monthly'. In London, a friend of hers, a member of the English Speaking Union, explained to Henry that Mrs Reese had for some years regarded her house as a sanctuary for authors where, she hoped, masterpieces would be written. *Had* any masterpieces been written there, Henry asked cannily. Not so far, was the answer. His informant told him that the creeks and rivers around her friend's house had fish in them, though she did not know whether they would be suitable for the subject of his study: evidently he had let it be known that he was planning a book on fish.

He accepted the invitation and at the end of February, 1934, travelled to Southampton to board the *Berengeria* for New York. Two years later he was to describe the voyage as 'one of the most desolate experiences of life so far'. He was expecting to be seasick all the time, he said, (all sea crossings aroused this fear in him: was this why he apparently never visited Lundy, an island that might have been expected to fascinate him, aboard one of the paddle steamers that for many years made regular crossings from Ilfracombe to the island in summer?) He claimed not to have slept for thirty nights; he had 'said goodbye to hope, to love, to life', and did not expect to see England again; in the train from Waterloo to Southampton the tears ran down his cheeks. It seemed to him that his soul had been slowly disintegrating for many years, though 'no one was to blame but myself – rather, my non-self'.

Two friends came to see him off. One was T. E. Lawrence, then still serving as Aircraftman Shaw and stationed at Southampton. The other was John Heygate, the writer and film maker, who was to remain a friend of Henry's for life.

Henry had first met Lawrence two years after the publication of *Tarka*. A profound admirer of *Seven Pillars of Wisdom,* he had been delighted when Lawrence wrote approvingly of *Tarka,* and came to visit him at Vale House in July, 1929 (not 1928 as Henry sometimes wrote). In *Devon Holiday,* Henry called him G. B. Everest. To Henry, Lawrence was not only one of those heroic figures for which he was always searching, but a Christ-like being: 'Like Jesus, Everest has completely realised himself, he has learned the enormous value of being his true or single self'. In later years, one of Henry's favourite fantasies was that Lawrence had slept in the hut at Oxford Cross – impossible, as it was not built in 1929; at least one friend, Maurice Wiggins, believed this, and wrote in his *Faces at the Window* that he had slept in the 'magic hut where Lawrence of Arabia had slept before me'.

John (later Sir John) Heygate was eight years younger than Henry, and had missed service in the First World War; he made up for it by spending some years as a bombardier in the Royal Artillery in the Second. He was educated at Eton and Balliol, had worked for three years as a B.B.C. news editor in the Savoy Hill days, and had written novels and a book about motoring round Europe, *Motor Tramp*. Before a recent illness he had been working for Gaumont British in Germany, supervising the production of English versions of films made in the UFA studios in Berlin.

Once in New York, Henry spent a few days there before being flown in an open-cockpit monoplane down the seacoast of the Carolinas to the Savannah River. His destination lay inland, some 75 miles from the sea. There, in March, it was as warm as an English July, and within a short time the sun had begun to heal him of some of his malaise.

Before leaving England he had signed a contract with Faber to write his salmon book, and received an advance which, he said, would keep his family for a year. Yet in the languor and heat of Georgia he found it impossible to think himself into the subaqueous world of his imagined fish. He turned back to the work he had begun the previous autumn, *The Sun in the Sands*. Starting afresh, he was soon deep in a happy evocation of his life in Georgeham between 1921 and 1924 – those years which were to remain for him a halcyon period to be looked back on with nostalgia. By transforming the unobtainable Barleybright into a character in his story, an adoring adolescent who sacrifices her life for him, he was able to exorcise her spell on him.

He wrote swiftly, and when he was not writing, played tennis, danced at the local Country Club, watched a golf tournament on the Augusta course, went fishing and explored rivers and creeks in canoes paddled by amiable, coloured boatmen. Their easy-going natures soothed the rapid tempo of his mind. 'I enjoyed being with the negroes; deep contentment flowed from them into myself'. He felt himself becoming a Southerner, 'the northern core of dream or introspection' being drawn out of him by the sun. It was an effort to begin work each morning, although 'the old world of the past is so real as I recreate its scenes, faces, and the actions of my old self which in retrospect seem so weak and vain and wasteful . . . But "if way to the better there be, it enacts (sic) a full look at the worst", as Hardy wrote'. Hardy in fact wrote, in his poem *'In Tenebris'*, 'it *exacts* a full look at the worst', but the quotation, or mis-quotation, was a favourite of Henry's, used more than once in his books and sometimes when talking to friends.

He met another writer and his wife, who invited him, apparently at the suggestion of his hostess – there is a hint that Henry had exhausted his welcome in her house – to join them at Valdosta, near the Georgia-Florida border. He travelled south in a Greyhound bus. Once among the orange groves he thought of Delius, whose music he loved, and who had spent part of his youth as an orange grower. With his new friends, Henry came to the fringe of the Okefinokee Swamp, and stayed cheaply at a big, run-down hotel, its many dim, empty rooms seeming haunted. The other writer is described as 'a world traveller in search of big game' who enjoyed life to the full and wrote stories which were 'read and appreciated by millions and paid for accordingly'.

Henry published two accounts, not quite identical, of his stay in the southern states; the first in *The Linhay on the Downs,* the second in *A Clear Water Stream,* which made use of material from several earlier books. In *The Linhay* he speaks of reading 'Hemingway's magnificent *The Sun Also Rises*' (the title would have appealed to him) as he lay in his Pullman sleeper, travelling back to New York. This might suggest that the fellow-guest in the decrepit hotel was Hemingway, who was in fact living at Key West at the time, and took delivery of his boat *Pilar* there in May, 1934. Yet, although it would have been possible for Hemingway to drive north and visit Mrs Reese, it does not seem he did so.

As usual when out of England, Henry was homesick, and this time he did not suffer from whatever doubts and uncertainties about returning that afflicted him on his first visit to America. 'I was desperate to return to England, which had been all my thoughts since leaving Southampton three months before', he wrote. 'Now my body is soaked with the sun, colour has meaning again, and Night is beautiful, tranquil for sleep once more.'

By the end of May he was at home at Shallowford, in the house full of children, five of them at this time – Windles, John, Margaret and 'The Twins', Robert, and Ann's daughter Rosemary. Rosemary was flourishing, but Robert was not. Loetitia was unable to feed him, no patent food suited him, 'he wailed and was thin . . . our little starveling baby'. In two of the more remarkable pages of *The Children of Shallowford,* Henry records his solution. He was dictating a story to Rosemary's mother when 'the grizzling cries of Robbie down below in the garden suddenly became unendurable'. Could nothing be done? Henry cried. ' "That baby's dying, why can't he have proper food? Why can't you feed him?" With that Robbie was fetched out of the pram, and glad of the excuse to leave the drudgery of words, I went to the river with my rod'.

The incident underlines the extent to which those drawn into Henry's orbit were expected to co-operate with his ideas. The outcome in this case was fortunate: Robbie rapidly gained weight 'and soon became as sturdy as his "twin" '.

If the river remained one of the places to which Henry retreated from domesticity, he was still not ready to begin that journey from sea to spawning grounds that he planned for *Salar.*

For a time after his return from his second American visit he must have hoped that an English publisher would accept *The Sun in the Sands* (he had already been told in New York that the story was too far back in time and too English for the American public.) The unmistakable fictional element in a book presented as auto-biography told against it over here; not until the late years of the Second World War would Faber decide to publish it.

The Linhay on the Downs came out in 1934, however, with a dedication to Henry's benefactor, Mrs Reese. It was a collection of essays on a variety of subjects, some of them dating back to 1928. Unusually for Henry, who did not have much patience with literary criticism, it contains a number of pieces on writers and their books. The longest is 'Reality in War Literature', which considers more than a dozen of the best war books published in the Twenties – most of them English, including Robert Graves' *Goodbye to All That,* Tomlinson's *Waiting for Daylight* and Masefield's *The Old Front Line* and *Gallipoli.* There are also two by French authors – Barbusse's *Le Feu* and Duhamel's *Civilisation,* from both of which Henry quoted at length. He gave most space to Edmund Blunden's *Undertones of War,* and explained that this was because J. C. Squire had asked him to write 4,000 words on Blunden's book for the 'London Mercury'. (It is interesting that he prints a telegram from Squire dated 6th December, 1928, but addressed to him at Skirr Cottage; this suggests that, three years after he had moved to Vale House, Henry still let it be thought that he was living in the romantic-sounding cottage. A similar use of the old address may be found in quotations from T. E. Lawrence's letters in *Genius of Friendship*. The reason may simply be thrift. During his Skirr Cottage days, Henry had a quantity of headed paper printed, and apparently continued to use it, without substituting his new address, until it was exhausted.) Henry added two postscripts to 'Reality in War Literature', listing more than twenty other books published since he first wrote the essay, among them Yeates' *Winged Victory,* which he urged anyone who was interested in his *own* work to read, and *A Soldier's Diary of the Great War.* The latter, for which he had written a long introduction, was published anonymously, but was the work of Captain Douglas Bell, like Yeates a former school-fellow. To Bell, Henry would later dedicate *A Fox Under my Cloak,* the fifth volume of *A Chronicle of Ancient Sunlight.*

This essay and its postscript are particularly noteworthy in that they show Henry's constant fascination with what others had written of the war; his compulsion to compare his experience with theirs and observe the way in which they had treated their subject. Knowing of his resolve, one day, to write his own account of the war, he remarked, 'It will need a titanic vitality to recreate the lost world of 1914-18'.

Henry included in *The Linhay on the Downs* an essay called 'Stag Hunting', which is virtually an obituary of Sir John Fortescue, who had died in 1933, just before the publication of his autobiography, *Author and Curator.* Henry recalled with gratitude the encouragement and help he had received from Sir John after the writing of *Tarka,* and spoke of him as 'that rare thing, a true sensitive'.

In the summer of 1934 an opportunity arose for him to learn to fly. An airfield was opened in June at Chivenor, beside the Taw near Heanton Court. Known as Barnstaple Aerodrome or Airport, the undertaking was the initiative of two experienced pilots, newcomers to the area, Robert Boyd and T. W. J. – Tommy – Nash. It was the home of a flourishing flying club at which, in the next five years, many members would obtain their civilian pilots' licences, some joining the Civil Air Guard. The remarkable airwoman, Ann Welch, says in her autobiography *Happy to Fly* that when she was seventeen, in 1934, she and her family spent a summer holiday camping, as she puts it slightly inaccurately, 'in Henry's barn in north Devon, on the hill above Barnstaple Aerodrome'. She had first met Henry two years earlier, while she was staying at Torcross in south Devon with an aunt. He visited her family often, she says, but his unpredictable behaviour – disappearing in the middle of a meal or arriving through a window – 'caused consternation to my father, who was never sure whether to appreciate a genius or complain about bad manners'. Nevertheless her parents consulted Henry when they were disturbed by their daughter's apparent obsession with all aspects of aviation, and at his suggestion she spent some time with C. F. Tunnicliffe and his wife, studying painting (though she quickly managed to find a nearby airfield where she could continue to enjoy going up for flights). Tunnicliffe at that time had just finished his work for the uniform edition of *The Lone Swallows, The Peregrine's Saga, The Old Stag* and *Tarka the Otter,* which Putnam brought out between 1932 and 1934.

At Chivenor, Ann Welch took flying lessons from Tommy Nash and went solo in September. Not to be outdone, Henry overcame his dread of airsickness and decided that he too would take flying lessons. They were not a success. By the end of the third – or perhaps it was only the second – he had exhausted his instructor's patience, and any idea of qualifying as a pilot was forgotten.

At the end of 1934 Henry turned to another potboiler, 'a mule of a book', as he called it himself, *Devon Holiday.* In August, S. P. B. Mais and his wife, Gillian, came to visit him, insisting that Henry had promised to walk all over Devon with them. Glad to leave his 'quiet, almost stagnant valley-life'. Henry abandoned the dam-building he was busy with, and they set off on a series of walks, described by Henry as being written 'in a spirit of slapstick and knockabout (but some of it what is called straight stuff)'. He renamed Mais Masterson Funicular Hengist Zeale, and called his wife Scylla. Windles joined the party for some of the time, with two others – a young American academic and a girl of eighteen who said that her father was Scots, her mother Swedish, and her birthplace Indiana. Slim, fair-haired and blue-eyed, she sounds like yet another version of Barleybright. She explained that she was a journalist, and began to act as a sort of part-time secretary to Henry. He was soon referring to her as Scribe, though she was unlike the 'devoted Scribe, Ann' of *On Foot in Devon* and other books. The latter is here referred to, in what sounds like a fit of pique, as 'a crazy secretary' who had helped him to make his first set of dams in the Bray during the winter before Windles' sixth birthday. The new Scribe, according to Henry, spent a few years of her early childhood with a spinster lady in Georgeham – i.e. Miss Johnson – while her mother, a pianist, was on a concert tour. The child recovered from a glandular complaint on a diet of raw vegetables, and Henry took her for walks.

Henry and his companions wander on Exmoor, Dartmoor, and the long beach of Saunton. They cross the estuary to Appledore. A pilot takes them on a flight in a twin-engined passenger aircraft – probably the Short Scion which Robert Boyd used for charter flights in the early days of Chivenor – up the valley of the Torridge to Petersmarland and on to Okehampton. The pilot was probably Boyd himself, though Henry identifies neither the airfield nor the pilot. His 'spirit of slapstick and knockabout' is much in evidence in his account of this episode. He says that they had met the pilot in the village pub the previous evening, and makes the preposterous statement, 'I believe he had stolen that kite; most of Zeale's friends are crooks'. By way of evidence for his suspicion of the pilot he observes that he wore a large diamond ring 'and had some platinum and gold cigarette cases. Moreover, his moustache ends were waxed'.

Possibly, with the fiasco of his flying lessons still fresh in his mind, he could not resist depicting an imaginary pilot in these unflattering terms.

Henry tells his companions a succession of tall stories about animals and people, including a preposterous description of a regatta at Instow and a long and serious tale about an escaped Dartmoor convict. Halfway through the book he has an idea for a story to be called 'The Maiden Salmon', which he reproduces as a final chapter, dedicating it to the Scribe 'for you inspired it, you are Love'.

According to Henry, 'maiden salmon' was the Taw-Torridge net fisherman's term for for a female grilse. The name appealed to him, and in using it as a title, he plunged into a mood of dolorous romanticism similar to that of *The Gold Falcon*. He wrote of a poet living in a hut 'near the river from which the moor takes its name' and writing 'an epic of the moor's ancientness and wisdom'. He makes a small salmon hatchery. Of the fifty or so alevins which emerge, all but one are eaten by a mullhead; the loss causes the poet to feel 'the doom of his previous life among men' overcoming him. A mysterious young girl visits the hatchery, but does not stay. The poet finds a minute gold star in the hatching tray, and when the surviving fish has grown to be a smolt, he attaches the star to its rear fin with silver wire before releasing it into the river. Two more years pass; the poet is unable to finish his epic. He dreams of his salmon, and walks to the coast where salmon fishermen are at work. In one boat is a girl with thick fair hair, 'strong in her maiden grace. The child he had seen by the hatchery four years before was a woman'.

Her father catches a salmon, but does not notice 'the gold it bore on its pennon-like fin'. The poet watches in anguish as it dies; he returns to his hut to finish his manuscript, and leaves it to be found when he has allowed the river to bear 'his useless body to the sea's oblivion'. However, the girl returns, holding the gold star, when Eosphorus the Lightbringer is in the eastern sky, and the poet knows that 'his search was ended, for on that brow was sunrise'.

Henry was approaching his fortieth birthday when he wrote this story, yet in it he reverted to the self-indulgent emotionalism and the lyrical, over-lush prose of his late twenties. Any satisfaction he felt in writing it must have been diminished by the knowledge that it was not a maiden salmon, or salmon maiden, that should have been occupying his imagination, but the strong male salmon, Salar.

CHAPTER EIGHT

A Fateful Visit to Germany: 1935

The beginning of anything always demanded much nervous energy, Henry remarked in *On Foot in Devon*. The nervous energy needed to begin *Salar* was so great that when at last he wrote the first words he was, he said, 'quivering like one setting out on an Atlantic flight, alone'. He would begin about 9.30 in the morning and go on for eight hours, sometimes twelve or more. He wanted to work like Arnold Bennett, whom he greatly admired, and who had once told him that he did not write as much as was supposed, but he did write *regularly*. Yet it does not seem that Henry could ever settle down to a measured routine as a writer; his tendency was to the sustained burst of creativity, followed by exhaustion and depression.

Henry claimed that he spent forty minutes out of every hour during the summer of 1935 protesting against the need to write for money, which was spent before it arrived, to keep his large family. The accounts he gives of his work on *Salar,* in *Goodbye West Country* and *The Children of Shallowford,* do not quite tally. In the earlier book he said that he sat out of doors at Shallowford typing, day after day, during June and July; then, knowing that his criticisms of Loetitia's housekeeping were unfair, withdrew to his hill-top hut and lived there alone until, one day in August, he felt that 'if the salmon did not die, I should; and so the ending was cut short'. In *The Children of Shallowford* he speaks of taking Windles to stay with him in the hut 'one summer when Loetitia was in the nursing home', and makes no mention of writing *Salar*. His son Richard was born on 1st August, 1935; it was at this time that Windles stayed at the hut, while Margaret and John boarded with the vegetarian Miss Johnson in Georgeham. Henry was not writing, but working on the hut, replacing some of the patent panels that lined it and treating the remainder with bitumen. *Salar* must therefore have been finished either before or after the birth of Richard; probably it was towards the end of August, after the children had returned home.

As Faber had already announced *Salar* in their autumn list, Henry had the uncongenial experience of having to send off each section of the book as he completed it, without a chance to indulge in the repeated revision that was his habit.

Jonathan Cape had very reasonably hoped that Henry's next book would come to him. Since bringing out *The Pathway* he had been the publisher of *The Village Book, The Labouring Life, The Linhay on the Downs,* and *Devon Holiday.* During these years he had kept up what Michael Howard, in *Jonathan Cape, Publisher,* calls a 'long and intimate correspondence' with Henry. On hearing that *Salar* was to go to Richard de la Mare of Faber 'to clear off an old promise', Cape wrote a reproachful and indignant letter pointing out that he had been more sympathetic to Henry's financial needs than either Putnam or Faber, had believed that Henry regarded Cape as his publisher for the future, and would have been prepared to make an arrangement to give him the rest from writing that he had complained of needing. He would even have made it possible for Henry to leave 'the Salmon book' aside for a while if he was not satisfied with it: 'it could have waited until after you had rested and could go back to it with a fresh eye. Now you tell me that it has not been read by anyone, but has gone straight to the printer as it was written! Good God!'

Despite Henry's complaint that the ending had been cut short, the story reaches its natural climax in the penultimate chapter, with the spawning of the salmon: the only question in the reader's mind is whether the author will choose to end with the death of Salar or show him returning to the sea to renew himself. Characteristically, Henry chooses death for the individual fish, while celebrating the continuing cycle of life for its species as the eggs it has fertilised hatch out.

Each stage of the salmon's journey from the sea to the upper reaches of the tributary in which he spends the last months of his life (the Bray near Shallowford) is seen with a filmic clarity and described with beautiful precision. Henry was able to make use of the thousands of images stored in his visual memory over four or five years of repeated watching of the estuary, the Taw, the Mole and the Bray; he would have had quantities of notes set down at intervals during those years. Nevertheless the imaginative labour of selecting and shaping all that he knew into a coherent narrative *in a limited time* must have been immense.

Tension is maintained as the salmon encounters each danger on its watery odyssey: porpoise, net fisherman, poacher, angler, heron, otter. Throughout the book Henry's unequalled awareness of weathers and seasons, and their influence on every aspect of natural life, enhances every scene and sharpens its sensuous impact. The views of underwater life are astonishing: this writer, with no snorkel or aqualung or waterproof camera to help him, somehow records what it is like to be a fish deep in the waters of the Bristol Channel, in the murky currents of the Taw-Torridge estuary in spate, in the broken water at the limit of the tidal Taw. Once he has brought Salar to the reaches of the Bray, Henry can write from his own experience of swimming there, sinking down in the deeper stretches to enjoy the pretence of being a fish or an otter in those places he had named soon after his arrival at Shallowford – the Fireplay Pool under the railway viaduct, the Wheel Pool and the Alder Pool. Until the story draws near its end, all human beings save water bailiffs are Salar's enemies, but in the person of Shiner, Henry is able to express his own compassion for the majestic fish. Shiner, once a poacher, now works for his 'chap' who is 'proper mazed about salmon, writing a book about 'm'; in his stratagems to outwit a gang of poachers and make fun of the water bailiff, he brings touches of humour to the book.

Salar the Salmon came out in November, 1935. Soon Richard de la Mare was able to tell Henry that it had 'beaten all records for his firm, selling 3,000 copies in one day'. It had sold just over 10,000 copies by Christmas. The large advance which de la Mare had persuaded his fellow directors to pay had been earned.

Two of Henry's friends had died during the previous year: Victor Yeates in December, 1934, and T. E. Lawrence in May, 1935. Henry dedicated *Salar* to them jointly. Yeates' death, because of his illness, had not been unexpected; that of Lawrence was a shock – not only to Henry, but to the British public in general, to whom the author of *Seven Pillars of Wisdom* had become a legendary figure. For Henry, the news was doubly appalling: it was after sending a telegram to him that Lawrence – as much a devotee of fast, powerful machines as Henry – had crashed on his motor cycle and received injuries that resulted in his death on 19th May.

Lawrence appears in chapter seven of *Devon Holiday* as G. B.

Everest. In a postscript, Henry said "The character called G. B. Everest has died . . . he crashed on his motor cycle a few minutes after sending a telegram in answer to a letter of mine in which I asked if I might go and see him and show him a proof copy of this book. That telegram is probably the last thing he wrote.

> 11.25 a.m. Bovington Camp 13 May 1935
> Williamson Shallowford Filleigh
> Lunch tuesday wet fine cottage 1 mile north
> Bovington Camp Shaw".

The cottage was of course Clouds Hill. Lawrence had been serving as Aircraftman Shaw until his discharge from the R.A.F. only two months earlier.

In July, 1936, Henry wrote an essay of some 18,000 words about his friendship with Lawrence – a friendship carried on almost entirely by correspondence. The essay makes it clear that the two men only actually met on two occasions: at Vale House, Georgeham, in July, 1929, and on board the *Berengaria* in February, 1934. Faber published the essay as *Genius of Friendship*: 'T. E. Lawrence', in 1941. Either in 1936 or, quite possibly, when revising the essay for publication, Henry gave a far more dramatic reason for his projected visit to Cloud's Hill. He had decided one day, he said, that 'It was time something was done about the pacification of Europe through friendship and fearless common sense'. With Lawrence of Arabia's name to attract them, ex-servicemen would gather in the Albert Hall and begin 'a whirlwind campaign which would end the old fearful thought of Europe (usury-based) for ever. So would the sun shine on free men!'

The original, simpler version sounds more convincing; the later one seems to belong to that fantasy world Henry so often inhabited, in which some magical, universal formula could be conjured up to wipe away all human miseries.

On 2nd September, 1935, immediately after finishing *Salar,* Henry was able to recuperate from the strain of writing against time by taking a holiday abroad. This was made possible by his friend John Heygate, who was working at the UFA Studios in Berlin. Although he thus helped to bring about the abrupt and decisive change in Henry's political ideas that would affect him, and colour his reputation, for the rest of his life, it should be stressed that Heygate himself was no sympathiser with Nazism. He liked Germany, had spent many years there in his youth, and found the Germans, in general, agreeable. In his book, *These Germans,* published at the

beginning of the Second World War, he expressed the opinion that
Hitler's domestic policies, in the mid-Thirties, had been of benefit to
the German people. But his final verdict on Hitler could hardly be
more condemnatory: he compares the dictator to a hideous medieval
torture machine, the Iron Virgin of Nuremberg. Germany, in
his view, resembled a prisoner enclosed in this repulsive device,
'skewered to Hitler's breast', its whole population 'pierced through
with propaganda' until nothing remained but to send it 'gibbering
and twitching to war'.

Heygate's own description of the Nuremberg Rally of 1935,
attended by 'my writer friend, H.W.', differs considerably in tone
from that of Henry in *Goodbye West Country*.

Surprisingly, for such an open-air countryman, Henry loved films
– 'the talkies', as he called them in the idiom of the Thirties. While
he lived in north Devon, he went often to one or other of the two
cinemas in Barnstaple – sometimes twice a week. (When he signed
the conveyance to buy his Norfolk farm, he took Loetitia to the
cinema to celebrate.) During 1936, he was broadcasting nature talks
regularly in both the Schools and Children's Hour programmes
from the B.B.C. station in Bristol.[1] It was part of his routine to
travel up, either in the Silver Eagle or by train from the little station
at Filleigh (now long closed, and demolished in 1987 to make way
for a new road) and, on arrival, walk to 'the usual picture palace'
near Bristol Bridge where he could be 'concealed in its darkness for
three hours for ninepence'. Afterwards he might eat a light meal in
the cinema's cafe. Films helped him to forget himself and live 'in the
sparkle and space of Beauty, gaiety, *life*'. At times he imagined
himself going to Hollywood as a script writer, and longed for the
excitement as well as the financial rewards. For many years he hoped
to see *Tarka* made into a film; in the entry for 16th October, 1936,
in *Goodbye West Country,* he outlined a possible scenario, based on his
search for the otter cub lost during his early Georgeham years. For
the central character, a war-disillusioned young poet, the search for
Tarka is to be the symbol of a search for 'the perfect love,
sublimated in the creation of a work of art. Food, sleep, comfort –
they matter nothing'. (This last is an interesting remark, since for
Henry, quite often, it seems that food, sleep or comfort, if they did
not 'matter nothing', mattered little.) Much as in his short story,
'The Maiden Salmon', a girl 'drawn to him in silent sympathy'
comes to his door after the otter has been found and then killed by
hounds.

Henry admitted that this would be a difficult film to make, but was deeply disappointed that no one was interested in the attempt. We had to wait until the end of his life for a producer determined to take Tarka into the cinema – though with a story-line following that of the book, rather than Henry's symbolic tale.

It would be exciting, Henry thought, to see how films were made in the UFA studios. He watched parts of a film being made in three languages; the star, the then very popular Lilian Harvey, played each scene in turn in German, French and English. Esmond Knight was the male lead in the English version.

His immediate work finished, John Heygate drove Henry in his open M.G. (leather helmets and coats worn, as in Henry's Silver Eagle) to Nuremburg for the Nazi Party rally. In the arena, Henry was outraged to find himself almost squeezed out of his seat by the 'bulky rump' of Frank Buchman, the leader of the Oxford Group which was later to develop into Moral Re-armament. Watching the arrival of Hitler, he saw the crowd's response as an 'eager gladness', and was moved by the playing of 'I had a Comrade' as the urns of remembrance were lit. Later, in the Adolf-Hitler Platz, he saw Goering and Goebbels. While Hitler took the salute there during the 'incessant march-past', Henry grew restless again, and wandered about, becoming exhausted by 'masses and movement'. Later, he said, he went to headquarters and saw Hitler quite close. The effect on him was extraordinary: projecting into the dictator qualities he admired, Henry described him as being 'a man of spiritual grace' and as possessing eyes that were 'falcon-like, remarkably full of life'. Any comparison with a falcon was always high praise from Henry; his Manfred had even told himself that Jesus was a falcon. Moreover, he was later to insist that the dictator's eyes were blue, in accordance with his conviction, implanted in him by his father at the age of three, that the most desirable colour for eyes was blue.

The whole history of Hitler's rise to power is evidence of his ability to exert an almost hypnotic effect both on those close to him and on huge crowds; not a few British observers in the Thirties were to succumb to this faculty. In April, 1989, articles and television programmes recalled the phenomenon, under titles such as 'The Seduction of a Nation' and 'The Fatal Attraction of Adolf Hitler'. In Henry's case there seems to have been a willed surrender of his critical sense, which was in any case idiosyncratic. His essay 'A Brave Book' in *The Linhay on the Downs* shows that he was prejudiced in Hitler's favour well before his visit to Germany: it contains the sentence, 'I believe that Hitler, through his poetic or moral power, will lead Europe to the new age of sunshine and peaceful strength'. Such meaningless utopianism was a dangerous vacuity. Henry filled it with the Hitler he looked on as a man of peace and beneficence because he *wanted* him to be a man of peace and beneficence. In *It Was the Nightingale,* a quarter of a century later, he was to show Phillip Maddison reflecting that he must always avoid what Conrad had called 'the terrible tyranny of a fixed idea'. Unfortunately Henry allowed the fixed idea of the benevolence of Fascism to tyrannise his life.

For the rest of his stay in Germany he was clearly determined to swallow Nazi propaganda whole, helped by a young party member provided as an escort, no doubt to ensure that he heard and saw all the right things, and talked to the right sort of people. He came back to Britain a convert to a dreamy, idealised Hitlerism (rather than Nazism) that had virtually nothing to do with the brutal, totalitarian reality. Unlike many contemporary political converts, whether of the far Left or the far Right, he did not lapse as time passed; the Hitler-shaped man of spiritual grace he had created was to remain yet another item in his fantasy world, a hero to be worshipped alongside T. E. Lawrence, incongruously enough.

Four months after his visit to Germany, he received from Faber the proofs of the one-volume *Flax of Dream* to correct; it ran to some 1,400 pages, more than half a million words in all. He included in *Goodbye West Country* the foreword he had written for *The Flax,* saying that he hoped it would suggest 'to the sensitive reader the parallel between the theme and intention of the book and the ideology of the new Germany'. For one sentence in this, 'I salute the great man across the Rhine, whose life symbol is the happy child', Henry was never to be forgiven by many readers, who were unaware that Henry's Hitler was as benign and divorced from reality as was the Stalin of political innocents of a different persuasion. In any case the sentence has to be read in the context of the one that follows, in which Henry goes back to his insistence that the theme of his novel is the unhappiness of the child.

Despite his tendency, in later years, to hint that he had met Hitler, it is noteworthy that he made no such claim in 1936, merely recalling in *Goodbye West Country* that he had amused himself by wondering what 'the minor country-writer' would say if brought before Hitler, and deciding that as 'those things which were fancied to be common or parallel experiences, should not be obtruded', he would have nothing to say.

During the summer of 1936 he visited my parents once or twice. Germany was still much in his mind. He talked of the new spirit of hope and confidence arising in the country, of the happiness of the blond, sun-burned *Wandervögel,* singing as they rambled in the countryside. As he was to write in *Goodbye West Country,* he had a German grandmother from Bavaria, and was proud of the fact. Born Adela Leopoldine Luhn, she was the wife of the grandfather whose Christian names Henry bore. Her son, William Leopold Williamson, gave his house, 11, Eastern Road, the name Hildersheim in her honour, but removed the name plate in 1914 – as Richard Maddison, in *A Chronicle of Ancient Sunlight,* named his house Lindenheim in honour of his mother, but also removed the name at the outbreak of war.[2]

Henry was thus predisposed to a fellow-feeling for all things German. Because this unfortunately included the Nazi regime, he and my father had a few political arguments for old times' sake; however I am fairly sure that no mention was made during the course of them, or at any other time, of an interview with Hitler.

I had missed most of the broadcasts he had been making from Bristol through being away at a school where no radio listening, even of Schools or Children's Hour Programmes, was thought of, but it must have been about this time that I first heard him read aloud something he had been writing. I can remember his soft voice, with its almost mesmeric quality, but not what he read: very probably a few passages from *Goodbye West Country,* as that was his work in progress.

I inflicted on him a school autograph book. To my dismay he wrote:

'Henry Williamson, Georgeham, 1936
Adolf Hitler is the only real pacifist in European politics today: and peace will come through him'.

This was not at all what I had hoped for from the author of the four novels making up *The Flax of Dream,* the last two of which I had just been reading with profound admiration. It was bewildering. Could he be right? I did not realise then how desperately he wanted to be right.

He talked to us of his latest plans. He was to move to Norfolk. It seemed almost a betrayal, as bewildering as his enthusiasm for a sinister, ranting demagogue. How could he, the devoted Devonian by adoption, move three hundred miles to the east? It was simple enough, he explained: there was nothing left for him in Devon; he needed the stimulus of a new county, a new way of life, the life of a man who worked with his hands, not his brain alone. He intended to become a farmer.

In the opening chapters of *The Story of a Norfolk Farm* he was to describe how he first cycled to Norfolk in August, 1912, when he would have been a few months short of his 17th birthday. (Elsewhere he wrote that it was during this Norfolk holiday that he saw his first otter.) He was reintroduced to the county by Richard de la Mare, his friend and publisher, soon after Christmas, 1935. De la Mare and his wife had a holiday cottage near Cromer. While Henry was staying with them, they took him to see an Elizabethan house that had been standing empty for some time, telling him that he could buy it cheaply; but he thought it too big, an unhappy house with a feeling of exhaustion about it. Instead he made enquiries about the farm land adjoining.

The idea of buying this land, working it, and writing a book about his experiences while doing so, seized him at once; he was encouraged, he said, by de la Mare. Faber's non-fiction list had always contained a fair number of books on agriculture.

In the mean time he could begin a book which would show him preparing to leave Devon. *Goodbye West Country* is presented simply as a diary of the year 1936. The entry for 1st January records a journey from Filleigh to Bristol by train to give a broadcast. How Henry has packed two days in London and several more in Norfolk into the post-Christmas period (as he was later to describe in *The Story of a Norfolk Farm*) is not explained. Arriving home at night feeling 'granulated, purposeless', he comforts himself with the thought that 'soon I'll be spreading muck, ploughing, harrowing, digging drains, making up roads'. Yet at that stage he had not had time to do more than look over the farm and contemplate buying it: there were to be months of discussions and negotiations before he did so. It is probable that much of the entry for 1st January was written later, when page proofs of *Goodbye West Country* were ready for correction.

Within a few days Henry was at Oxford for a farming conference, after which he went down to Kent, and from there drove to Sussex to see the grave of Victor Yeates. Although dissatisfaction with his life at Shallowford had evidently increased his habitual restlessness, the prospect of a move seemed to increase it still further. The pages of *Goodbye West Country* show how often he was away from home during 1936, in Kent, in Norfolk, in South Devon, in London, in Paris at the invitation of his Georgian hostess, Mrs Reese or 'Miss Louise', in Brighton with his friend John Heygate, or simply at his writing hut. An additional reason for these absences was that he was very well aware of the harm his irascible behaviour, and what he himself called his ranting, inflicted on his family. Repeatedly he deplored his own conduct, yet remained incapable of controlling or correcting it. From a distance he pictured his home, and 'It always seemed so lovely, it made my heart ache – but only when I was away'.

The reason he gives for one of his visits to London makes it clear that his plan for the novel sequence that would develop into *A Chronicle of Ancient Sunlight* was very much alive in his mind, years after he had first conceived it in Georgeham. On 27th January he travelled up to watch the funeral procession of George V, 'to get a full-dress scene for my London trilogy'. His companion on this journey was Ann, who was living in Kent. A month later he drove to Shoreham, to stay the night with S. P. B. Mais, and afterwards went on to Kent 'to help Ann with her novel, to be published pseudonymously'.

Henry's publisher, Faber, bought out this novel the following year under the title *Women Must Love,* and the pseudonym chosen was Julia Hart-Lyon. That Henry wanted to hint at a connection between himself and the author of *Women Must Love* is indicated by the fact that in the second edition of *The Gold Falcon* there is a passing reference to 'Julia Hart-Lyon, who writes the literary gossip in one of the Sunday papers'.

In outline, the novel's story is simple. Susanna Fair, an eighteen-year-old secretary, has a short-lived affair with a composer who happens to be her uncle by marriage, and a longer one with Richard Scotforth, an author whose novel *Heaven Without Horizon* she has just read and greatly admired. She leaves her London job to work as secretary-household help in Richard's house in Cumberland, and soon feels that she has made a mistake. Richard is a lover at night and an exacting, fault-finding domestic tyrant by day. He rails constantly at his patient and weary wife, and quickly begins to undermine Susanna's self-confidence. He goes on a journey, ostensibly abroad, but is soon writing to say that he is spending his time in Cornwall with a slim sixteen-year-old girl who has hair 'bleached barley-coloured by the sun'. Susanna finds that she is pregnant and goes back to London, first to her mother – who tries to persuade her to have an abortion – and later into squalid digs. After the birth of the baby, Ruth Rosemary, Richard rents a cottage for Susanna in Dorset, visits her there, and scandalises the village by bathing naked. A telegram to say that his younger son is very ill recalls him to Cumberland. The boy dies, and Richard cremates him on a hilltop pyre at night. He has written a radio play, 'The Sun is Risen', to be broadcast on Christmas Eve; driving his Bugatti too fast, he is killed on his way to the studio.

Henry's ideas, written and spoken, his characteristic behaviour when world-weary or in high spirits, are clearly displayed in the person of Richard Scotforth, and a sympathetic portrait of Loetitia is provided in his wife Alethea. Chapter 21, 'Ménage', may be read as a brief but closely-observed complement to *The Children of Shallowford*. Evidently Henry read and approved – and perhaps contributed to – the portrayal of Richard. (Two sets of corrected proofs of *Women Must Love,* with six pages of additional typescript, exist in Exeter University's Henry Williamson Archive.)

On 9th March, Henry drove back to Devon. It rained all the way; characteristically he endured in his open car for seven hours, but at Exeter 'gave in, and put the hood up'. This is an interesting example of his pleasure in enduring discomfort. Sometimes he did it from a desire to test himself, as he put it; at others from what sounds like a self-punishing impulse; at others again from a sense of egalitarianism. Resting comfortably in de la Mare's Norfolk cottage, for instance, he had asked himself why he had a 'faint inner objection to relaxation . . . was it right to be so comfortable, when most people on the earth existed in circumstances which were a disgrace to anyone with imagination?' And always, at the back of his mind, was the memory of the trenches in December, 1914: compared with that, anything was bearable.

Later in March he drove to Bristol for a broadcast. Ann was now staying at Shallowford again, and went with him, wearing borrowed leather coat and flying helmet. They got back at midnight. It was cold, with a white mist in the Exe valley, yet for Henry it was 'a point of honour not to put the hood up'. Anyone who travelled in the Silver Eagle had to be prepared to be as Spartan as its driver – and to have strong nerves, when Henry was in the mood to demonstrate his skill at driving fast.

The next time he came back from Bristol at night, fortunately alone, he overturned the car when only a few miles from Filleigh. It tipped on to its offside, and Henry climbed out, unhurt, as he had from a crash on Bagshot Heath three years earlier. The next day a photographer from a local paper took pictures of it; one is included in *Goodbye West Country,* showing the car without its silver eagle mascot, which Henry had removed after the accident in case anyone stole it.

For some time, while the Alvis was being repaired, Henry drove an old Crossley left with him by a relation as settlement for a debt, but he was not satisfied until he had his own car back; his affinity with and affection for it caused him to write later that it did not seem to him fanciful to speak of particular machines having a spirit that was in sympathy with their owners.

He wanted to take life more easily during this year, which he saw as an interim between the mental labour of writing *Salar* and the physical labour of becoming a farmer. He had already written much of what he was then calling *Tales of My Children,* which would be published in 1939 as *The Children of Shallowford;* he had contracted to prepare 'a pemmican biography of Richard Jefferies with extracts from his books', as well as a re-arranged and annotated version of Jefferies' *Hodge and his Masters;* there were radio talks to be written each month, and newspaper articles. The material for *Goodbye West Country* he assembled as he went along. All kinds of things went into it: not only many observations of birds, fish and animals, but the substance of several broadcast scripts, including one on red deer given in full as first written, as re-written, and as finally broadcast; appreciative or indignant letters from strangers about his books, and letters from his American publisher and other friends; recollections of his boyhood; and the long account of his visit to Germany of the previous year.

His constant sense of the need to earn money by writing oppressed him. In the essay 'Moonlight' in *The Linhay on the Downs* he had said that his trouble was that he had got into the habit of using himself as a receiving apparatus for natural impressions, in order to render them into words and so obtain money. The camera of his mind was tired, 'abused by a demoniacal photographer'. There were nearly a dozen people entirely dependent on him. In 1936 he came back to this, claiming that for three years he had been 'the support, or part support, of five families, comprising in all seven adults and twelve children' . . . thank God, since *Salar,* editors no longer reject most of what I write'. Even if he was overstating the case, implying responsibility for several relations by blood and by marriage that was not strictly his, Henry's self-martyring tendency made it real to him. The knowledge that in planning to take over a run-down farm he was gambling with his family's future added to his anxiety.

One day at the beginning of May he drove to his writing hut in the Crossley and walked across Pickwell Down to look at the little goyal or combe which he had imagined as the site of Willie Maddison's tumbledown cottage. With distaste he noted the new houses above the shore, and the two hotels (one of the latter burned down a few years later and was not replaced; the other, rebuilt and greatly enlarged, has now been converted into holiday flats). On the beach he felt 'a sudden poignancy for friends I had known on these sands; faces I seldom saw now'. Whether or not my parents were among those friends, he certainly renewed his visits to them, as has been said, and in August he enjoyed days with S. P. B. Mais and his wife, who were staying at Woolacombe.

Henry recorded that the hill-top field was now a happy place: 'Loetitia and Ann are here, and all the children, and Mary their cheerful Irish nanny'. He included a photograph of Loetitia and Ann on Woolacombe sands, in which the head of Petre Mais can just be seen.

An addition to the party in the field was a young man who ate with them in the loft over the woodshed. 'I think he is a fan. Always a young man is there – sometimes with a different face, but always the same ideas. I feel like an old stag squired by a staggart . . .' (This staggart has identified himself in the pages of the Henry Williamson Society Journal as Guy Priest.)

Henry had been increasingly pursued by fans since the publication of *The Pathway*. (Some of them might have taken note of Dr Johnson's rejoinder to the lady who expressed a wish to increase her acquaintance with authors, 'conceiving that more might be learned from their conversation and manner of living than from their works. "Madam," said he, "the best part of an author will always be found in his writings".') Often they were serious-minded young men who wanted to be writers, or at least wanted to write novels in the manner of Henry Williamson. Their reception varied. The entry for 24th June, 1936, in *Goodbye West Country*, provides a satirical account of what was probably a fairly typical visit, and implies Henry's gratitude to Loetitia for playing a large part in the entertainment of difficult and humourless would-be writers. Sometimes Henry might allow the eager fan to talk to him while he carried on with some practical work, adopting one of his down-to-earth no nonsense guises; on one occasion a young poet came to see him 'with perfervid poetry in his eyes, and departed with scorn in them' because Henry had gone on trying to get the three carburettors of the Silver Eagle synchronised, showing no enthusiasm for art, literature or Communism. To be allowed to become a temporary member of the Williamson household, a fan had to show some sign of talent, to which Henry was always generous.

It was during those August weeks of 1936 on the hill-top field that the conveyance and mortgage documents of the Norfolk farm arrived. Loetitia and Henry read them through while the children went down to play on the swings opposite Miss Johnson's house. The staggart was called in to witness Henry's signature. It was appropriate that this signing should have taken place on the first piece of land that he had ever owned – and now he was the owner of the 240 acres of Old Hall Farm, Stiffkey, which in his books is renamed Old Castle Farm, Creek. (Possibly the 'Castle' element was irresistible after eight years as a tenant of the Fortescues at Castle Hill, Filleigh.)

The following month, at Michaelmas, Henry gave notice to vacate Shallowford. As it was a twelve month's notice, it would be September, 1937, before the family finally left the cottage – but in his imagination, Henry was already a Norfolk farmer. He had spent eight years in Georgeham, and by the time he left would have spent eight years at Shallowford. It so happened that in Stiffkey, too, he would spend eight years.

CHAPTER NINE

Old Hall Farm, Stiffkey

In the last months of 1936, Henry was in a state of acute nervous fatigue, finding it difficult to sleep, as in the months before his visit to Georgia. In the small hours of the night his brain would begin 'its old trick of churning up past mortifications, miseries, thwartings, work undone, misjudgements, etc., all the old semi-rotten compost of the past'. He saw himself as 'rudderless in the stream of life, mentally barnacl'd, a hulk'. In the chapter 'Innocent Water Buttercup' in the original version of *The Children of Shallowford,* which was among those he cut from the second edition, he described one waking nightmare, which concerned his planting of water crowfoot in the Bray not long after his arrival at Shallowford. On impulse, as he did so many things, he brought some stems of the plant from a chalk stream in Wiltshire. (There are thirteen British species of crowfoot; Henry calls his *ranunculus fluvitans,* so probably meant *ranunculus fluitans,* the River Crowfoot.) He had noticed that it formed a home for nymphs and larvae of ephemera, the food of trout. Local experts on river life assured him that the stems would be washed away by winter spates. They were wrong; the plants took root and spread rapidly. Some years later (apparently in 1937, as he says Windles was eleven) someone told him that the fishing in the river Clwyd in Wales had been ruined by the planting of Canadian pond weed.

This information threw Henry into a panic. His imagination showed him the Bray, the Mole and the Taw clogged with the weed, impassable to salmon; the capital value of the fishing destroyed. Wildly he calculated what the salmon beats brought to their owners. Having come up with the improbable total of £300,000, he decided that he might well be sued for that amount – 'and I was £300 overdrawn, the father of half a dozen children, and had written almost my last book'.

At three o'clock in the morning he went out with rake, mattock and scythe to begin the task of removing the crowfoot from the Bray. (When he gave a shorter account of this episode twenty years later in *A Clear Water Stream,* implying that it happened before the writing of *Salar,* he said that he felt like the legendary Cornishman Tregeagle, condemned to empty Dozmary Pool with a leaking limpet shell and twist the sands of Lyonesse into ropes.)

Somehow or other he cleared much of the weed from the Bray, and persuaded himself that he had not in fact done any lasting harm, but his irrational anxiety is an indication of his mental turmoil, as he later perceived, asking himself whether his worry had been 'a symptom of something else, which an active life in the open air would remove'.

Yet the active life in the open air was merely to add physical fatigue to mental. The title he chose for chapter 19 of *The Story of a Norfolk Farm,* describing how he took possession of the farm on Old Michaelmas Day, 1937, was 'I am a Melancholy Farmer'. For much of the next eight years, this was to be an all too accurate self-description.

In the early chapters of the book Henry explained how he was able to afford to buy the farm and work it for the first year or two: Loetitia offered him money left to her by her father, and Henry, on the death of his mother in 1936, received money left to him in trust by his grandfather. Believing that he needed a manager, he persuaded Loetitia to write to the youngest of her brothers, whom he rechristens Sam, and invite him to return to England (from Australia, which Henry for some reason changes to Africa) to take the job. It is at this point that the serio-comic episode of Henry's intervention in the business affairs of the Hibbert brothers, referred to in chapter 3, is outlined; in his usual confessional style, he showed himself over-riding Loetitia's diffidently offered warnings that it might be difficult for 'Sam' to work amicably with him.

During this period, Henry was filled with contradictory impulses. He insisted that writing was not a living: 'I wanted to *do* something. Words were not enough'. Yet at the same time he told himself that he could always write and so earn any capital needed to run the farm in the future; going further, he pictured the farm becoming so successful, after three years, that he could go away, leaving the running of it to 'Sam', and 'Lie in the sun on some far sandy shore, or idle by a trout stream; and find the freedom I had not known since the old days at Skirr Cottage'. Elsewhere he cut the three years to one, after which he would write the books which had been 'waiting within my hidden mind for many years now' – in other words the sequence that was to become *A Chronicle of Ancient Sunlight*.

On a visit to Norfolk when he was negotiating to buy the farm, he told himself that the county was his home. 'I was always a stranger in Devon, but here I am among my own sort of people'. He needed to convince himself that East Anglians were his sort of people, but eastern England was never to become his sort of countryside, as the west had been. He made his farewells to Devon in two books. At the end of *Goodbye West Country* he said, 'Now that I have to go – I *have* to go – it is as though a tree were being uprooted'. In the chapter in the first edition of *The Children of Shallowford* called 'Ancient Sunlight', he spoke of seeing 'the golden ghosts of the children playing by the summer river, or under the lime trees' rustling leaves. There is no return; and as I am made, and always have been, I long to return. Only in the past has my being a sense of form'. Dreaming backwards into time, he saw himself planting aubretia between the stones of the path of 'the early cottage' (Vale House), while Windles stands by the gate. He claimed to have lived in Devon for 23 years, discounting the seven years of war and life in London that intervened between his idyllic brief holiday in Georgeham in May, 1914, and his return to settle there in 1921.

Throughout 1936 and the early months of 1937 he read all he could about farming. He took the 'Farmers' Weekly' and the 'Farmer and Stockbreeder'; he talked to farmers and asked their advice. However much he may have abominated the 'mental barbed wire' of his school curriculum, when a subject caught his imagination he was a tireless learner. (Possibly he would have approved today's educational vogue for the heuristic approach.) Bird, animal, plant; the life cycle of otter and salmon: he had spent thousands of hours absorbing knowledge of all these. Now he became a student of crops and stock and the fertility of the soil.

He could afford to take a rest from writing, except for occasional newspaper articles: he had two books ready to come out in 1937. Putnam, the publisher of *Tarka* and his other early nature books, had accepted *Goodbye West Country*, while his edited selection from

Richard Jefferies' writings was to be published by Faber. He had
also re-arranged Jefferies' *Hodge and His Masters* for Methuen, and
written an introduction for it.

Henry would have seen much that he wrote in his introduction to
Richard Jefferies as applying to himself. In moments of inspiration,
he said, Jefferies believed himself to be 'a prophetic thinker and
writer of the world . . . the theme of his work was the creation of,
the burning hope for, a better, truer, more sunlit world of men'. His
pages 'glowed and shone with ancient sunlight'; he was a genius, a
visionary, and a prophet of 'an age not yet come into being – the age
of sun, of harmony'. Although he might not proclaim it quite so
openly, Henry believed that all these things were true of himself.
Incidentally, this is one of the passages which indicate the way his
perennial rejoicing in sunlight had developed into a symbol of or
metaphor for his own huge, vague, idealised yearning for an
impossible blissful world of harmonious humanity.

It is more startling to read that Jefferies was not only 'a little
brother of Jesus' but showed Hitler-like characteristics: 'literary
criticism of a future age will discover many similarities in these two
men. Both grew up solitaries, unaffected by schooling, learning only
from the natural self. One withered away; the other acted, fulfilled
himself'. This apparently preposterous comparison between two
men who could hardly have been more dissimilar is simply further
evidence of the ectoplasmic, benign Hitler who had emanated from
Henry's impressionable imagination in Nuremberg.

He deduced that Jefferies had possessed very keen eyes and ears:
'all writing of the first class comes from exceptional sight and
hearing: and insight arises from stored physical impressions of sight
and sound'. Throughout the first half of his writing life, at least,
Henry's sight and hearing were evidently excellent; all his most
enduring writing, especially in *Tarka* and *Salar,* came from stored
physical impressions of sight and sound, but especially sight.
Although by the late Thirties he was ready to acknowledge that
several of his books written during the decade, though 'as good as
most country stuff', were 'not much good', and although he might
refer to himself in print as 'a minor country-writer', he was usually
confident that at his best he was a writer of the first class.

He knew that he would not be able to write about his farming
adventure until he had had a year or two of practical experience. He
was impatient to begin, and made careful plans of the work to be
done on the neglected acres he had acquired. He bought a lorry and

trailer; he bought three old dilapidated cottages in the village of Stiffkey; he leased a gravel pit from which to take materials for making new roads on the farm.

In May, 1937, four months remained before he was due to take possession of Old Hall Farm, but the bankrupt tenant had already gone, and he was free to start work. As the farmhouse had been sold separately, he had as yet nowhere for his family to live; there were two cottages on his land, but they were tenanted, and he was to experience great difficulty in persuading the tenants to leave. His three derelict cottages – bought for £190 – would need much work before they were habitable. Loetitia and the children therefore remained at Shallowford while Henry set off for Stiffkey, towing a caravan behind the Silver Eagle, while 'Sam' drove the lorry towing a trailer loaded with a quantity of timber, lathes, tools, and the little sailing dinghy, named *Pinta* after Bevis's boat, which Henry kept for several years in the Taw-Torridge estuary, and hoped to sail in the cold waters of the north Norfolk coast.

He was in his forty-second year. He told himself that he was lucky to have escaped into middle age; that his sort of writer, 'almost useless for anything else in life except digging into himself and turning feelings into words', usually came to an unhappy end 'through tuberculosis, starvation, suicide or drink'. In spite of the phases when he had supposed himself to be ill (especially during the Skirr Cottage years, and in 1933) he now acknowledged that he had sound lungs (never, as he sometimes suggested, damaged by gas), was well fed and had too much tenacity to kill himself. As for drink, he said that he loathed much of it – though many friends were to bear witness that he could be a hearty social drinker as he grew older.

From the start of the journey east, things did not go well. Henry makes it clear, in *The Story of a Norfolk Farm,* that he quickly began to justify Loetitia's warnings that he would be critical and impatient with 'Sam', whose nature was so unlike his own. Shouldering the blame in retrospect, he enlists the reader's sympathy for 'Sam', and quotes his reasonable protest, 'The trouble is you want me to think with your head all the time, instead of letting me do things my way'. Yet Henry contrives to leave the suspicion that, if he had it all to do again, he would show no more restraint.

Despite the need to provide accomodation for his family, he decided that road-making came first. In his usual fashion, he tore into the job and became exhausted, but after a few days took on two unemployed men who worked well, and the roads crept steadily across his land and around the outbuildings.

In July he drove the lorry to Kent; Ann, his 'faithful scribe' of the early Shallowford years, had agreed to come to the farm, bringing some of her furniture. On hearing that she had been in contact with mumps, Henry at once remarked that if she became ill, and passed on the infection, 'our whole scheme may be wrecked'. When she did in fact develop mumps, she submitted to being banished for six weeks (or so Henry said) to a tent on what had been named Pine Tree Camp, her food pushed to her at the end of a pole.

The work on the decayed village cottages was by now being done by a local builder, more slowly than Henry had anticipated. The weather grew cold. In November, 'Sam' left to go to a factory job; as his sister had foreseen, working with Henry had become intolerable. Henry and Ann moved into the farm's old granary, with an anthracite stove by way of heating. When the east wind blew sleet through the leaking roof and rickety doors, this was not enough, and Henry noted that Ann's face was often set and white.

During these bitter weeks of early winter, Henry was visited by a neighbour, Dorothy, Viscountess Downe. (With his solar obsession, he renamed her Lady Sunne in his book.) She was a member of the British Union of Fascists, and invited him to join the party and speak on its behalf. After some hesitation, he agreed and so, as he approached his 42nd birthday, became a committed follower of Sir Oswald Mosley. He found it a strange feeling to go out at night in Lady Downe's car, which had a platform and microphone on its roof, to speak to 'flint and brick walls of almost empty squares and deadend streets'.

Meanwhile he went on with the work of the farm. He was lucky enough to employ two knowledgeable, honest, kindly and unfailingly helpful farm workers, father and son, to whom he paid grateful tribute in *The Story of a Norfolk Farm* and elsewhere (they appear in *A Chronicle of Ancient Sunlight* as Luke and Matt). He bought two horses, a variety of implements, and threshed out the corn stacks left by his predecessor. Finally he bought a Ferguson tractor. This was the third machine for which he was to feel a real affection – but whereas the Norton and the Silver Eagle had been primarily for pleasure, this was a valuable working tool, of a design which he extolled repeatedly, in his books and to friends. It was small and light, half the weight of an ordinary tractor, ideal for every type of soil. Henry called it a work of genius, and happily began his autumn ploughing with it.

Since the lease of Shallowford had expired in September, Loetitia and the children had been staying with a friend elsewhere in north Devon. Just before Christmas, Henry sent for them come up to join him in the granary, as the cottages, though structurally complete, still needed some internal work.

They came, and Henry exchanged his grass widowhood for his former position as head of an extensive household. Its members are listed in the dedication to *Goodbye West Country:* 'To the migrants – Loetitia, Ann, Robin, Windles, John, Margaret, Robert, Rosemary and Richard'. (Robin was Loetitia's youngest brother.)

Although the makeshift life in the granary may have delighted the children at first, the cold of that winter, and the contrast between the mildness of Devon and the sharp East Anglian air is still remembered by their adult selves. While his family slept in the loft on Christmas Eve, Henry went out into a clear frosty night and, as he so often did, recalled the early months of the First World War and the strange Christmas Truce of 1914 which, in retrospect, he saw as the great transforming event of his life. His autobiographical books celebrate it again and again; even his foreword to the one-volume edition of *The Flax of Dream* begins with an account of it, and claims that 'the seed-idea' of that novel sequence was 'loosed upon the frozen ground of the battlefield'. The fulfilment of that idea had been the mainspring of his life ever since, he said, and he was hopeful now; 'the vision of a new world, dreamed by many young soldiers in the trenches and shell craters of the World War, was being made real in Germany'.

So he insisted on believing – and perhaps the chapter called 'A Vision of Christmas' in *The Story of a Norfolk Farm* was indeed written at the time it describes, the end of 1937. Yet as the Second World War had begun by the time he was well into the book, it is more probable that the chapter belonged to the time when he knew all his hopes of peace were vain, although he was never to concede that his 'pacifist' Hitler was a chimaera.

CHAPTER TEN

The Story of a Norfolk Farm

At the beginning of January, 1938, the Williamson family moved into the reconditioned cottages in Stiffkey, and Henry had the garden cleared of rubble and replanted. He was now beginning to farm in earnest, buying bullocks to be fattened, some turkeys and laying pullets. He also began to sow his first crop of barley and oats. At the same time he was hard at work on a draft of the original edition of *The Children of Shallowford*. In answer to a letter from my parents, he wrote, in February, 'Funny, I was writing about you when the post came . . . Birth of Windles, Trojan, nursing home, Aubrey trying to take the hills on top, very engine proud: Gipsy passing out in back, me super-anxious. Your kindness. I must write something to try to get some money to pay these enormous and, probably-to-be-lost, expenses. It's been a continual strain, not knowing what to do and always conscious of the race against time, or the season'. Having summarised his road-building and cottage renovating, he went on, 'I took on three men's work, to be done from a jangle of growing children and fear of failing and letting them down, and I shan't turn back: tho often the little hill of Ox's Cross seems like heaven, for its smallness, & simplicity & peace. Tho I'd be lonely now, with all the best gone out in books. I've given away almost all of myself, I suppose, and feel poor thereby. It doesn't come back: unless one is a Faustus, and takes some young woman to love one. How lovely to be on the sands as in 1921-22-23, and do nowt but play and muse and swim and have no cares. And here I am billed to speak at British Union meetings, and working so that I can free myself to join Mosely (sic), whom I like much, and who is desperately in need of personal reaffirmation and help. No new thing this: the books, and especially the Flax, were only an intermediate step in my destiny. You may recall the revolutionary desire always there: only it had to pass through the reactionary and subversive stages . . . It's now 9.50 a.m., and I haven't been down to farm, *where we haven't yet really started farming*. (His italics) I've overspent on improvements, concrete yards, drains, roads, etc., and neglected the farming. But we've ploughed five-sixths of our arable, tractor and horses (little farm doesn't justify this elaborate tractor, really. £300 – Ferguson, hydraulic implements). Ten bullocks came today (£17 each) to be fattened. I must go. The problem here is hills. If 'twere level, all would be easy. But the buildings are down low and I've got to take muck up the soft fields and it's too costly. Tractor slips. Both towing bars of the big new two-ton rubber-wheeled carts are broken. No roller. No harrows. Rats eating expensive seed barley. Reconstruction work half-done, neglected. Drains in, and all under concrete, but no tops to sump. I'm fed up and can't do a thing except easy simple labouring work. I don't want responsibility, but rest'.

He complained that all his first editions were somewhere in damp sheds or barns, and original illustrations were lost or rat-eaten. However, although he said he had no photographs of the farm, he sent us a snap of himself on the Ferguson tractor. When my father, by a slip of the pen, referred to this as a Fordson, Henry was quick to correct him. 'Tractor is a Ferguson. Fordson, no sir!!'

Before he told us of his struggles with the farm, my mother, with maternal partiality, had sent him the typescript of an adolescent novel I had written, and in the midst of his energy-sapping work he found time to read it, write letters of criticism and encouragement, and even show it to Richard de la Mare of Faber. It was too immature for acceptance, and Henry exhorted me to start another book and write 'more of things you've known, seen, experienced . . . Fiction is a trade and you mustn't start a shop until your goods are saleable for their practical value'. In another letter he urged me to 'stick it, the way is hard hard hard all the time'.

For him, the whole year was evidently hard. Confronted by mounting debts, he returned to the mental labour of writing simply for money, producing, he said, 22 newspaper articles and 18 radio talks, as well as completing *The Children of Shallowford*. He lamented that whereas in the old days he had been able to write all night, now, after a day's physical work, he could not go on beyond midnight. (How many established authors would have undertaken to write at all in such circumstances?) Things were made worse by the fact that he was having to do his own correspondence and keep the farm books, as Ann, evidently feeling that it was time to live her own life, had gone to live in Wiltshire.

He was so shaken by her departure that he left the farm to go on without him for a week or two while he recuperated in Devon. During his stay at the writing hut he visited my parents; once more they became his confidants. Back in Norfolk, he wrote them a long, agitated letter, saying that on his journey home he had met Ann by chance near her cottage and had, he thought, effected a reconciliation – only to find that, on reflection, she insisted that she wanted no more to do with him. He promised to send us a copy of *Women Must Love,* saying that 'When you read it, you'll see how to me it seemed impossible that such a break could occur. I mean, the door shut in the face of a friend in deep exhaustion and trouble . . . I expect it was wrong somehow, else there would have been harmony between us except irritation and strain on my part, so often . . . It is finished, and the incredible has happened. Silence, dear Shado, will best thy grave become. It seems rather like the penultimate chapter of The Pathway, come again. And, the poignard twisting in its throat, it was the spirit of the book that drew that life, wholly in dedication, to me. And it was the inner conflict and disintegration of Maddison that finally embittered and almost destroyed that life. I know it'. He was thinking of giving up the farm and allowing Loetitia to divorce him, but saw the impracticability of such a move. 'The trouble is, No money, and the only place to go is the hut; & that in winter, no, I couldn't bear it. The old haunts, no, they are impregnated with the past. Germany? The mountains? A far cry from 1921 and the Decca trench gramophone & all hope and all illusion. However, there's work to be done'.

He then added some verse:

1914-18

Shall life renew these bodies, of a truth
All death will he annul, all grief assuage
And fill those void veins full again with youth,
And wash, with an immortal water, Age?
When I do ask White Age he saith not so,
My head hangs weighed with snow!
And when I hearken to the Earth she saith,
My fiery heart sinks aching: it is Death.
Mine ancient scars shall not be glorified,
Nor my titanic tears, the seas, be dried.'

We assumed, as he evidently meant us to assume, that this was original. Many years later, re-reading this letter, I realised that it was not: it comes from a sonnet by Henry's favourite war poet, Wilfred Owen, entitled 'The End'. By no means one of his best poems, it was understandably assigned to the section 'Other Poems, and Fragments', included at the end of his *Collected Poems*. The first line is 'After the blast of lightning from the east'. In our ignorance of the poem's source, we found it surprising: however poetic his prose might be, we had not thought of Henry as a writer of verse.

He followed his quotation with a paragraph showing an extraordinary change of mood. Knowing that the boarding and breeding kennels my father had set up some years earlier was not financially successful, and that there was a possibility that we would soon move away from Devon, he went on:

'Ha ha ha, he he he, little brown glass I'll quaff of 'ee. Your problem is real: mine is PHONEY. I shall be sorry to pass, on my crutches, Streamways and find it changed, and you all gone away, away, away. Eheu, fugaces, fugaces! (Bring me my dictionary, Jeeves!) I'll send the book. Meanwhile, my best love to all of you. Wish I were with you to put back a beer or two'.

(Had he perhaps already put back a beer or two before finishing his letter?)

Later that year the friendship between Henry and my father was interrupted. In the Twenties, my father had taken a postal course in free-lance journalism (in at least three of his books Henry had made fun of one of the consequences of this, but luckily my father had not read those particular books, and my mother, who had, did not pass on the information). Now, however, hearing how well Henry was able to solve his financial difficulties by journalism, my father recalled his earlier attempts, and discussed with him the possibility of writing a series of articles for a national daily paper on the care and breeding of dogs. Henry encouraged him, promised to mention his name to an editor, and kept his promise. Unfortunately he then succumbed to his tendency to gossip. (He often referred to his own garrulousness, and made short-lived resolutions to curb himself.) On this occasion, perhaps during a convivial evening, he talked too freely to an acquaintance, whom he and my father had in common, about my father's affairs. The acquaintance passed on the information to my father, who was understandably incensed. He wrote Henry an angry letter, although my mother, trying as usual to act as peacemaker, persuaded him to moderate his original draft somewhat.

Knowing that any reply made directly to my father might not be read, Henry wrote to my mother as intermediary; in the course of his letter he said: 'As for the tone of A's letter to me, that was of course his own idiom, and it was caused by my remarks which pierced to his soul or essence. His only reply was rough music and a barrage of everything handy at my head, and I am inclined to think, with a sense of humour which has never quite abdicated, quite right too! Anyhow it was presumption on my part to make any sort of criticism; and as for the discussing of him with others, this has been my habit for many years; just as it has been his to discuss others also; but we have both done it in our different idioms . . . I promise you A as a subject of conversation will in future be out of my head, for ever and ever; tho if we meet by chance and he is friendly, I shall be the same. I am still fond of him, tho you may not think so, and do not think the past amity has been so one-sided as he seemed to think when he wrote his riposte!'

This disarming letter did not entirely mollify my father when it was handed on to him to read. He was in any case seriously disturbed by Henry's refusal to alter his belief that Hitler was a man of benevolence, and became more so at the outbreak of war. At the age of forty-two, my father joined the army as a private soldier but, perhaps because he had held a commission at the end of the First World War, was soon on one of the very short officers' training courses of the period. Commissioned in the R.A.S.C., he went to France at the beginning of March, 1940, and was promoted to captain. On 1st June he was among those brought back safely from the beaches of Dunkirk. During a subsequent spell of sick leave at home in Georgeham, he met Henry and, shaken by his experiences and angry at what he had heard of Henry's unchanging political stance, refused to acknowledge him. It was their final encounter; a year or two later, my parents moved away from Devon, and they did not meet Henry again.

It would seem that Henry remembered the slight all too clearly. When he came to write *Lucifer Before Sunrise* he showed Philip Maddison, in the summer of 1940, visiting the south Devon village of Malandine, which represents Georgeham. He encounters and is ignored by George Pole-Cripps, a character who appeared briefly in the early chapters of *It was the Nightingale,* and was an ungenerous caricature of my father (different in tone from the portrayal of 'Valentine' in the first edition of *The Children of Shallowford*, on which this part of *It was the Nightingale* is based). George is a lieutenant in the army and claims, falsely, to hold the rank of captain and to have been at Dunkirk, although in fact he has never been out of England. No doubt it gave Henry satisfaction to include my father in the list of military impostors who appear now and then in his novels, beginning with Captain Colyer in *The Dream of Fair Women,* but in this case the falsity is his own. It is an interesting instance of the way in which, while following his own experiences fairly closely in the *Chronicle,* he might reconstruct events to accord with his view of them.

At about the time of the Munich crisis, Henry had the satisfaction of harvesting his first crop of barley and oats; he enjoyed seeing his children playing in the corn fields, the older boys leading the horses to the stacks. Yet the price of barley dropped sharply that year, and when Henry drew up a balance sheet at the beginning of winter, he found that he had lost money. He told Loetitia that, as the mortgagor, she should foreclose 'before the whole damn thing goes bust', but she assured him that it would not go bust, and he had done splendidly; he praised her generosity.

The tenants of the two cottages which Henry had bought with the farm had at last moved out. Despite his anxiety about his overdraft, Henry employed a builder to begin work on alterations. To celebrate the end of his first year of farming, he gave a party in the granary in which, during the first winter in Norfolk, three adults and six children had camped out and shivered around the inadequate stove. The food – cold turkey, pheasant, ham and salad – was set out on the eleven-foot-long oak table which Henry said was seventeenth century, and eaten by the light of many candles. The guest of honour was Robert Donat, who was just about to begin his part in 'Goodbye Mr Chips'. With his usual sense of the glamour of all those connected with the film industry, Henry did indeed feel honoured by his presence.

The autobiographical *The Story of a Norfolk Farm* in fact concerns only the first two of his eight years at Stiffkey. For a vivid depiction of the war years, one must turn to novels written later: *The Phasian Bird,* published in 1948, and three of the volumes of *A Chronicle of Ancient Sunlight,* published in the mid-Sixties – the final chapters of *The Phoenix Generation* and the whole of *A Solitary War* and *Lucifer Before Sunrise.* In these fictional but diary-based versions of his experiences, seen through the eyes of Phillip Maddison, there is often bitterness and anger, whereas *Norfolk Farm* ends on a note of achievement and happiness. It is dedicated 'To all who have worked and suffered for the land and people of Greater Britain'. The reader may wonder what was intended by that 'Greater'. The Empire, perhaps? Or was it that imagined post-war land in which all would be ordered according to Henry's ideas of a healthy and happy society?

The title of its last chapter, 'Return to the West', is prophetic: in six years' time Henry would indeed return to the west. Moreover there is irony in the fact that he should have chosen to summarise his early years as an East Anglian farmer from three hundred miles away on his north Devon 'hill of winds'. Near the beginning of the book he had remarked that he had never been happy in Devon, yet must have known as he wrote the words that they were not true: the fact was that he was seldom happy – as far as he was capable of any lasting happiness – anywhere but in Devon.

The chapter is dated '21st May, 1939', the second anniversary of his arrival to begin work on Old Hall Farm. Henry, at ease in the farmhouse now comfortably converted from the two cottages, rejoices in a recital of pleasures: an electric cooker 'which delivers the best food I have tasted. Thank you, Loetitia'; the food itself, home-produced ham and bacon, eggs, beef, chicken, honey, home-baked bread from corn grown on the farm. To all this was to be added the health of the creatures that provided the food, and of the reclaimed fields. He asked himself whether he was wise or foolish, glad or sorry, to have taken the farm, and could find no answer, although he did know that he was glad the two years of grinding labour and worry would not come again.

All was so well with the place, in his view, that he drove off to Devon in the ageing Silver Eagle – coatless, the windscreen flat – happy to be free. 'I began to see a new West Country as I travelled towards the sunset. I had left it a weary writer. I was returning a keen farmer'. He drove through Braunton and 'up the steep sunken lanes to the village I knew better than any place on earth . . . I was home again, on the dear earth of Devon'. He claimed to find a new comradeship in Georgeham. In the King's Arms the landlord, Charlie Ovey, and his wife, made him welcome, 'friends of whom the rare word *faithful* can be used'. On the beach at Putsborough he wandered 'light as a wraith in the sunlit air, and was myself again', as he had been on that May of 1914 when his footsteps were the only ones on the sand; he lay in the grass of his field 'and came as near to bliss as any man can come in this world. I had earned my holiday; I had worked for this field; I had worked for my farm'.

When he went back to Norfolk, he told himself, he would start work again 'and harm no man in the world by that work – growing food for my own sort, English people'.

The pride in this passage is justifiable – yet *Norfolk Farm* was not completed until the autumn of 1940; he would have known by the time he wrote it that he had been suspected of harming English people by his political ideas; that the new war he had dreaded and tried to persuade himself could not happen, had begun, and part of his farm had been requisitioned for military purposes.

Faber would not agree to publish the book in its original form; they insisted that Henry should rewrite some parts of it and cut others which were not considered essential to the story of the farming venture, but were 'likely to excite a controversial interest at odds with the main theme of the book'. Although he hoped that the passages would be restored 'in the happier and healthier age following the end of the War', this did not happen. Whatever hobbyhorses he had been riding – almost certainly political – were by then best forgotten.

In an afterword dated June, 1940, Henry offered a brief summary of the crops grown on his farm in 1939, and the work done to reclaim his land and restore its fertility. The book came out in 1941. By that time Windles was at work with his father; in February, 1939, he had celebrated his thirteenth birthday, and at the end of the summer term Henry took him away from his public school 'which was educating him for a way of life which was dead', and recorded that the boy spent his fourteenth birthday ploughing. It was to Windles that Henry, in *The Children of Shallowford,* attributed the idea of becoming a farmer. Having asked the boy what he wanted to do when he grew up, he received the answer, a farmer. ' "A farmer? The finest work on earth! Let's take a farm," I said, jokingly'. From this developed the idea of working the land by day and writing about it by night. Nevertheless, the account of events he wrote later, in *The Story of a Norfolk Farm,* makes no mention of his decision being influenced by any suggestion from Windles.

The Children of Shallowford had appeared in October, 1939, an unfortunate month for the publication of any book. However, as the war went on, the demand for books steadily increased among civilians forced to spend long evenings at home and servicemen enduring weeks or months of boredom in camps or barracks or aboard ship, when not in action. Henry's picture of his growing family and their life, first in a remote village and then in the even more remote deer park of an ancient estate, held an appeal for many readers – as did his picture of his farm two years later, with its reminder of the English countryside that waited for the return of peace.

Stiffkey Church – from the farm.

CHAPTER ELEVEN

Return to the West

With the outbreak of war ensuring that food-growing was essential work, Henry's new occupation became one of value to the country. Henry himself, however, was regarded with suspicion. Having arrived at Stiffkey as an incomer, his apparent ability to pour money into his neglected farm had aroused some resentment – even rumours that he was in the pay of Germany. His theories about agriculture, drawn from his reading, were equally resented by practical men who had worked on the land since childhood. At the beginning of Part Four of *The Story of a Norfolk Farm* he included a chapter entitled 'Misfit', in which he spoke of beginning to dread walking down the village street, conscious of being a 'foreigner' disapproved of by his neighbours. He even implied that in their minds there was some comparison between himself and the late eccentric vicar of Stiffkey, who had attracted newspaper notoriety for neglecting his parish for the attractions of Soho and, after being unfrocked, had joined a circus and been killed by a lion shortly before Henry took over his farm.

His membership of Mosley's party and his speeches on its behalf understandably did nothing to improve his reputation. He, the country watcher, was watched in his turn. If he used binoculars to observe birds, he was spying; if he went out on his land at night, he was suspected of signalling to the enemy. By the spring of 1940, when the 'phoney war' ended with shocking suddenness, local gossip arising from enmity and mistrust ensured that Henry should be questioned about his loyalties, even though his known political affiliations might have brought this about in any case.

Much of *The Phasian Bird,* begun probably towards the end of the

war, gives the impression that it was written in a mood of great
bitterness; in it the central character, known as Wilbo, is arrested
without charge and kept in prison without trial, not knowing
'whether he would be allowed to live or die, whether or no he
would ever again see his loved ones'. However, by the time he came
to write his final draft of *A Solitary War* in 1965, Henry could depict
Phillip Maddison's brief detention under Section 18b of the Defence
Regulations with reasonable restraint. One morning in June, 1940,
Phillip is taken to a local police station and locked in a cell. He is
treated with courtesy and friendliness by the station sergeant, given
food and a newspaper to read. In the afternoon he undergoes a mild
questioning by a group of officials. Afterwards his wife is allowed to
visit him and give him a book; he even has pencil and paper, on
which he writes an article intended as 'an exposition so clear that all
men would understand it' of the need for peace. The next day he is
taken by car to another town and interviewed by the Chief
Constable – somewhat of an anti-climax after his wild imaginings,
during the journey, of imprisonment in Wormwood Scrubs for the
duration of the war, internment in the Isle of Man or Canada, or
even execution for treason. The Chief Constable tells him that he
does not believe he is a spy, though plenty of people do; that as his
farm has been searched and nothing has been found 'of what we
were led to believe we might find' he is to be released: 'Now be a
good fellow, and don't get into trouble, will you?' Phillip has been
detained for no more than a day and a night. This may be taken as
a fair representation of what happened to Henry himself, even
though occasionally, in later years, he might hint at longer and more
dramatic questioning and less gentlemanly treatment.

The picture of life on Phillip's farm given in *A Solitary War*
shows Henry's other self longing, during the first year of the war,
for a manager to take the running of the place off his hands. There
is a good deal of humour in his account of Phillip's attempt at a
solution: a fellow officer from the First World War, Teddy Pinnegar,
a widow named Mrs Carfax who is Teddy's friend but not
apparently lover, Phillip and his eldest son Billy are to form what is
called a Combined Household while Phillip's wife Lucy and the
younger children go to live with her younger brother in a suburb of
Gaultford (Bedford). (Lucy is the mortgagor of the farm, as Loetitia
was of Old Hall Farm.) It is proposed that Teddy shall go into
partnership with Phillip, but during the winter the Combined
Household dissolves in acrimony.

Before the break-up there is a tragi-comic episode. Phillip has been carrying on a correspondence with a girl called Laura Wissilcraft who has read his books and with whom, in *The Phoenix Generation,* he had a brief and disconcerting encounter. (Having anticipated 'another Emily Bronte, a girl Shelley, from her letters and poems to him, he had been disappointed when she turned out to be a rather plain, unkempt and neurotic girl.) Phillip is incautious enough to send her a letter complaining of 'his present unhappy position' in that his wife and children have left him. This brings Laura from Suffolk – a forty mile ride – on her bicycle. Finding the whole Combined Household in residence, together with a visiting friend, Lady Penelope, she accuses Phillip of lying to her, and cries, 'Who are all these people?' Offered food, or whiskey, she merely repeats, 'Food! Whiskey!' When dinner is ready she refuses to leave the chair in which she has been sitting, eats nothing and will not answer when spoken to. She is carried bodily to a car and transported to a room booked for her in a pub in a nearby town. Next morning she walks back to the farm and behaves as on the previous night.

'Finally it was Billy who induced her to mount the saddle of her bicycle in the road outside'. (How he does this is not explained.) '"I suppose you think my behaviour is unconventional?"' she asks the boy. '"Oh no,", replied Billy. I think it is quite conventional for our farm"'.

While it is undoubtedly true, as some critics have objected, that Henry's work is in the main lacking in humour, and that he slid into facetiousness when trying to be funny, by the time he came to write *A Chronicle of Ancient Sunlight* he had developed the power to regard himself and those around him with more objectivity than in the books of the inter-war years; as a result he could at times achieve genuinely comic effects.

At the beginning of the war, Henry had been dismayed to find that the fairly regular income he had earned from free-lance journalism was threatened as newspapers shrank in size. Even contracts for broadcast talks were not easy to come by for a time. However, the series of talks about his farm which he had broadcast during 1938 and 1939, and which had been reproduced in 'The Listener', had given his reputation as a writer on country matters a new dimension, and must have attracted listeners to buy *The Story of a Norfolk Farm* when it was published in January, 1941. In August of the same year Faber brought out *As the Sun Shines,* a selection of passages from his novels and non-fiction works, as one of a series they called Sesame Books. (Among other titles in the series were *The Picnic and Other Stories* by the poet Henry had venerated as a young man, Walter de la Mare, and *Harvest by Lamplight* by that other farmer-writer, A. G. Street, whose advice about the probable future of agriculture Henry had sought before he bought Old Hall Farm.)

In July, 1941, Henry travelled to Devon with a companion who, in Part 2 of *Lucifer Before Sunrise,* 'Woodland Idyll', becomes the willing Cockney worker, Bert Close. In the Thirties, Henry had bought a small wood near Georgeham, and in a letter dated 1st September, 1941, he told me 'The woods visit was an attempt to make a little money, tho' it just broke even with 120 trees a day felled and sawn up by the two of us, hard work on war food and blazing sun but so *easy* – 7.30 a.m. – 5.30 p.m. – after the complicated hazards and sloths and time-lag of farming, plus the present pus in the body politic which inverts all the virtues of peace into the vices of war . . .' During that visit he had encountered a suspicious reserve among Devon villagers comparable to that which he had experienced in Norfolk: 'The Gadarene swine is a very real thing; I felt the trotting beat of the feet of the unimaginative and mentally fearful several times this summer, while merely cutting tons and tons of wood', he observed in a letter a few weeks later.

He lamented that after the strain of the four previous years, a potentially bumper harvest was threatened by the weather: '. . . wheat (pedigree Squarehead II) sprouting in the ear and so lost: and clovers undersown in barley for next year's hay as high as the June-drought-shrunken barley and the problem of drying before putting in a stack – for clover green and barley sere just go up in smoke and lambent flame. Never known such a harvest, 46 days of rain rain rain. £994.18.5 overdraft . . . and the fear, Am I beaten?'

To make a little extra money he had not only cut down his wood, but undertaken to read manuscripts for Faber. Through Henry I submitted to them a book I had written on my experiences in the ATS during the first eighteen months of the war. Henry recommended publication, and Faber accepted his advice, subject to my making some additions and alterations; they sent me a contract in February, 1942 and – somewhat precipitately, I feared – set the book up in galley proofs, having obtained the necessary war-time clearance from the Censor. Unfortunately, as I was still in uniform, the proofs had to go to the War Office to be read by the then head

of the ATS, Mrs Jean Knox. She considered that it would dis-
courage recruiting (conscription for women had not then been
introduced). As a result, in July, 1942, the Director of Public
Relations wrote to the Officer Commanding the division of the ATS
in which I was serving to say that it was 'not considered fitting for
an auxiliary of the Auxiliary Territorial Service to write a book of
this nature during the progress of the war', and regretted that
permission to publish could not be granted. Faber lost the expense
of having the book set up, and a very young writer experienced a
sharp disappointment.

However, in the months between Henry's first reading of my
typescript in September, 1941, and the arrival of the War Office
veto, he somehow found time, in spite of his heavy work load, to
write me more than a dozen letters of advice and encouragement. In
one he reminded me that 'A writer *begins* to work on his book when
the first draft is completed. He amplifies, changes about, cuts and
rearranges' was one piece of advice he reiterated in various forms,
once using the analogy from the film industry that he always found
so fascinating: 'Remember the art of writing lies in *selection afterwards,* just as a good film is always made by its cutter . . . who fits it
together, shifts and cuts and joins up, & in the end produces a
perfect story from the viewpoint of the *audience,* who after all are the
chief part of the film, for if they walk out, all the finest camera work,
acting etc etc is wholly wasted. This is what you have to learn, bit
by bit, if you wish to become an artist in complete control of your
material *and of your inspiration.*'

He also reminded me of Faber's excellence and said that he
wished he had been published by them from the beginning: 'all the
others have made me feel awkward and frustrated: curious, Faber
alone has consistently done well from the start with all the books
he's published. His name is tops: quality first, for all the directors
and staff are cultured people first, not money-grubbers first'.

These letters also contained descriptions of the continuing
difficulties of running his farm. 'I'm bailiff, tractor driver, engineer,
buyer and seller, manager, house designer, clerk, secretary, all in
one, and things pile up and up and there's no end to the hateful
homework as it were – and I want to lie on the ground and sleep for
a thousand years, and feel the hawkbit and the thyme & the gulls'
feathers trembling & the sea & the salmon & the sands & all the
laughter and joy in the world . . .'

Some ten days later he wrote: 'I've been working 14 hours a day

& am rather limp at the end so forgive this sketchy letter. Must go to bed now, Long day tomorrow. I never find an Englishman who keeps his word, especially in business if by doing so he will lose perhaps a little money. I can't elaborate but it's always so. But life – 'business', personal, active – will be instinct with honour in the future of the after-war. People now are afraid. Did you hear "St Joan" last night? It's all there'.

The assurance that after the war life would be 'instinct with honour' was typical of Henry in certain moods. He enjoyed the role of prophet, and his prophecies might be profoundly pessimistic or unrealistically optimistic. The optimistic ones indicated what amounted to a belief in a magical transform- ation of humanity, and were uttered as though they themselves were magic spells: as though, if proclaimed fervently enough, they would come true.

Soon he was to learn that his excellent foreman was leaving to work elsewhere for more money (this was the helpful worker who is named Bob in *The Story of a Norfolk Farm* and Luke in *A Chronicle of Ancient Sunlight*. Henry claimed to be 'looking after 5 children indefinitely, while Gipsy rests'. He had hoped, he said, to be able to go to his writing hut during the winter 'and into a book which the publisher badly wants'. This was probably to have been a continuation of *The Story of a Norfolk Farm*, with the title *A Norfolk Farm in Wartime*. In December, 1941, Henry remarked in a letter to me, 'I expect the book I am doing now will have to be so much cut that it won't be a book when it's done: libels; subversive; pro-peace and anti-war; and what would be mildly approved in 1941 would cause rage in 1942 if Singapore were in the hands of the honble yellow peril. Oh dear, what a mess it all is'. Evidently his fears were realised, since no war-time farm book of his appeared, but it is probable that he re-used revised passages of the material in *The Phasian Bird* and the volumes of *A Chronicle of Ancient Sunlight* dealing with the war years. It's possible that some of it was also used in a series of articles he wrote for the 'Eastern Daily Press' in 1943, under the pen name Jacob Tonson. (The choice of pseudonym is interesting. Jacob Tonson was the remarkable late 17th/early 18th century bookseller who published *Paradise Lost,* as well as much of the work of Dryden, Pope, Addison and Steele. When Arnold Bennett began to write a column called 'Books and Persons' in the literary periodical, 'New Age', he did so under the name Jacob Tonson. Henry's adoption of the same pseudonym was almost certainly made in homage to Arnold Bennett, whom he liked and admired – partly, perhaps, because Bennett had praised his own work.)

In the letter quoted above, Henry spoke of being tempted to get out of farming, yet lacking the courage, in spite of wearing himself out 'in order to turn £1,000 or so into £990 at the end of a season's cycle'. Nevertheless, in another mood he would assert that 'nothing is done without constant work. The easy things of life are false. The hard, narrow, momentarily unpopular way – leadeth to salvation, even if life is lost meanwhile'. In him, a profound belief in the Protestant work ethic was exceptionally puritanical – and as an unresting perfectionist he often demanded too much of himself and others. Moreover his work load in the war years, struggling by day to keep the farm going, and by night to persevere as a writer, might have brought a man with a more stable nervous system than he possessed to the verge of collapse.

Yet he was still willing to give time to helping other writers. One of these was Lilias Rider Haggard, a daughter of the public servant who wrote not only such best-selling novels as *She* and *King Solomon's Mines,* but also books on rural life and agriculture. It is interesting that Sir Henry Rider Haggard, who had lived in Norfolk, had himself worked to restore a run-down farm in that county in the late nineteenth century. Henry would almost certainly have read his books, *A Farmer's Year* and *Rural England,* in which he would have found Sir Henry anticipating his own struggles, observing, for instance, that a Norfolk farm he had taken over in 1889 was 'in so scandalous a condition that now, after eight years cleaning and manuring, it has only just recovered its fertility. The heart had been dragged out of it, the arable was a mass of docks and weeds'.

Lilias Rider Haggard had for some time been writing, anonymously, a weekly article on Norfolk country life in the 'Eastern Daily Press'. Henry first began to read these in 1939. Struck by their quality, he wrote to the editor, discovered the writer's identity and offered 'the use of what small skill I possessed to help shape (a selection of the articles) into a book'. Faber published the result with an introduction by Henry, in 1943. Evidently his help was not, in the long run, appreciated; in a letter written in 1945 he complained, after observing that he had tried, with varying degrees of success, to help about twelve young writers into print during the past few years, that *'Norfolk Life,* unwanted old newspaper articles for years, sold 20,000 copies. Then, flushed with success, the author declared I had spoiled her book. No one would look at it until I rewrote and recast it. What a joke life is!'

At about the time *Norfolk Life* appeared, his money worries were eased by the re-issue of several of his early books, and he quickly gave up his work as a reader for Faber. The letter recording this is undated, as his so often were, but probably belongs to 1944. Jubilantly he confided, 'There is to be a limited edition of 4 early nature books, all subscribed on the merest whiff of mention, 750 sets at £4 each. Royalty, £600; and not a pen to paper to earn it! The old work of Skirr (Cottage) and Vale (House) coming to roost, in fact'.

This would appear to be a reference to the boxed set which was announced in 1945 but for various reasons not ready for sale until 1946. The title was *The Henry Williamson Nature Books,* and the set was in fact limited to five hundred, priced at six guineas each. It contained *Tarka, The Lone Swallows, The Peregrine's Saga, The Old Stag* and *Salar the Salmon.*

'As for the antient (sic) Flax,' Henry's letter went on, 'that is sold out, all 10,000 copies, and the RAF pilots apparently feed on it. 1929-39 didn't want it; my post-war; but the second brood apparently does. 20 years before its time. It cleared £600 in 6 months' royalties: before this war, it made £6 a year'. The farm, he said was now worth about £15,000. 'I mention cash only as an indication of the progress apparently made, tho to me it has been a battle, with never a moment of relaxation. Perhaps others may have it; I'll be content if they do . . . Gipsy is a bit tired. The children grow. Margaret is now almost a young lady. Going to Wantage school next term. John is at Walsham, near Norwich. Windles wears RAF cadet's uniform. Bombers thunder all night and all day, hundreds, thousands of them. I hope I don't miss the post-war: what a swing-away there will be. The war books of 1922-29 will seem pale in comparison by the reaction this time. Lids, I fear, Will fly right off this time; not stop at 1926 General Strike fizzling out. History shows that after every war there were high hopes and words and arms raised for blows . . . ironic to reflect that we are now a proper totalitarian efficient state, while others are quite out-classed and passé, rapidly becoming the "decadent democracies". But I wish the spirit were or could be different. Among civilians, I mean. The money-makers. I know an ex-gipsy who nets £150 a week for 6 hours on an aerodrome & who has not paid any tax or ever signed a cheque. . . . '

(The sentence about totalitarian state and decadent democracies is echoed in *Lucifer Before Sunrise,* where Phillip, imagining a writer achieving 'a novel of our times, transcending *War and Peace',* says that he must deal with 'compre- hension and clarity' with the 'inner or psychological processes by which the "decadent democracies" become totalitarian in their efficiency for destruction by war and the totalitarian states fall apart into "decadent democracies"').

Like many prophets, Henry tended to be wide of the mark. Virtually no war book of the post-1945 period had the revelatory impact or justifiable anger of those published between the wars, and the Labour election victory of 1945 brought about social change of a sort Henry had not foreseen, though he heartily approved the betterment of living conditions for large numbers of people in the decades after the war.

At about this time he went into Cromer hospital for a minor operation. (In *Lucifer Before Sunrise* he gives Phillip Maddison an experience of hospital in 1943 as the result of being accidentally shot by soldiers on his land.) In his absence the running of the farm was left to Loetitia and the increasingly rebellious Windles, who had celebrated his 17th birthday in February, 1943. The spell in hospital and a stormy dispute with Windles seems to have weakened Henry's resolution to carry on with the farm. Whether or not it really had been a childhood remark by Windles that had stimulated Henry to consider becoming a farmer, he had certainly, during the early years in Norfolk, pictured Windles succeeding him at Old Hall; at times he even told himself that all four sons might later run it in harness. Now, while he had to acknowledge that his longed-for respite, when he would hand over the running of the farm to *someone* – brother-in-law, friendly partner, bailiff, son – would never come, he resolved to return to the life of a full-time writer. At the beginning of the East Anglian venture he had told himself that writing was not enough: he wanted to *do* something. In the intervening years he had done a great deal, shredding his nerves and those of his family in the process, forcing himself to the limit of his physical, mental and nervous resources. At last he recognised that, for him, writing took precedence over any other activity. He had ample material; all he needed was the opportunity to work on it.

Several years earlier he had converted an old barn into a writing place, calling it his studio. The artist Edward Seago, who lived for much of his life in Norfolk, visited him there while on leave from the Royal Engineers, and painted his portrait. He wanted to paint him holding a fishing rod, but Henry objected that to get the proper atmosphere they would need to go to a stream, preferable in Devon, on a hot summer's day. However, he had to be content with going out into the sunlight on the farm. Seago completed the head in one sitting, and did not want to touch it again. Henry, duly holding the fishing rod and smoking the very short pipe which he claimed was necessary to keep off flies when he fished, gazes into a remote distance far beyond any river, as though intent on that visionary world in which he spent so much of his life. Afterwards, Seago made a study of his hands in the studio, and noted the orderliness of the place, 'with its books and scythes and hoes and neat built-up rows of thorn logs felled by himself'.

It was in this studio that Henry wrote the first drafts of the early novels of *A Chronicle of Ancient Sunlight*, and also much of *The Phasian Bird*. In an article published in 'Women's Illustrated' in February, 1946, (the first of fifteen autobiographical articles under the general title 'Quest') he said that he had 'during an enforced rest after coming out of hospital, worked as hard at my writing as I had previously worked on the farm. In twelve months I had written seven books' (an astonishing creative frenzy, even for Henry). Yet at the same time he was once again earning a modest regular income from free- lance journalism. Between February, 1944 and December, 1945, the 'Evening Standard' published more than eighty of his articles. Many tell of the stresses and uncertainties of farming. More lightheartedly, he observes and records the activities of his children, with a fond, fatherly eye. And the sharply observant nature writer is always there, describing or speculating on the behaviour of partridges, snipe, magpies, owls and even the semi-domestic robin.

As 1945 went on he spent more time at his writing hut above Georgeham. In May he had some sort of temporary breakdown. (In a letter written seven years later he referred guardedly to having had 'a collapse' on the farm at that time.) It was evidently precipitated by a breakdown of another sort: his sturdy little tractor, the Ferguson he had valued so highly, was worn out, like its owner, by eight years of very hard work. When its camshaft broke, it seemed a symbol of the destruction of all that had once been hoped for. To recuperate, Henry fled to the one place in which he had always found some measure of peace. Before long he received a letter from Loetitia saying that she had left the farm, taking the younger children with her. Henry recalled that '. . . although we had discussed the encessity of giving up the farm on scores of occasions, always they had ended in my saying that I would never give in'. Now the decision had been taken for him.

Yet he was still not quite ready to give up. He set out for Norfolk without delay. Halfway home the Silver Eagle – fifteen years old by this time – overheated. The next day he coaxed it as far as a Suffolk village, where it again broke down, sixty miles from Stiffkey. In the village, by chance, he saw a house advertised for sale and bought it on impulse – making up his mind in three minutes, he said. He wrote of knowing that it was right for him to work only at his writing, and to bring the family together again.

But it was too late. Loetitia had evidently recognised some time earlier that her marriage was effectively at an end, despite the fact that her last child, her daughter Sarah, was born in 1945. She obtained a divorce and settled down, with her younger children and her brother Robin and his wife, in the house Henry had chosen for them in the Suffolk village. Henry's first marriage, like his life as a farmer, was at an end.[1]

(When this house was sold a few years later, Henry, in characteristic fashion, was not present; he was on holiday in France. He was thus able to lament, in a letter, that the house had been sold well under the advertised price, and that its contents had gone for derisory sums. However, his daughter Margaret had rescued for him 'the three-leg walnut table on which *Tarka* was writ', paying just six shillings for it.)

Yet although he said that 'when finally I had undertaken to sell my farm I turned away from the telephone and wept', in the longer run he recognised that the sale was a release. The grief was for the loss of an imagined future: 'My dream of founding a yeoman family, to last for centuries, was over in eight short years'.[2]

In a letter dated 26th August, 1945, from Old Hall Farm, Henry wrote, 'I have always been unhappy here; only unhappy at times there. (That is, in Devon). Of course Devon is a fearfully uncultured place. The secret is to have no contacts with the people; only slight touches . . . I am tired of people. I seem to have known only wasters, liars and egoists. This is of course but a moment's mood. My farm is sold; it has gone back to weeds again. The family life is moribund; there was not the spirit here. I am a littler Hitler whose dreams are smouldering as a petrol-soaked corpse. I have bought them a house and there they will live untidily as they like.

In October I leave, as in 1921, for a small hut in Devon. After War One all was fresh; after War Two is is (sic) known. All one can do is to try to recreate the past in ancient sunlight . . . Brothers and sisters have I none, and no parents; and I have no children, either. And no wife. The artist is alone; always. Rarely there is a companion, who *knows*. It is rare in artistic history'.

Referring to my effectually banned book about life in the ATS, *Feminine Plural,* he went on, 'Let me know how you get on. There is no reason why, one day, FP should not see print in covers. But don't rush things. All things have their seasons. I rewrote a book for someone recently, it comes out soon with Jarrolds, called *What Hope for Green Street?* After that, the first-author (whose work was jejune and only partly readable) must dree her own weird. I'll give no more advice. It isn't acceptable to amateurs; only to professionals. After say 7 years of hard work, then they begin to *realise*. Good luck to you. I sit here; my cook (Robert, aged 11) has just left. Gipsy has left; and Margaret, and Richard, and Sarah. I have just averted a foolish and terrible proposed action, sponsored by relative fools, which might have transcended Stiffkey Scandal No.1, of the late poor silly Rector. But I am still and always will be Henry Williamson – living in the country of the Blind'.

In another letter Henry explained that it had been one of his brothers-in-law who had proposed the 'foolish and terrible action', the handing over to the 'proper authorities' of letters Henry had written to him over a period of years 'as evidence of a state of mind which should be certified'.

No doubt the shock of his divorce, and the wretchedness of the abandonment of his farming hopes, had much to do with the shrill self-pity of the first of the letters just quoted, and the unfairness of the remark about family life, the spirit of which had been, and would be, so staunchly maintained by Loetitia. Yet all his autobiographical books – which include his two novel sequences – indicate his enduring sense of being a man against the world.

The departure of Windles and the troubles of the final years on the farm left a deep mark on his mind. As late as 1952 he wrote from Georgeham, 'Windles is in Canada; married. He refused the offer of farm of 240 acres and all stock in 1945, to carry it on for his mother, who had disappeared while I was resting here. My farm was A Class in 1941 and all smashed up by 1945; the farmer was beaten up and smashed about early in that year, following the breakages of tractors, ladders, trailers etc etc. It was all very tragic; but the spirit of spivery etc in a county of 80 airfields all built on a cost plus 10% basis, ruined all the ordinary life of work, except among the old,

who were tired, underfed, and bewildered. This creature fought
against it, damned as a traitor from the start. The farm was filled
with escapists who came and beat me down and stayed and took
wages and got it the name of the Convalescent Home. Nobody
seemed to care; a priceless yeoman farm being built up for someone
who saw only the war-time values of big money: many a lorry
driver, exempt, took £20 a week for driving his shambling old
vehicle let out at an extra £3/10/- a day hire to contractors who got
10% more if their labour and costs were the greater. The end was
like Zola: a microcosm of the macrocosm in Europe. Only a few see
it even now, with Russia and Asia at the gates of the house divided
against itself . . . The farm, I hear, is now a pedigree milk farm
worth 1000% what I paid for it in 1937, to start Windles as a
farmer'.

I had met Henry not long before he wrote this letter, and he had
told me of his second marriage, and the birth of his son Harry, but
had said little of his work, despite the fact that he was well into *A
Chronicle of Ancient Sunlight,* and the first two novels of the series,
The Dark Lantern and *Donkey Boy,* had already been published. The
letter refers to the disappointments he had experienced when first
Faber and then Collins had rejected his post-war work: 'Well, my
savings or capital are all gone; and I'm back in 1921, less the élan
vital, and starting as an author once more; with a new publisher,
two others having decided that my work submitted between
1947-50 wasn't any good. We shall see'.

'Less the élan vital'. Yet during the next twenty years he would
work on steadily, completing his second tetralogy – fifteen novels
averaging 150,000 words each, a total of more than two million
words – and one last 'animal book', on the subject of racing
pigeons, until, at the age of seventy-seven, his creative vitality
would at last falter.

Henry Williamson on his much-loved Ferguson tractor: Old Hall Farm, Stiffkey, 1938.

Henry Williamson with Christine, his second wife: the Rock Inn, Georgeham, c. 1948.

At Ox's Cross, looking south towards the Taw-Torridge estuary lost in haze, 1958.

Henry at Ox's Cross, July 1958.

Inside the 'Studio' at Ox's Cross. Edward Seago's portrait of Henry can be seen on the cabinet under the stairs, which led to the upper room in which Henry often slept. In winter, he said, heat from the pipe of the iron stove (out of shot) helped to warm this bedroom.

In the caravan at Ox's Cross which provided additional space after Henry's second marriage.

CHAPTER TWELVE

A Stubborn Phoenix

In each of the three decades of his writing life, Henry wrote a remarkable animal book: about a mammal in the Twenties, about a fish in the Thirties; now, in the Forties, about a bird. Although *The Phasian Bird* was not published until 1948, when he had been back in Devon for three years, and its later drafts were written there, it is probable that he originally outlined it during his Norfolk years. (In a letter written in the year of its publication he said, 'I wrote my book *Phasian Bird* 24 times, & nearly died in the doing of it; that's how it was built up to be clear & omissive (sic) and maybe comprehensive'.) It may therefore seem relevant to the final period of his East Anglian life.

On Old Hall Farm, as on many in Norfolk, pheasants were numerous, and shoots were organised every year. Henry, however, knew of a bird of even more resplendent plumage and exotic origin than the familiar *phasianus colchicus;* he chose to write of a Reeves's pheasant, *Syrmaticus Reevesii,* a more recent introduction to Britain; intended as a sporting bird, it proved too fast and high for the guns. The Chinese, Henry wrote, called it Chee-kai, the Arrow Bird; some considered it to be the origin of the phoenix myth. Slightly larger than the common pheasant, it had a tail six feet in length; its swift flight 'was as a golden rocket' until it fell 'like a whisk of fire, like a comet made animate in grey, brown-barred smoke and flame, a prince of birds in chain mail of black and gold . . .'

Concentration on a living embodiment of the phoenix concept that had occupied his life for so long stimulated his imagination and released the creative energies that had been comparatively idle. Once again his projected series of novels about Phillip Maddison was postponed while he wrote of the brilliant pheasant Chee-kai, which comes to symbolise 'resurgence and beauty' in the eyes of the painter turned farmer who is known throughout the book by the nickname given him by his farm workers, Wilbo.

Thus Chee-kai is not, like Tarka and Salar, simply an indigenous British wild creature whose ways of life are studied and recorded with all the accuracy and empathy of which this writer, with his exceptional visual sense, was capable. Certainly the careful observation and lovingly precise depiction of the bird and its surroundings, and its interaction with other creatures, are as vivid as ever. But the life of this wild thing is closely interwoven with the life of a man, becomes his personal symbol to be protected at all costs, and dies when he dies.

The egg from which Chee-kai hatches is one of several with which a farmer replaces the eggs of an ordinary hen pheasant. All the chicks hatch, but while they are still small are attacked by a moorcock and a cat. The hen pheasant and all the chicks save Chee-kai are killed. He is fostered by a pair of partridges, but when the partridge and all *her* chicks save one are killed by a hay cutter, the cock partridge, Pertris, continues to care for his own surviving chick and Chee-kai. The farmer, near bankruptcy and harassed by the bank, shoots himself. His successor, Wilbo, watches the strange partridge-pheasant family. He does not want to admit the local game syndicate to his farm; he is appalled by the wholesale slaughter of wild life – not merely pheasants are shot, but owls, teal, wood pigeon, snipe, moorhens, hawks, rabbits and hares.

Wilbo's idealised picture of the farm as he wants it to be is similar to that of Henry himself in *The Story of a Norfolk Farm* and of Phillip Maddison in *The Phoenix Generation*. He sets himself to get rid of 'the remnants of sloth and decay. The weeds, the neglected horses and implements, the general dereliction of the place were but manifestations of inferior human thought, of fatigue in the body politic; these visible thoughts in decay had to pass away, to be succeeded by those of resurgence, this old order had to be succeeded by new order'. The men who work him and the local villagers are puzzled by his attitude, disapprove of his methods, and become suspicious of him. His workers see him as a man 'who seemed, for some reason, to be a man working against time'; he is 'all wire'; they watch his 'nervous hurrying figure' with some concern. His stockman, a helpful and useful ally, advises him to enjoy himself by 'knocking over' a few pheasants. Wilbo prefers to watch the living birds, or to sketch out of doors.

His activities arouse rumours. In June, 1940, come his arrest and imprisonment. While he is away his wife, 'an equal-minded woman, with a power of endurance which was the greater for a limited imagination', works hard to try to carry on the work of the farm and helps village women by forming a branch of the Women's Institute and distributing orange juice and rose-hip syrup.

Wilbo is released – apparently in late 1944 – in a highly nervous state. The farm has been run down, and he fears that the County War Agricultural Committee is likely to take it over under emergency powers. His son, an only child, tells him that Chee-kai has survived; Wilbo regards this as a miracle and a portent, but he believes that if he loses his farm, the bird will die.

When he is in fact dispossessed, he has some kind of breakdown; his wife calls her doctor, who examines Wilbo in his studio and pronounces him physically sound, but privately considers that he needs 'straightening out by a psychiatrist'. However, he notices Wilbo's paintings and exclaims, 'My dear fellow, there is genius in the hand and mind that painted those pictures!' He advises him to do nothing but paint. He also decides to introduce him to a young American pilot from New England who is a poet.

After the doctor's visit, Wilbo leans against the outer wall of his studio in the sun. 'Trying to see all things clearly, with balance, without bitterness', he feels a balance coming 'like a benison between the two sides of his mind which had been in division, even as the spirit of western man'. He asks himself by what strange accident 'had this Arrow Bird come upon the field of a small Norfolk farm, by what chance had it found friendship with a common partridge, by what fate had it escaped destruction in a countryside of men uprooted and restless with death? A bird radiant with the sun, born in an age of darkness . . . watched over by the brave, the dun, the lowly English partridge, true spirit of the soil of England'.

Friendship develops between himself and the young American, who asks him to paint a picture of Chee-kai on his bomber. Wilbo does so. On a bombing mission, the pilot thinks of the bird 'of phoenix legend and of resurrection'. He crashes and his plane catches fire; as he dies he sees a golden bird flying to him, 'bringing upon its breast the sun of far Cathay, the azalea groves and deep rocky ravines noisy with rushing waters, broadening into the wide and reedy valley of the Phasis, a river in Colchis'.

There is a fall of snow. On Christmas Day, Wilbo goes out on skis. Unknown to him, a number of characters representing everything that he – like his creator – regards as deplorable are trespassing on the farm. They include a pheasant poacher, a money lender, a small-time dealer known ironically as the Flockmaster (who has his counterpart in the prying busybody, Horatio Bugg, in *A Solitary War* and *Lucifer Before Sunrise*) and some members of the local shooting syndicate. The Flockmaster has promised to prove to two American soldiers 'of emigrant Eastern stock, probably Levantine' that a gamecock he owns can kill Chee-kai. From the distance Wilbo sees the birds fighting, and skis down to protect the pheasant. The soldiers, though presumably off duty, for some reason are carrying sub-machine guns. They fire at Chee-kai but hit Wilbo. He is found dying by his faithful stockman. On another part of the farm a member of the shooting syndicate fires at Chee-kai and hits him; he dies in the top of a pine tree that has often been his roost.

At Wilbo's funeral the parson declares that the dead man 'in his own way and according to his own conscience had lived for his country; and who was to say that he had not died for it, he whose last words . . . had striven to lay the blame for what had happened upon himself . . . thinking only of others, in the consciousness of that magnanimity, or greater love, which must be shown to all men, to friends and enemies alike, if mankind was truly to inherit the earth as the kingdom of God'.

(If the beginning of this sentence expresses the kind of thing Henry would have wished for his own obituary, had he died in some accident of the kind described, the ending expresses the New Testament values which he regarded as paramount, however difficult to achieve, during the whole of his adult life.)

The considerable differences between the stories of Tarka and Salar, and that of Chee-kai, are clear to see. Quite apart from the bird's function as a symbol, the element of natural history in the book becomes increasingly subservient to the chronicle of Wilbo and his troubled war-time experience. Nevertheless, *The Phasian Bird* offers a picture of the north Norfolk countryside and the birds of its fields and skies, as brilliantly sharp and delicate as those of the Devon river valleys in the earlier stories, though constantly darkened by the shadow of war.

It is a book distinguished by a remarkably consistent level of heightened prose. The unsympathetic critic might complain that it is patched with purple. Yet like other writers who have suffered this accusation, Henry was a believer in inspiration, and in the artist as the instrument through which creative work flowed from some external world of the spirit; under the influence of this inspiration, he said, he wrote rapidly and did not need to revise. For all that, it may be assumed that *The Phasian Bird* underwent its due measure of revision, and every page was written with deliberation as its author's temperament dictated: that temperament, unfailingly romantic, governed his use of language.

Henry's 'collapse' on Old Hall Farm in May, 1945 is undoubtedly reflected in the descriptions of Wilbo's increasing nerve strain and sense of alienation. Certainly Wilbo, after he has been dispossessed of his farm, is in the same situation as was Henry during the months he remained at Old Hall Farm after he had sold it.

By bringing about the death of Wilbo, Henry for the third time killed off that 'detachable psychic part of himself' of which he had spoken in the Thirties. Willie Maddison and the Manfred of *The Gold Falcon* had each represented a stage of his life (and each, incidentally, had been mourned with fulsome praise by surviving characters.) Now his persona as a Norfolk farmer was dead, but his dogged phoenix self was very much alive, and almost ready to begin that long-planned novel sequence. For that, the two acres of his field above Georgeham was room enough.

CHAPTER THIRTEEN

Beginning Again

The field above Georgeham can seldom have felt more like a sanctuary than in the time after Henry's return from Norfolk. Yet in October, 1938, he had written in a letter 'the only place to go is the hut; and that in winter, no, I couldn't bear it'. Now, exactly seven years later, he resigned himself to regarding the hut as his base, even with winter approaching. For extra accommodation he had a caravan, and there was always the one-up-and-one-down building once known as the wood store, but now called the studio, in which, in the Thirties, the young man Henry referred to as a staggart had joined the Williamson family at meals.

In any case Henry did not intend to spend all his time in Devon; there were always visits to friends in various places, including London, where he sometimes stayed at the Savage Club (in *A Chronicle of Ancient Sunlight* this becomes the Barbarian Club), and sometimes at the National Liberal Club. And there was, as for Henry there had always been, the pursuit of love, leading to his second marriage, in 1949, to Christine Mary Duffield. *How Dear is Life,* the fourth volume of the *Chronicle,* bears a dedication to her, using her initials only, C.M.D.W., 'without whose help these novels might have remained unwritten'. It does not seem that he could settle to work steadily on them until he was once again reassured by the presence and support of a wife.

Many young women might have jibbed at being expected to begin married life in the limited accommodation available in the Ox's Cross field, but Henry was fortunate in that his second wife, like his first, was prepared to accept comparatively spartan living conditions.

Harry, the only child of this marriage, was born in 1950. In view of Henry's life-long love of listening to music (and although he never played any musical instrument, he had a pleasant light tenor voice and as a young man liked to sing) it is interesting that the youngest of his children should have developed musical talent, and become a composer.

During the years immediately after the war, Henry was appearing as a busy author. In 1945, Faber brought out *The Sun in the Sands,* written eleven years earlier; in 1948 they followed it with *The Phasian Bird* and a revised and re-illustrated version of *The Starborn.* In sharp contrast to the melancholy of *The Phasian Bird* and the wispy mysticism of *The Starborn,* the only story Henry wrote specifically for children – although by that time two generations of children had read *Tarka* and his other nature writings – came out in 1949. This, called *Scribbling Lark,* sounds as though the Hugh Lofting of the Dr Doolittle books had joined forces with the boisterous Henry Williamson who had written the original version of *Dandelion Days* in the early Twenties. It is an exuberant fantasy about an old carthorse, Prince – renamed Scribbling Lark – two escaped monkeys, a retired ex-alcoholic jockey and his tame fox. By devious means Scribbling Lark wins the Derby, helped by the intervention of the fox, which allows itself to be pursued across Epsom race course half-way through the race.

As has been said, *The Starborn* originated in the Skirr Cottage years and was first published in 1933. It shows Henry at his most serious, even portentous. He called it a pendant to *The Flax of Dream:* it is the book Willie Maddison is writing, and quotations from it appear in *The Dream of Fair Women* and *The Pathway,* as well as in *The Sun in the Sands.*

Although Henry was never as attracted to Dartmoor as he was to Exmoor, he loved Lydford Gorge. A note on a Christmas card he sent to my parents in 1923 said, 'I go to Lydford tomorrow', and the purpose of this visit may have been to recapture the atmosphere of the place for his planned re-writing of the original draft, which he said had been lost.

The Starborn, who has a twin sister, Mamis, is the son of Esther, recently widowed; her husband, an embittered poet, drowned in Lydford Gorge. Taken from his cot in a storm by some entity called the Mother-Maiden, the Starborn is brought up in an owlery in the ruined Lydford Castle by attendant Spirits of Beyond: Air, Water, Leaf, Quill, Fin and Fur Spirits. There are also the Mind Spirit and something, or someone, called Wanhope. In *The Pathway,* Willie explains, mystifyingly, to Mary Ogilvie that Wanhope represented Thomas Hardy, but Henry would have known that *wanhope* is an archaic word for despair, used more than once by Chaucer – in his *Testament of Love,* for instance, and in that long, serious prose sermon which ends *The Canterbury Tales.*

The Starborn is eventually returned to the human world, as a young man, by the Mind Spirit. Allowed to take one spirit with him, he chooses Wanhope, previously regarded as 'the despised, the outcast' among the Spirits, but now acclaimed as Master Spirit 'who had sat at the feet of the All'.

Having endured hunger and cold (he is naked), the Starborn borrows clothes from a scarecrow (one of the 'oddmedods' to which Henry not infrequently compared himself, loving to wear old clothes). Various people see him on the moor and take him for an escaped criminal or lunatic. Esther meets him near the Gorge; not surprisingly they do not recognise one another, but she takes him to her house and cares for him. He behaves, as she says, as a child of nature, rescuing animals, offending the local schoolmaster by preventing him from caning a boy, and telling stories to the children.

He and Mamis spend much time together until she marries her cousin Robert. The Starborn is recalled by the Mind Spirit to an assembly of 'Voices, Shades, Phasms (sic), Spectres, Apparitions and Spirits'. Wanhope, whose form and appearance alter to that of 'a Stranger, around whose shining head a crown of thorns was deeply set', leads the Starborn to join 'the company of poets', among whom, inevitably, are Shelley and Jefferies. Esther goes out into the snow to search for the Starborn, and is found with 'a smile of deepest peace' on her dead face.

That he should wish to revive this early work, even in a revised form, twelve years after its first publication, indicates how much Henry still valued it. Yet it seems one of his least satisfactory books; it gives the impression of straining after mystical effects beyond his reach and slipping instead into a vaporous, sentimental whimsy. The best passages, predictably, are those in which he briefly forgets his other-worldly dreaming and concentrates on depicting aspects of nature. The reader is left with the feeling that once he re-introduced the Starborn to human society, his invention failed him.

Largely, it seems, because he thought he could use it as a platform for his political ideas, Henry decided that he wanted to edit the quarterly magazine, 'The Adelphi', which had been founded in 1923 by his friend John Middleton Murry, and edited by him throughout its existence. Murry, whose birthplace in Peckham had been only a mile or so from Henry's, was the elder by six years. He had no experience of active service; during the First World War he worked at the War Office in Political Intelligence. By 1919 he was Chief Censor; he received the O.B.E the following year. Thereafter his life was devoted, quite literally, to literature, as editor, critic and biographer. He had a lasting admiration for Henry's work, and wrote a long essay on his novels which appeared posthumously in 1959. During the Second World War he, like Henry, farmed in Norfolk, at Thelnetham; he later wrote an account of this, *Community Farm*. Henry visited the farm several times during the war, and portrayed it in *A Chronicle of Ancient Sunlight,* where Murry appears as Wallington Christie, and Phillip Maddison takes over from him the editing of a magazine called 'The New Horizon'. *Donkey Boy* is dedicated to Murry.

The first of the three issues of 'The Adelphi' to appear under Henry's editorship covered the October-December quarter, 1948. It included what he described, in a letter, as 'some poems and prose by a great poet killed in 1944, aged 20 years'. This was the work of the remarkable youth, James Farrar, an R.A.F navigator, whose writings Henry read aloud to friends. He arranged a selection from Farrar's diary of R.A.F. life, with sketches and poems, and secured its publication by Williams and Norgate in 1950 under the title *The Unreturning Spring:* one more example of his willingness to recognise and celebrate talent, even though in this case the celebration was, tragically, posthumous. (James Farrar's manuscripts and notebooks are now, like Henry's, in the care of Exeter University Library).

'The Adelphi' was described as 'A magazine with a policy of reality in the resurgence of Western civilisation, based on the values of soil and work' – characteristically Williamson values – but unfortunately the tone of some of its contents caused the cancellation of many subscriptions, and by 1949 Henry had had enough; he handed over the editorship to B. Ifor (later Sir Ifor) Evans and concentrated on his novels.

To cast around for a new publisher because neither Faber nor Collins would agree to take on his *Chronicle* was a harsh experience for a long-established author in his mid-fifties. However, Henry was fortunate in one literary friend, Malcolm Elwin, who has left it on record, in the 'West Country Magazine' for the summer of 1946, that he regarded Henry as a writer of genius. A biographer and essayist, Elwin had been a fellow author in the lists of both Jonathan Cape and Collins in the Thirties. He shared with Henry a deep admiration of Richard Jefferies; somewhat surprisingly it was he, and not Henry, whom Cape commissioned after the war to edit and introduce the volume in their 'Essential' series devoted to Jefferies. He knew and loved north Devon; for a number of years he lived in one of the houses built in the Thirties above Vention Sands. A keen cricketer, he revived Lynton Cricket Club in the late Forties; the club played on a ground in the Valley of Rocks, which is the setting for the farcical cricket match in *The Gale of the World* which immediately precedes the final drama of the storm and flood.

In 1947, Elwin joined Macdonald as general editor of a series of illustrated classics. They had just published two collections of his essays, *The Pleasure Ground* and *The First Romantics*. As soon as he had read the first novel of the *Chronicle, The Dark Lantern,* he recommended that Macdonald should take it. (In appreciation, Henry dedicated the book to him.)

Malcolm Elwin remained Henry's adviser, editor and encourager for several years (and incidentally persuaded Macdonald to continue with the sequence in spite of disappointing initial sales). Nevertheless, Henry eventually rebelled against suggestions that he should cut and tighten up his work; there came one of the fallings-out that marred so many of his relationships. In spite of this, Macdonald kept faith to the end of the *Chronicle,* and Henry never again needed to go in search of a publisher.

Another admirer was Waveney Girvan. As early as 1931 he had published a 'bibliography and critical survey of the works of Henry Williamson'; possibly he was one of Henry's inter-war staggarts. His devotion to the west country and to literature was expressed in practical ways: he established the 'West Country Magazine' in 1946 (Malcolm Elwin edited the first two issues) and soon afterwards set up a small publishing house, the Westaway Press, based in London but concentrating on books about the western counties by west country writers.

Out of these two ventures grew, in 1951, the West Country Writers' Association, which happily continues to flourish, although the Westaway Press and the 'West Country Magazine' had comparatively short lives. Henry became a founder member of the Association and when Eden Philpotts, its first President, died in 1960, accepted the invitation to succeed him. Although he gave up the presidency after five years, he remained a Vice President. The Association's annual two-day congresses were, and are, held sometimes in various cities in the six south-western counties – Bath, Bristol, Plymouth, Exeter, Taunton – and sometimes in smaller towns such as Barnstaple or Lyme Regis. Henry attended them regularly, and enjoyed himself, meeting old friends and making new ones. He was not averse to being mildly lionised by writers younger or with more modest and localised reputations than himself.

Although I had been a member of the West Country Writers' Association from the beginning, I was living in London during the first two decades of its existence, and attended few congresses, but once or twice in those years I was able to meet Henry with my husband and our young children. On one occasion he showed us a snap of his second wife with a small boy and girl. The boy was his son Harry, but he allowed us to think that both were his. He greeted our son and daughter gravely, and thereafter, if he saw us without them, enquired after 'the nips' (to him, small children were 'nippers').

At one meeting he seemed in an agitated state, and began to speak of having averted an action for divorce which would have drawn to him much adverse publicity; mentioning the divorce of a member of the peerage then being contested, he said that his would have created an equal stir.

I last met him when the West Country writers met in Exeter in 1973. He had recently made up the difference between himself and Kenneth Allsop (it had arisen as a result of a television interview during which Allsop asked a question to which Henry took exception) and they were once more together on good terms. Henry must have felt very glad of this when the news came, some two weeks later, of Allsop's sudden death.

As J. C. Trewin was to write in his obituary of Henry in the West Country Writers' Association newsletter, in social gatherings he was liable to 'let the boyishness in his nature take over'. This boyish, prankish streak never deserted him, except perhaps in the last sad months of his life. It was a trait that annoyed and alienated a number of those who met him and knew him only superficially. Henry would attend lectures on literary subjects given at the congresses, but he never liked being offered information he had not specifically asked for, and so was a poor listener. He might chat to companions; if these were male, he might suddenly lean forward and stroke the hair of some young woman within arm's reach. If he found the startled face turned to him pleasing, he would seek to further the acquaintance later. Until he was in his seventies he continued to be attractive to women.

It was inevitable that after a few years in his hilltop field he would grow restless. He had seen a good deal of Ireland during visits to his friend John Heygate, who had inherited his baronetcy during the war and from then on described himself in *Who's Who* as 'writer (retired)'. His extensive estate at Bellarena, near Limavady, Co. Londonderry, was a magnet to Henry; perhaps, he thought, he might go and live in Ireland. Yet he could not actually bring himself to leave England for long. For a while the thought of the little village of Appledore, on the Taw-Torridge estuary – only six miles as the gull flew, although more than twenty by road – attracted him; in 1953 he nearly bought a cottage there. Finally he learned that 4, Capstone Place, Ilfracombe, was going cheaply, and bought it. Although only eight miles from Oxford Cross on the B3231, it offered a contrast to his writing hut and studio. After his second wife left him in 1962, he spent increasing amounts of time in the cottage. He was sometimes solitary, but by no means always so. There might be visits to or from members of his large family – by the time his *Chronicle* was finished, in 1969, all the children of his first marriage were independent adults; even his youngest daughter, Sarah, was in her twenties, and Harry was no longer a schoolboy. Unhappily, it seems that he was still capable of creating friction with those closest to him; he had never lost his tendency to weep easily, and would sometimes do so as he confided to friends that he had quarrelled with one or other of his children.

Other relationships could be more fortunate. Some of those who knew him well in the Sixties have written accounts of time spent with him. Kerstin Hegarty not only cooked his meals and typed his manuscripts, but accompanied him on walks to Baggy Point and across Saunton Burrows, finding him 'an amusing, lively companion', full of anecdotes and quotations. After she had returned to London he continued to be a fascinating escort when she met him occasionally for meals or theatre visits. She went with him to France in 1964, with a press photographer, when he was writing a series of articles on the First World War for the 'Evening Standard'.

The following year, when Henry would have been seventy, Sue Caron met him somewhere near Georgeham; he offered her a lift in his 'tired Austin A 40'. (The aged Silver Eagle had been sold by this

time. A remarkable car, it still exists; having been rebuilt with care
by its most recent owner, it was still running well in 1983).[1] The
affair that followed was, she says, 'a torrid relationship', although it
evidently had many tranquil moments, when Henry talked at length
about his life and his novels, or read aloud as he loved to do, and
did so well. At the time he spoke to her of ending his *Chronicle* with
Lucifer Before Sunrise because 'it seemed best to stop at October
1945' – an opinion he must have changed almost at once, since he
was later to record that he had worked on *The Gale of the World* for
four years. He confided to Sue Caron details of a 'shattering' affair
with a woman writer who had called him Prospero; this would
presumably have been his relationship with the original of Laura
Wissilcraft in *The Gale*. It is possible that the young novelist Ann
Quin, author of *Berg* and *Three,* contributed something to the
character of Laura as she appears in *The Gale,* though not to her
earlier incarnation in *The Phoenix Generation.*[2]

Alexandra Burgess, who first visited Henry at his writing hut in
1957, during the period of his second marriage, returned in March,
1968, to work for him in what she calls a 'secretarial/Girl Friday
position' while he was working on *The Gale of the World,* with the
usual re-writing of every passage. Although she sometimes found
him difficult to work for, he was also 'compelling, delightful, great
fun, with a wicked sense of humour, and invariably kind and
generous'.

All three of these writers, of a generation so much younger than
Henry's, pay tribute to the profound effect on them of knowing
him. Kerstin Hegarty calls his friendship 'one of the greatest
and most rewarding of my life'; Alexandra Burgess says he was
'undoubtedly the greatest influence on my life'; Sue Caron, who
observes that she has had many lovers but few real friends, claims
that she had 'never known such love in my life'.

Apart from companions such as these, during his last twenty
years Henry made many friendships as a result of his interest in
and support of the 'Aylesford Review', a literary and theological
quarterly published by the Carmelite Order. Father Brocard Sewell
of the Order has told how this came about, following an invitation
to Henry to contribute to an issue of the magazine, to be devoted to
his work, in the winter of 1957-58. Henry duly contributed, and
later wrote other articles and reviews, refusing payment; he also
offered an essay 'In the Woods' (the basis of the chapter 'Woodland
Idyll' in *Lucifer Before Sunrise)* to be published as a booklet, royalties

going to the 'Aylesford Review'. He paid visits to Aylesford Priory in Kent, and attended literary conferences at Hawkesyard Priory in Staffordshire, delighting in meeting many young artistic people. They included Michael Hastings, Michael Horovitz and his wife, the poet and actress Frances Horovitz, Laura Del Rivo, Jane Percival, Nicola Wood, Penelope Shuttle and Oswald Jones (the latter, a photographer, was a close friend of Henry's during these years). Frances Horovitz visited him at Ox's Cross in 1965 when his son Robert and his daughter Sarah, who was twenty, were also staying there. She found Henry exhausting yet stimulating; characteristically he read aloud to her his work in progress, *The Phoenix Generation,* by the hour. She observed that 'Henry is at loggerheads with Sarah over a number of things and I am the point of communication between them – awkward at times'.³

Although not a Roman Catholic (it would be difficult to imagine Henry submitting either to instruction or to discipline) he admired sincere believers of any faith; his portrait of Father Aloysius in *The Golden Virgin* is a testament to this admiration.

One might suppose that the writing of the fifteen novels of his *Chronicle* would have absorbed all Henry's creative energies during the Fifties and Sixties – yet during those years he found time for much occasional journalism. Between April, 1958, and January, 1962, he wrote more than forty short essays under the title 'From a Country Hilltop' for the Co-operative Society's monthly publication, which then had the title 'Home Magazine'. When changes in the magazine's make-up meant that his column was no longer required, he became a contributer to the 'Out of Doors' series of the 'Sunday Times', for which he wrote fifteen pieces during the next two years. The 'Home Magazine' articles are very varied – rewritings of material from books produced in the Thirties; incidents having something in common with his work in progress, *A Chronicle of Ancient Sunlight;* new observations of birds; glimpses of his son Harry as a choir school pupil; accounts of visits to friends such as the poet and dramatist Ronald Duncan at Welcombe near Hartland and John Heygate at Bellarena.

Ronald Duncan had lived at Welcombe since 1937. In his introduction to *Henry Williamson: The Man, the Writings,* he remarked that 'One of Henry's most constant attachments was to my wife, Rose Marie. "I think she is the most beautiful woman I ever saw," he told me. Their relationship remained wholly platonic, and thus endured. It was to her he ran, with tears in his eyes, when his wife,

Christine, left him'. Soon after this, hearing that Duncan was taking his wife and daughter on holiday first to Sicily and later to places on the Italian mainland, Henry went to his friend's travel agent in Barnstaple and booked on the same flight and in the same hotels. Duncan recalls that 'we squabbled mildly a good deal on this journey', yet it seems that he and his family accepted the unexpected addition to their party without protest. They were used to Henry's ways, which included 'a kind of childish perversity, which generally . . . punished himself more than others. Frequently he would motor over for dinner, then march up the hill again before the meal was served, only to return later to beg for a hunk of cheese'.

As has been said, Henry wrote articles for the 'Evening Standard' for the fiftieth anniversary of the outbreak of the First World War. For the 'Daily Express' he marked the fiftieth anniversary of the opening of the Somme battles with three pieces published on successive days. From March, 1967, to the spring of 1971 he wrote more than thirty articles for the 'Express'. A few dealt with the First World War: the battle of Vimy Ridge, the Somme again, and that never forgotten experience, the Christmas Truce. He wrote of visiting one daughter in Cornwall, and watching seals; of visiting another in Dorset, and rescuing an injured lapwing; of visiting his son Richard, warden of Kingley Vale Nature Reserve, where he saw a hobby striking at butterflies or listened to his son talking about fallow deer. Material from books of the Thirties reappeared, about starlings, the courtship of rooks, owls in Skirr Cottage and peregrines on Baggy. Several of the articles make anguished pleas for the protection of otters (this was before the passing of the act to protect them), whales, birds and wild flowers. In the Twenties he had lamented the effect of the pressure of human numbers, as the fields he had loved in boyhood had vanished under thousands of houses; now he was aghast at the effects, world-wide, of the vastly increased human population armed with the power to annihilate one species after another – and finally, only too probably, its own.

Although almost certainly not by any deliberate or conscious planning, in the very last article of the series, 'After the Storm – the Dance of the Phantoms' (27th March,1971) he came to resemble a kind of steadfast and uncomplaining Lear. Walking on the shingle of a south Devon beach, lashed by gale and hail like 'white gravel', while thunder rolls over Dartmoor and the sea, he *lies down* to watch, in a lull in the wind, 'Lambent blue phantoms . . . St Elmo's fire' dancing across the beach. Few men, and certainly few writers,

can ever have welcomed the elements in all their moods as did
Henry.

Apart from his freelance journalism, he prepared television
scripts, including the lovely, elegaic 'Vanishing Hedgerows', written
at the request of David Cobham, who directed the resulting
documentary and was later to direct the film of *Tarka*. Earlier, after
completing *The Golden Virgin,* he had broken off to produce a book
on fishing, *A Clear Water Stream,* despite the fact that he had
abandoned an attempt to write a nature book in 1955. In this he
took the opportunity to reproduce, little changed, a number of the
finest passages of river observations from *Goodbye West Country* and
the original edition of *The Children of Shallowford,* while re-telling the
story of his years at Shallowford, his experiences as a breeder of
trout and salmon and as a fisherman in England, the Hebrides and
Canada. Faber published *A Clear Water Stream* in 1958, the year in
which Macdonald brought out *Love and the Loveless,* the seventh
novel in the sequence *A Chronicle of Ancient Sunlight.*

Henry also gave a number of talks and readings from his work at
various places, including the Beaford Centre for the Arts (a
Dartington Trust foundation not far from Great Torrington) and
the Lobster Pot at Instow, where a member of one audience shouted
out 'Fascist!' Henry merely paused while the interrupter walked out,
and then went on reading.

In 1953, with the help of the Arts Council, north Devon staged
an ambitious Festival of the Arts (also called the Taw-Torridge
Festival), with performances by the English Opera Group, among
others. (A belittling parody of the event appears in *The Gale of the
World,* when Lynton and Lynmouth stage a very inartistic Festival
of the Arts). Ronald Duncan, who was chairman of the festival
committee, saw to it that Henry was given the opportunity to give a
lecture. The title he chose was 'The Two Rivers of my Youth'. He
referred once more to the seventeen re-writings of Tarka, 'every
word chipped out of my breastbone', and read passages from *The
Children of Shallowford.* Recalling the paradisal beauty of Saunton
Burrows, as he had known them thirty years earlier, he spoke of
seeing them 'on the most still day of summer, when the vast blue of
heaven is as the ultimate truth of God'.

By that time both *The Dark Lantern* and *Donkey Boy* had been
published. Despite his picture of himself, only a year earlier, as an
author starting afresh 'less the élan vital', his mental energy clearly
remained prodigious, and he had the satisfaction of knowing that,

however strenuous the creative effort ahead, he had solved some of the problems that had faced him in planning his last long sequence of novels.

CHAPTER FOURTEEN

A Chronicle of Ancient Sunlight

When Henry began his *Chronicle* he had been meditating something of the sort for more than a quarter of a century. In one of his earliest published stories, 'Aliens', from *The Lone Swallows,* he had introduced a boy called Phillip living in Lewisham, with a country-born father, a friendless man embittered by the necessity of living in 'an alien and crowded suburb' and working in a London office. A year or so later, writing the original version of *Dandelion Days,* Henry made John Maddison, Willie's father, tell the boy, 'Your Uncle Richard lives at Brockley, a very depressing place in the south-east of London and inhabited, if my memory serves me, by people still more depressing'. This passage was cut from the revised version.

Now at last the character of Phillip could grow and flourish, and however depressing the young Henry Williamson had found Brockley, his older self knew that he had in it a rich source of interest.

There was so much material – not only all that was stored in his remarkably retentive and visually exact memory, including family anecdotes told him in boyhood by his mother, but his accumulated diaries. He had kept a diary of sorts since his schooldays, and had continued it, though perhaps sporadically, during the First World War. From then on he had filled a series of thick notebooks with detailed accounts of his experiences, observations of the natural world, the progress of his writing, character studies of people he met, happenings in the world at large and fulminations against many of them. In a letter written to me in 1942 he exclaimed 'Little notes, how they bring back authenticity!'; in another he insisted, ' . . . if you keep a notebook or a diary, and note down things which strike you, every day, you will find this INVALUABLE in the years to come, when your real work begins . . . observe and think, note down and store up . . .'

At the end of both *The Phoenix Generation* and *A Solitary War* he even stressed the fact that he had used his diaries in writing them: in the former one finds: 'Journalised: Devon 1935 – Norfolk 1941. Drafted: Devon 1952-56. Recast: Devon 1952-56' and in the latter: 'Journalised: Norfolk – Devon 1941. Novelised: 1949-57 – Devon. Recast: London 1965'.

Yet throughout the *Chronicle,* personal experience and invention intermingle: Henry Williamson the novelist used his imagination freely on the memories of Henry Williamson the child, youth and man to construct the life of Phillip Maddison.

Although he had always intended that the First World War should be the high point of the sequence, he had been indignant when Edward Garnett, Jonathan Cape's literary adviser, had suggested he should start in 1914. It seemed to him essential to begin in the 1890s with the first meeting of Richard Maddison with his future wife, Hettie. The marriage certificate of Henry's parents indicates how closely the description of the clandestine marriage of Richard Maddison and Henrietta Leaver, which appears in *The Dark Lantern,* follows reality. William Leopold Williamson, bachelor, aged 27, a banker's clerk living at 19, Cranfield Road, Brockley, was the son of Henry William Williamson, a surveyor. On 10th May, 1893, at Greenwich Register office, he married Gertrude Eliza Leaver, spinster, aged 25, living at Westpelaer, Cavendish Road, Sutton, Surrey; her father was Thomas William Leaver, a manufacturing stationer. The witnesses were Henrietta Leaver and W. C. Cornish.

When Henry was born, the couple were living at No. 66, Braxfield Road, a turning off Brockley Road, Lewisham. The next street is Comerford Road, and this, it seems, was in Henry's mind when he gave Phillip a house at the end of 'Comfort Road' as his birthplace. Phillip's parents soon move to the newly-built No. 11, Hillside Road nearby, as Henry's parents later moved to No. 11, Eastern Road.[1]

Henry thus had no need to invent a topography for the opening novels of his sequence, only to rename the streets of Lewisham, its open spaces and the little dying river Ravensbourne. His urban landscape is recreated as convincingly as are the Five Towns of Arnold Bennett – whom he had met in the 1920s and admired as a

writer and a man. There is much in his presentation of places and
people, in *The Dark Lantern* and *Donkey Boy* especially, to suggest
that he was seeking to depict his 'Wakenham' in a spirit of
Bennettian realism.[2]

As for characters, they lived with him in vivid recollection:
members of the Williamson and Leaver families – parents, grandparents, aunts, uncles, sisters and cousins – waited to be reshaped
and transformed as members of the Maddison and Turney families,
and the occupants of certain houses in Eastern Road waited to come
to life again as the Maddisons' neighbours. Henry, who wrote so
often of his sense of loneliness, and who, like most writers, sought
solitude for his work, was very far from experiencing the isolated
only childhood he attributed to Willie Maddison in *The Beautiful
Years;* on the contrary he was surrounded in his boyhood by a large
circle of relations, friends and acquaintances. Nevertheless he
undoubtedly had so little in common with them – with the possible
exception of one of his father's sisters, that aunt, already mentioned,
who wrote *The Incalculable Hour* and introduced him, in his late
teens, to Shelley and Francis Thompson – that he developed a
strong sense of being an odd one out, even a misfit, which he never
lost.

At one time he meant to treat his Wakenham/Lewisham and its
people satirically, but he had come to see that he must present every
individual with sympathy and look without rancour at all aspects of
the expanding suburb in which they lived. At the same time, he was
still determined to demonstrate that it had been the outlook, ideas
and values of families such as his that had made the Great War
possible, even inevitable.

The title of the first volume derives from a type of light, also
known as a bull's-eye lantern, much used in the days before electric
torches. (Robert Louis Stevenson, in *Across the Plains,* recollected
the popularity of a cheap tin variety of bull's-eye lantern among
boys of his generation in the 1860s.) Richard Maddison, a Dorset
countryman by birth who has settled reluctantly to work in
London, uses his dark lantern to go out at night to visit moth traps
on an open space, grazed by sheep, called the Hill, near his lodgings.
One night, just as he believes he has glimpsed a butterfly long
extinct in the London area, a Camberwell Beauty, he is attacked by
some of the roughs who frequent the Hill, and has to fight them off.
It is a symbolic moment: the probably illusory sight of a creature
that recalls the once rural villages now vanished under acres of

buildings, coinciding with an episode of human violence. A ravaged countryside, a lost peace: these are to be the predominant themes of *A Chronicle of Ancient Sunlight*.

In essence, the first half of *The Dark Lantern* is a late Victorian romance. Richard meets Hetty Turney, the daughter of a partner in a successful printing and stationery business; they fall in love, difficulties are put in the way of their courtship (in which the dark lantern plays an important part during evening meetings in the Turney summer-house) and they marry in secret. From that point onwards the story grows harsher. Hetty dares not tell her father she is married, because he disapproves of Richard; Richard dares not tell the bank he works for that he is married, because they stipulate that employees must remain single until their salary reaches a figure considerably higher than his. The couple live apart, Hetty at home, Richard in digs, until as a result of a secret holiday together, Hetty becomes pregnant. On hearing this, her choleric father promptly knocks her unconscious. She goes to live with Richard, first in digs, then in a rented house. Almost at once their marriage settles into the pattern of disharmony it will always follow. It is a marriage of dissimilar natures which, in happier circumstances, might have been complementary. Hetty is an optimist, generous-spirited, warm-hearted and somewhat feather-headed. Richard is a pessimist, an introvert, obsessively tidy, punctilious and basically a cold man. Before his meeting with Hetty, his hobbies – butterfly collecting, playing the cello, walking and cycling in the countryside – were all enjoyed in solitude. Once married, he becomes fault-finding and domineering – the more so as the unfortunate Hetty, devoted to his well-being, is childishly submissive and anxious to please. Richard seems to have little to offer save a constricting sense of responsibility for his wife, and, in due course, three children.

Once he and Hetty are together, the dark lantern has a new use; by its light he addresses envelopes in the evenings to earn extra money. His employers discover he is married and dismiss him, but he soon finds work as an insurance clerk, accepting a drop in salary. When his father is killed in an accident, he inherits the then considerable sum of £2,000 from a trust set up by his grandfather. In April, 1895, Hetty gives birth to a son, Phillip; it is a forceps delivery, she is ill for some time afterwards and unable to feed the baby. Richard nurses him at night so that she can sleep. Various baby foods are tried without success until an aged neighbour offers donkey's milk, whereupon Phillip begins to thrive, and so becomes 'the donkey boy'.

Out of his legacy Richard buys, for £650, one of a row of fourteen semi-detached houses being built along the side of the Hill on which he once hunted moths and butterflies: the No. 11, Hillside Road already mentioned (Henry saw no reason to change the house number of his own home.) Thereafter, although Richard presumably still has nearly two-thirds of his £2,000, he continues to behave as though he is a poor man, and enforces domestic economies. His difficult, exacting nature, utterly unlike those of his wife and son, ensures that the boy is made unhappy – the more so when a sister, Mavis, is born, and Richard shows a preference for her.

Phillip, with dark hair and blue eyes, combines his parents' colouring: his father is said to be a tall Nordic type, in contrast to the small, dark-haired Celtic Hetty. The boy, indulged by his mother, is clinging, fearful and weeps easily. Because he has rather more than the normal inquisitiveness and meddlesomeness of small children, his father punishes him, so that he becomes 'as aggrieved in spirit as was the father'. However, he lives in the midst of more tolerant adults: servants, neighbours, as well as Turney relations. When, to Richard's disgust, Hetty's parents come to live at 12, Hillside Road, visits from a wide assortment of diverse characters, married and unmarried uncles and aunts, offer Phillip lively if not always welcome alternatives to the cramping tensions of his own home. *Donkey Boy* ends with his winning a scholarship to a local grammar school, largely on the strength of a good essay.

No doubt Henry felt that he had made ample use of his schooldays in *Dandelion Days;* little is heard of Phillip's classroom experiences. The emphasis is on his spare-time activities. As a member of a small gang of boys who play on a few acres of waste ground known as the Backfield, he becomes a bully by proxy: he fears to fight, but on his behalf one pugnacious member of the gang pummels into submission anyone Phillip dislikes or is afraid of. When parental intervention ends this behaviour, Phillip hears of the movement newly founded by Baden Powell. The section of *Young Phillip Maddison* recording his career as a boy scout is a sequence of hilarious absurdities, beginning when Phillip, in the absence of any established local troop, unofficially sets up a patrol called the Bloodhounds with himself as patrol leader; his authority over his raggle-taggle followers, all younger or from a poorer background than himself, is never secure. Later he joins a troop set up by a rumbustious would-be cleric named Purley-Prout, and goes to chaotic camps and to a jamboree at the Crystal Palace. Allegations

concerning Purley-Prout's pederastic leanings cause the disband-
ment of the troop. During his last years at school, Phillip seeks
happiness as a nature watcher in the Kentish countryside. Having
somehow passed School Certificate, despite failure in many subjects,
he is found a place in a branch of the insurance firm for which his
father works. (These chapters offer a version of Henry's own
experiences in the interval between leaving school and being called
up as a Territorial – that interval he had denied for so long, in his
fantasy of fighting in the trenches at the age of seventeen.)

Predictably, Phillip takes no interest in the work. His fooling
about and reports of imaginary activities, described in the first half
of *How Dear is Life,* amuse some of his seniors and irritate others.
He joins a Territorial Battalion of the London Highlanders (in effect
the London Scottish) in order to earn the four pounds paid to
recruits. In his spare time he still sometimes cycles out into the
country; for his summer holiday he goes to Devon – not to the
Georgeham of Henry's enchanted fortnight in May, 1914, but to
Lynton, where his Aunt Dora has a cottage.

In August he is called up. After a short period of training, his
battalion arrives in France in time to be involved in the confused
fighting near Messines Ridge at the end of October – part of the
battle known as First Ypres.

The chapters describing this action are as convincing as any in
subsequent scenes of the war – yet are not written from first-hand
experience, since Henry enlisted in the Fifth Battalion of the London
Rifle Brigade, which was not drafted to France until November.
However, that crucial event in Henry's life, the Christmas Truce of
1914, is another matter: he was undoubtedly present during the
remarkable spontaneous pause in hostilities which, although not
universal throughout the Western Front, lasted in some areas from
Christmas Eve until New Year's Eve. During those days, German
and British soldiers (members of what Henry, who had a German
grandmother on his father's side, liked to call the 'cousin nations')
wandered together across No Man's Land, exchanging remi-
niscences, photographs and presents, sang songs and played football
matches.

Henry's astonished discovery that German youths believed as
fervently as did British youths that they were in the right and had
God on their side was the first of the two principal transforming
experiences of his life (the second, linked to it, came twenty one
years later in Germany, when his emotional nature transmuted the

base metal of Hitlerism into a golden chimaera, the Führer's will to peace). Also from the Truce originated Henry's fascination with the planet Venus, seen rising over the German trenches: that planet which is known as both the Evening and the Morning Star; which was Eosphorus to the Greeks and Lucifer the lightbringer to the Romans.

The climax of each of the four novels that follow *How Dear is Life* is one of the main life-wasting episodes of the war: Loos in September, 1915, in *A Fox Under my Cloak;* the first hours of 1st July, 1916, on the Somme in *The Golden Virgin;* wretched weeks of 1917 in the murderous morasses of Passchendaele in *Love and the Loveless;* ³ and the last great German offensive of Spring, 1918, in *A Test to Destruction.*

In an author's note at the beginning of *A Fox Under my Cloak,* Henry acknowledged that a number of scenes in the novel were based on incidents recorded in the *Official History of the Great War, Military operations,* compiled by Brig. General Edmonds and Captain Wynne. He added that each of the characters in his story had an existence in the 1914-18 war, 'though not all necessarily acted or played their parts in the times and places mentioned'. He dedicated the book to Captain Douglas Bell, M.C., who was wounded at Loos, and whose *A Soldier's Diary of the Great War* was published anonymously in 1929, with an introduction by Henry.

It seems evident that he again referred to the Official History while writing the remaining three war novels; he may also have made use of some parts of his extensive collection of books on the war, a number of which he discussed in his essay 'Reality in War Literature'. It has been pointed out by Peter Cole (Henry Williamson Society Journal No. 14, September, 1986) that it is clear that he found both *The History of the London Rifle Brigade* and *The London Scottish in the Great War* of considerable use to him.

Nevertheless, the pictures he paints of the war are his own; whether powerfully imagined or deriving from personal observation, they are brilliantly sharp, impressionistic recreations of battle in varying conditions, weather and terrain. It is a matter for conjecture at which points in each novel after *How Dear is Life,* invention and research take over from first-hand knowledge of events, although it is fairly sure that the military career of Phillip Maddison, though paralleling Henry's in certain respects, quite often differs, especially in 1918.

It seems that Henry, like Phillip, served as a private soldier for the

FACTS

MERS
SAVE
£400,000,000
A YEAR
ON IMPORTS
WE CAN SAVE MUCH
MORE IF THE GOVT.
WILL LET US

At a point-to-point meeting in the sixties: supporting the cause of agriculture.

Henry Williamson on Putsborough beach in 1969: Baggy Point can be seen in the background.

On the rocks at Putsborough, 1969.

Henry Williamson in London, c. 1970, at an anti-Vietnam war rally.

Outside the writing hut at Ox's Cross. Reading aloud from his work to an attentive young visitor, 1965.

first six months of the war, and was invalided to England with
dysentery and trench feet early in 1915; that, also like Phillip, he
obtained a commission in the spring of that year. The Army List
shows that H. W. Williamson was gazetted as a second lieutenant in
April, 1915, in the 10th (Service) Battalion of the Bedfordshire
Regiment. (Phillip is commissioned in the Gaultshires, and Henry's
name for Bedfordshire was Gaultshire.)⁴ He had the good fortune to
receive a temporarily disabling but comparatively light wound on
the first day of the Somme; by the late summer he was spending sick
leave at Georgeham. He later attended a course for transport officers
at Belton Park, Grantham, and served with the 208 Company,
Machine Gun Corps – as a transport officer – at the time of Third
Ypres (Passchendaele). It is interesting that a Lieut. Maddison, who
survived the war, was commissioned in the Machine Gun Corps in
1915; can it have been from this officer that Henry borrowed the
fairly unusual surname for his central character?

In the last months of the war Henry was on home service, acting
as adjutant – though as he himself recorded, in a very desultory
way – at a Rest Camp. In October, 1918, he had been expecting
to experience service in India, but the Armistice caused the
cancellation of this posting. He spent much of 1919 in Folkestone.
One of the notebooks preserved in Exeter University Library is
stamped 'No. 1 Dispersal Unit, Shornecliffe'. It contains a short
story dated February, 1919, a reference to his love affair with a girl
he calls Mignon, who would therefore be the original of 'Evelyn
Fairfax', and some nature notes dated as having been written in the
orderly room of No. 3 Rest Camp, Folkestone on 9th April, 1919.
Later nature notes on birds are dated Brocton Camp, Staffordshire,
in September of that year. It was at Brocton that his army service
ended.

The theme of the novels making up the First World War section
of the *Chronicle* is courage in its various forms. Courage was a
subject of considerable importance to Henry, the more so as he
insisted on referring to his boyhood self as a coward. In his essay
'Out of the Prisoning Tower' he remarked that at school he had
regarded himself as a coward 'without undue concern'. When war
came, it was a different matter. He saw courage as synonymous with
honour, and both deriving from a boyhood in which the child
received the right kind of love from both parents – a kind which he
considered he had not received. This opinion was clearly unfair to
his mother, at least. If Hettie Maddison is to be regarded as a

portrayal of Gertrude Williamson, and there is no reason to suppose it is not, Henry had a constantly devoted if somewhat over-fussy mother. The genetic chance that produced in Henry a child whose nature was wholly unlike that of his father may have been unfortunate for them both, and their lack of mutual sympathy evidently oppressed a sensitive small boy. Yet in calling himself a loveless child, Henry overstated his case.

Phillip Maddison is presented as a man who, initially lacking courage, gradually begins to disregard his own safety; an officer called West, nicknamed Spectre or Westy, demonstrates a steadfast bravery at all times; another officer, Bill Kidd, is the gung-ho type who indulges in reckless bravado. There is also an example of non-combatant self-sacrifice in Father Aloysius, in *The Golden Virgin,* who tends wounded soldiers on the Somme and later dies of wounds.

Phillip is self-willed, resistant to either authority or discipline; he is also still timorous and emotional, both as a private soldier and when, not without difficulty, he has obtained his commission. His behaviour with a regiment on home service in the early summer of 1915 is so absurd, noisy and impertinent that his fellow-officers administer fairly harsh unofficial punishment on three separate occasions. During spells of active service in the next three years he does his best to avoid the hazards of the life of an ordinary front-line infantry subaltern; thus he applies for and obtains slightly safer occupations, such as gas officer and transport officer. Nevertheless his unquenchable curiosity leads him to wander about during lulls in active warfare, virtually sight-seeing; he wants to 'stand and stare and let his feelings possess him, so that he could lose himself in a dream that was beyond nightmare – the romance of war, the visual echoes of tragic action'. He keeps a diary of events and of his own experiences (a practice forbidden by regulations, though many more literate soldiers ignored this.) He resembles, in fact, a man collecting material for a book about the war. More than once he is suspected of being a deserter or an impostor, and on one such occasion carries out a particularly extravagant exploit: carrying reports given him by the wounded Spectre West, he seizes the horse of a suspicious Provost Marshal and gallops to G.H.Q., where he is allowed to report to no less a person than Sir Douglas Haig. Twice taken prisoner by the Germans, he escapes each time. Faint echoes of Baron Münchausen may be heard in episodes such as these.

Phillip's inability to assume conventional military attitudes earns him the disapproval of his superiors; he receives a number of adverse reports, and is passed over for promotion until, in 1918, he is promoted lieutenant-colonel in the field, commanding the remnants of a battalion, following the death in battle of senior officers.

Spectre West, Phillip's mentor, hero and forbearing friend, has meanwhile earned steady promotion, the D.S.O. and bar, the M.C. and two bars, and lost an eye and a hand. On the eve of the German offensive of April, 1918, West tells Phillip to hold Wytschaete, on a ridge near Messines, at all costs. Phillip's fire-eating second-in-command, Bill Kidd, provides support, advice and devil-may-care example. Kidd sets up a machine-gun post in a pill-box called Staenyzer Kabaret, holds out there and refuses to move when Phillip passes on orders for withdrawal. (A Lieut. Hodgson performed a feat similar to this at St Quentin Cabaret, near Messines, during this action.) Phillip goes to consult Spectre West at brigade headquarters; both are wounded by a mustard gas shell. Temporarily blinded, Phillip is transferred to Boulogne, and makes repeated efforts to speak to West, without success. Both are aboard a hospital ship torpedoed in the Channel; Phillip is rescued, but West drowns, having given his lifebelt to a messenger sent by Phillip.

Phillip thereupon persuades himself, during his convalescence, that he is responsible for West's death; on being notified that he is being awarded the D.S.O. – the recommendation having been West's last kindness – he feels that he is a fake. The specific act for which he has been decorated is his success in destroying a German machine-gun nest which had been preventing the withdrawal of West's headquarters during a British retreat in March, 1918. However, during the preceding years he has performed a number of valorous deeds (as well as foolhardy ones during his sightseeing tours): a raid on a German trench and capture of a prisoner (who dies of mysterious causes); the rescue from No Man's Land, in the aftermath of a failed British attack, of a wounded fellow officer; the destruction of a German field gun while escaping from captivity during a British bombardment. Despite all this, he remains convinced of his own inadequacy.

Recovered from the effects of mustard gas, he is appointed adjutant of a Rest Camp near Folkestone. Here he has an affair with Evelyn Fairfax – the Evelyn of *The Dream of Fair Women*. In the earlier novels in the sequence a good deal has been heard of his emotional life, beginning with his adoration-from-afar of Helena

Rolls, who lives in Hillside Road but cannot be persuaded to show
any interest in Phillip. Early in the war he had what appeared to be
his first sexual experience with his precocious schoolgirl cousin,
Polly, whom he does not much like. Since then he has been in love
once, with a girl called Lily Cornford, who worked in a laundry and
was a part-time prostitute; she has 'large blue glistening eyes and a
loose smiling mouth', and performs the difficult-sounding feat of
'swimming into his aloofness from the lakes of her eyes'. She is
killed in a Zeppelin raid. The amorous advances of an aunt by
marriage cause Phillip to withdraw in alarm; on leave with Spectre
West at a hotel called Flowers, which sounds like Rosa Lewis's
Cavendish, he was unable to respond to a married woman called
Sasha, who came to his bed on two occasions. Throughout the
Chronicle, in fact, Phillip is usually presented as a diffident lover,
liable to be afflicted with impotence. The affair with Evelyn has
none of the ardour of Willie's pursuit of her in *The Dream of Fair
Women,* and is soon over.

Transferred to a camp near Cannock Chase, Phillip consults a
doctor who tells him that he has been drugging himself by
repeatedly returning to France to escape from some underlying
repression, probably from his early years. His indifference to his
duties causes his colonel to tell him that his papers are to be sent in
for immediate demobilisation. A civilian again, with a disability
pension of some £75 a year, he rapidly regresses to the immature
and erratic behaviour of his pre-war and early war-time years,
with the difference that he seems like a man on the verge of a
nervous breakdown – hardly surprisingly. The condition then
usually referred to as shellshock (later battle shock and in today's
jargon post-traumatic stress disorder) was common enough among
ex-soldiers, especially those whose dispositions were particularly
nervous and sensitive. Although Phillip has spent more than half
the war in England – on home service, on leave, in hospital with
trench fever or other forms of sickness, or wounds – he has
experienced enough, during months of mind-shattering bombard-
ments, constant hazards, and the sight of innumerable deaths and
maimings, to increase his innate tendency to instability.

He refuses to go back to the insurance office – which has been
paying his salary during his service – buys a Norton motorcycle and
rides aimlessly from one place to another. At home he has violent
disputes with his father about the true nature and causes of the war,
after one of which he rushes into the street, flourishing a loaded

revolver. The climax is a drunken walk with Tom Ching, his hanger-on from boyhood, one-time member of the Bloodhound Patrol, along the course of the Randisbourne. Ching sets fire to a watchman's hut; Phillip takes the blame, is charged with arson, and serves a month in prison.

This is a strange episode, almost a travesty of Phillip's gallant exploits at the Front. It is as though the author wearied of his character's assumption of a heroic stance. Phillip even pretends that the Randisbourne is a Flanders river he once crossed during a retreat; the ruined former countryside through which it flows, its trees felled to make way for building sites, becomes a sort of No Man's Land. His first act, on being charged, is to write to *Buckingham Palace* to ask that his name be removed from the register of holders of the D.S.O. – much as Manfred Cloudesley, in *The Gold Falcon,* requested the War Office that his numerous awards should no longer be credited to him. Did Henry become uneasy at having endowed his central character, this avowed version of himself, with an award he did not, in fact, receive? (Indeed, as Daniel Farson established in his *Henry Williamson, A Portrait,* he did not even receive the M.C., although he sometimes allowed friends to think that he had, and was not above allowing an M.C. medal to be seen, in a small glass-fronted case – as Mrs Kingsman in *The Golden Virgin* keeps her dead son's M.C. on the wall in her sitting room).

The anti-climactic final chapters of *A Test to Destruction* see Phillip beginning a job selling advertising space in Fleet street. After a final row, his father forbids him the house, and he moves into the room in his grandfather's garden where his uncle Hugh Turney died a few years before the war, of syphilis – a disease which Phillip briefly and erroneously believes himself to have caught from a seventeen-year-old prostitute. The novel comes to a quiet close with the death of grandfather Turney. His house become Hetty's property, and she at last has a little independence from the repressive Richard.

Throughout the five novels which, in whole or in part, make up Henry's long-projected picture of the war, there is a counterpoint between life at the Front and life on home service or among civilians. Through the eyes of Hetty, Richard, Grandfather Turney, Aunt Dora and others, impressions are built up of the distorted and grief-ridden years between 1914 and 1918. (According to Hugh Cecil, Henry 'quite shamelessly' lifted whole episodes from Michael Macdonagh's diary, *London in the Great War;*[5] yet even if this is conceded, the material has been assimilated skilfully into the close-knit narrative and adopted to the lives of the *Chronicle's* characters.) In addition, in contrast with the resigned stoicism of the average serving soldier, are set the figures of the deserter, the lead-swinger, the uniformed impostor, the conscientous objector whose only conviction is fear, and the civilian clinging to his reserved occupation until conscription forces him into uniform.

The novels thus offer a wide over-view of the war as it affected the British people most closely and alarmingly. To take in the many other theatres of war would have required an altogether different and even more demanding fictional scheme, and had never been part of Henry's intention; he was above all an author who wrote of what he knew.

He was nearly sixty-five when he completed *A Test to Destruction,* yet his younger self evidently remained very close to him – perhaps too much so. It is one of the weaknesses of these five novels that so much of the writing is intensely subjective. Another is that Phillip's hero, Spectre West, is never a rounded character; beginning as a colourful, irascible company commander, swigging whisky for dutch courage, he later abjures alchohol and grows increasingly correct and lacking in personality. Apparently presented as the epitome of military virtue, he dwindles into a wooden figure, while Phillip's metamorphosis from excitable non-hero to daring battalion commander does not quite succeed in suspending disbelief.

THE GOLDEN VIRGIN: ALBERT: 1917

CHAPTER FIFTEEN

The Chronicle Continues

Henry's autobiographical books of the Twenties and Thirties provide much of the material for the next four novels of his sequence. Usually this material is rearranged and recast, but sometimes passages are repeated almost word for word, apart from the substitution of third person singular for the first person. Despite considerable geographical, chronological and emotional changes, Phillip's life, and the lives of his close relations, follow a course not unlike that of Henry and his family during the years from 1920 to 1945.

The source of many chapters of *The Innocent Moon* is *The Sun in the Sands,* published only sixteen years earlier, although written during Henry's second visit to the United States in 1934. (The final page even bears the note 'March 1934 – March 1961, Florida – Devon'.) Some episodes are considerably expanded, and many extracts from Phillip's diary are quoted. The jobs in Fleet Street, love for a girl nicknamed Spica, visits to a literary club, months spent in a cottage in Devon with Julian Warbeck, meetings with Irene and her daughter Barley and with Sophie and her children Queenie, Annabelle and Marcus, all appear for the second time, although the cottage is near a south Devon village called Malandine. Phillip goes on a walking tour in France with friends from the newspaper for which he is writing articles, and makes a foolhardy crossing of a pass in the Pyrenees; however, this time Barley does not – as in *The Sun in the Sands* – die while trying to reach him, he only dreams that she does. They fall in love. Back in Devon, Willie is drowned in the Taw, as in *The Pathway*. (From this point onwards, Henry was rid of the slight awkwardness of having, in effect, two dopplegängers in his chronicle.) Immediately after Barley's eighteenth birthday, Phillip persuades her to marry him by special license at Caxton Hall instead of returning to her finishing school. They spend their honeymoon in his ramshackle cottage in Malandine. In this departure from personal experience, the imaginary marriage to a very young wife, of which Henry had told the rector's wife in Georgeham in 1919, attained a new kind of fictional reality; moreover the unattainable schoolgirl who had enthralled him in the Thirties became at last accessible to his other self. Yet because he wanted to continue the record of his own life, in which the real Barley was only a frustrating interlude, she could not be allowed to live. At the beginning of *It Was the Nightingale,*[1] Phillip and Barley spend a holiday in the Camargue, where they find an otter cub and smuggle it into England. Later that year, Barley dies in childbirth. Many of the details leading up to the birth, including the doctor's game of skittles in the village pub and the unsympathetic north-country midwife, are as described in chapter one of the original version of *The Children of Shallowford*. Phillip, in what is made to sound a heroic and very painful process, acts as a blood donor in an attempt to save Barley, but she dies of a haemorrhage. The baby, named Billy, is looked after by Phillip's next-door neighbours in Malandine, a family based on the Thomases of Georgeham, with whom Henry used to take his meals in the early Twenties after being advised by his doctor to eat more regularly.

Phillip moves into his cousin Willie's old cottage in north Devon, and is introduced, by Mary Ogilvie of *The Flax of Dream,* to her cousin Lucy Coplestone, who lives with her widowed father and three brothers – 'Pa and the Boys' – in Dorset. The brothers run an engineering works adjoining the house. Having thus moved what is in effect Loetitia's family into a neighbouring county, Henry offers an unflattering picture of their way of life and lack of business sense, recalling chapter five of *The Story of a Norfolk Farm*.

By now Phillip has had a number of short stories published, as well as three novels about a man called Donkin, who is said to be based on Willie. He begins a story about an otter; the cub brought back from France was lost soon after Barley's death. His uncle Hilary, a man of means, has bought the Maddison estate at Rookhurst lost by his feckless father. (Uncle Hilary – Sir Hilary Maddison, K.B.E., C.M.G., Captain, Retd., R.N.R. – is evidently based on the unhappy ex-sailor uncle, without title, honours or landed estate, who visited Henry at Vale House when Windles was only a year old, and again briefly at Shallowford, and died a few years later.) He offers Phillip the opportunity to become a pupil under his land steward, with the tenancy of Skirr Farm (the home of the Temperleys in *The Beautiful Years*). Phillip accepts, and marries Lucy; the novel ends with their honeymoon, which begins on Exmoor and closely resembles that of Manfred and Ann in *The Gold Falcon*.

There follows in *The Power of the Dead* some account of Phillip's farming apprenticeship, though he spends much of his time with friends in London or Devon, or writing; he produces a war book of some kind – passages from *The Wet Flanders Plain* are quoted – as well as the final volume of his tetralogy about Donkin, and *The Water Wanderer,* about Barley's otter, the theme being symbolic of his lost love. This last wins a literary prize, the Grasmere; the Donkin novel, *The Phoenix,* sells more than 20,000 copies.

At a party Phillip meets a girl called Felicity Ancroft and begins to fall in love with her. He becomes friendly with Piers Tofield, a character based on Henry's friend John Heygate. As Heygate married the former wife of Evelyn Waugh, it is interesting to find Phillip visiting a young writer called Anthony Croft, whose wife, Virginia, later leaves Anthony for Piers. (Evelyn Waugh's diary for 11th November, 1928, records that a friend had brought 'a man called Henry Williamson to see us'. Having noted that he had won a prize with *Tarka,* and had great success with a novel – i.e. *The Pathway* – Waugh makes the surprising remark that he is 'quite elderly – though I find him coupled with me in reviews as promising young writers'. The 'elderly' Henry was a few days short of his thirty-third birthday at the time, while Waugh was twenty-five. Waugh's comments on Henry are characteristically acidic; he found him wholly without culture, very gauche and 'suddenly earnest-minded, but capable of fun'. Henry took away a copy of *Decline and Fall* with him.)

When *The Power of the Dead* ends, Felicity is in love with Phillip and is to become his secretary. He is no longer even a dilettante farmer; his uncle has sold his estate to the War Office and is to marry Irene, Barley's mother.

The next novel, *The Phoenix Generation,* covers a longer span of time than any other in the sequence: from the General Election of 1929 to the eve of the Second World War. It shows Phillip and Lucy living in a long thatched house in a village called Flumen Monachorum – in effect Filleigh, although it is said to be not far

from Skirr Farm. It has two miles of fishing; Phillip is preparing to
write a book about a trout. Details from Henry's autobiographical
books such as the fiasco of a new hearth, the employment of an
alcoholic ex-soldier as a servant, the buying of a hill-top field and
building of a shelter on it, reappear. Phillip's affair with his
secretary, Felicity, results in the birth of her baby at about the time
that Lucy also bears a child. He finds Felicity a dilapidated cottage;
she settles in and begins to write a novel.

Already interested in the ideas of the Mosley figure, Sir Hereward
Birkin, leader of the Imperial Socialist Party, Phillip visits Germany
with Piers and becomes a fervent admirer of Hitler, whom he regards
as a phoenix. (The chapter describing this visit, entitled '*Hakenkreuze*'
– Henry preferred to use the German word, *Hakenkreuz,* for the
crooked cross, rather than swastika – is virtually a repetition of the
long entry for 2nd September, 1936, in *Goodbye West Country.)*

Phillip's book, *The Blind Trout,* is published, and sells well; it has
as its theme an intense sense of loss in the reduction of the
once-clear stream, the Randisbourne (Ravensbourne) to a befouled
runnel of dead water; there is an echo here of Henry's story,
'Aliens', written in London in 1920.

Phillip moves to East Anglia to farm; Felicity rejoins him as
secretary. Articles he writes about his farming experiences bring an
assortment of 'acquaintances and pests' to the farm, which is
sometimes referred to locally as the Convalescent Home. Phillip
joins Birkin's party and, in late August, 1939, has a plan to fly to
Germany on a peace mission, but Birkin tells him it is too late; 'the
curtain is down'. Phillip returns to his farm, and the patient Lucy,
turtle dove to his phoenix. By now they have four children.

Having moderated his affair with Felicity to a platonic friendship,
Phillip's emotional life is now focussed on Melissa, a cousin of
Lucy's. She appears briefly in *A Test to Destruction* as a blond,
blue-eyed child who talked to Phillip while he was convalescent in
1918. He has met her again at a Dorset Yacht Club (based in part on
the North Devon Yacht Club, Instow, of which Henry was a
member in the 1930s).[2] She is in her last term at school. While her
surname, Watt-Wilby, is not one of Henry's name jokes, it is a play
on words: for Phillip, she is indeed what will be, the woman who
will be his companion at the end of *The Gale of the World,* the final
volume of the *Chronicle.*

Not only in its title, but also in the body of the book, Henry
displays his liking for symbolism. The 'blind, black and ageing trout'

represents the dying Europe; moreover Phillip begins to regard his derelict farm as a microcosm of the European macrocosm; its reclamation, when achieved, is to be a token of the resurgence of the continent. Although he allows Phillip to acknowledge to himself that this latter idea is a fantasy, it is typical of Henry's tendency to present the actions of the individual as symptomatic of humanity at large. During his first years at Shallowford, when councils in rural areas made no arrangements for refuse collection, he bought three dustbins and set them outside the kitchen door; they were labelled COMPOST, BURNING and BURIAL, and he was frequently heard to lament when broken glass and china were found in BURNING, or broken toys in COMPOST. In *The Gold Falcon,* Manfred describes similar bins to Barbara Faithfull, and tells her that they are 'symbolic, to me, of a tidy world after the formless human chaos called war'.

In *The Phoenix Generation* and the two novels that follow it, Henry also made much use of the fable of the tortoise and the hare – Phillip being the too impetuous, too impatient hare, constantly at odds with the slower, more cautious 'tortoise' minds about him, although he is finally able to admit that they have often been in the right. (The joking title of the chapter in *A Solitary War* describing Phillip's brief imprisonment under Regulation 18B is 'Jugged Hare'.)

By comparison with the ten-year span of *The Phoenix Generation, A Solitary War,* dedicated to Oswald and Diana Mosley 'in friendship', covers only about ten months; as has been said, it describes the fiasco of Phillip's partnership with Teddy Pinnegar. The novel ends in the early autumn of 1940, with Phillip, having assured Lucy that he will be 're-arrested and removed to a barbed-wire cage somewhere, if invasion comes', going out at night to lie on the hill above his farm. The concluding sentences contain concepts familiar from many of Henry's earlier books, including his favourite phrase 'The sun saw no shadows'. Phillip watches the rising of the morning star, remembered still from the Christmas Truce of 1914: 'Lucifer the lightbringer of mythology; Lucifer the fallen angel, Lucifer the prince of darkness'.

So the penultimate novel of his sequence received its title. *Lucifer Before Sunrise* runs to some 200,000 words. Henry's note at the end of the book, '1941-1967', suggests that he began work on a draft of it not long after completing *The Story of a Norfolk Farm*. It contains many lengthy entries from the diary ostensibly kept by Phillip, carrying forward the story of his farming and family life from the end of 1940 until the autumn of 1945. Expansively, Henry

chronicled in detail the activities of Phillip's farming years, which
were in effect those of Old Hall Farm, Stiffkey. Ploughing, hay-
making, harvesting, threshing; growing and lifting and processing
sugar beet; caring for sheep, pigs, store cattle and poultry – all these
are seen against the harsh background of the fears and changes and
outrages of war. In the harassed and harassing Phillip, Henry
presented his own view of himself during his Norfolk period,
possibly distorted by his ever-present tendency to self-denigration.
And in the remorse of Phillip, as he observes that his eldest son,
Billy, has become alienated from him, the reader may hear the voice
of Henry acknowledging his mistakes and misjudgements in his
treatment of Windles.

There are lighter moments, when Phillip relaxes with his children
and shares their pleasure in various pets – a fledgeling owl, cats and
other creatures – but repeatedly he notes with chagrin that on his
entry into a room where his family are talking and laughing
together, a silence falls as they wait apprehensively to judge his
mood.

Phillip writes a book called *Pen and Plough;* he continues to yearn
to begin his novels about his parents and the First World War; he
builds himself a studio in which to write and towards the end of the
novel is said to have produced nearly a quarter of a million words
in six months. He reads *War and Peace* and considers that 'the entire
motive for the Napoleonic War was missing from the work. The
original impulse of genius, the vision of Napoleon clenched to his
clear and unequivocal will-power, where did it appear, in character,
upon the pages of the book?' Therefore, Phillip decides, 'the
gradual divergence in time between Napoleon's spiritual ideals and
the physical reality of his actions' was not shown; Tolstoy simply
did not understand why Napoleon had gone to war.

Here, not for the first time, Henry developed one of his own
political notions. From the mid-Thirties he projected upon dictators
of the Right (but emphatically not of the Left, despite his admiration for Lenin in his youth) an idealistic aim, the unification of
Europe for benevolent purposes, refusing to acknowledge self-
aggrandisement and thirst for power as motives.

As the novel comes to its end Billy, who has joined the R.A.F.
and been posted to an operational bomber squadron, is killed when
the aircraft of which he is a crew member crashes over the Alps.
(Henry could not resist 'writing out' this boy, whose real-life
counterpart, Windles, had struck him during a quarrel and, after the

war, had left England – not to die, but to make a successful new life for himself in Canada.)

Lucy leaves Phillip, explaining that she knows he would never give up the farm if the decision were left to him, and she wants to force his hand; moreover, at the age of 44, she is pregnant again, and there is both the baby and her younger children to be considered: if the latter are not to lose their respect for him, he must have his freedom and she must have hers.

Her brother Tim tells Phillip that he has showed letters and extracts from Phillip's diaries, which reveal 'the same mentality as that of Hitler', to the police, 'with a view to considering that treatment for your mental condition should be inaugurated'. Phillip visits Lucy and, admitting that he has been 'a dreadful person' to her for years, promises to give her grounds for divorce if she will 'call off the cruelty case', which he fears may ruin 'what is left of my reputation as a writer'. (The accusation of cruelty arises from an appalling incident in the middle years of the war when Phillip, in an excess of near insane fury, kills two kittens and then makes a violent attack on Lucy.) He has sold the farm for three times what he paid for it; the money will be made into a trust for her and the children; he has bought a house in Suffolk which she and the children and – despite his actions – Tim and his wife and family can share.

Phillip's reception of the news of Hitler's death is strange. As is his habit, he listens to a German radio station, and when Doenitz announces that 'the Führer is fallen', Phillip at once thinks 'This lets me out'. The whole passage describing this episode was evidently taken from Henry's journal, an extract from which, corresponding almost word for word with pages 481-2 of *Lucifer Before Sunrise,* is presented under the title 'An Affirmation', as Appendix 2 of *Henry Williamson, The Man, the Writings,* the symposium prepared by his friends after his death. Henry, like Phillip, remarked 'This lets me out'. In what way did Hitler's death let him out – and out of what? A secret vow, an imagined allegiance, a schoolboyish make-believe bond of brotherhood to that wholly imaginary Hitler he had created for himself in the vacuum of his longing for a benign superman to solve the problems of humanity?

His Damascus-road conversion in Nuremberg had been so complete that even in the late Sixties, writing *The Gale of the World,* he could include, again as a diary entry, Phillip's ludicrous suggestion that an 'eager writer of genius', wishing to produce a *War and Peace* for this age, might 'show truly the luminous

personality of Adolf Hitler . . . this Lucifer, this light-bringer . . .
one in those early years of the 'thirties possessed harmoniously by
the highest spiritual force, gentle and magnanimous, yet also the
man of cool calculation, of immense patience and understanding of
all problems'.

Such passages are as chilling as his reference to himself, in the
letter quoted in chapter 11, as a 'littler Hitler'. Despite his tendency
to rant, frequently referred to in his books, and his failings as
husband and father, Henry was never a Hitler of any size or shape,
and his obsession with the dictator remains a deplorable but
ineradicable flaw. The tragedy lies in the phenomenon of a man of
good will attributing to a man of ill will his own idealistic, if vague,
aspirations.

Towards the end of *Lucifer Before Sunrise* Phillip, although
carrying on or supervising farming operations, turns more and
more to other activities; he restores a polluted stream, cycles about
the countryside, bathes with his younger children, plans and writes
notes for his projected novels, and visits Malandine, where he finds
his converted linhay in ruins – the area has been used for battle
practise – but rescues a chest containing his notebooks 'over twenty
volumes, one for every year since 1919' as well as his father's dark
lantern. 'Lantern and journals – he was safe'. Having been wounded
by soldiers firing live ammunition on his land, he has had a spell in
hospital; since then he has seemed to live in a state of prolonged
convalescence, his almost frantic resolve to make the farm a success
dwindling away as very gradually he drifts back into the life of a
whole-time writer.

His relationship with his children is less tense. It is shown that in
earlier years he expected, with surprising Victorian stuffiness, to be
addressed as 'Sir' by his sons; now the younger ones, at least, call
him Chooky. Phillip pays tribute to Lucy's constant patience and
hard work, her 'endearing consideration' for him; after the news of
the end of the war in Europe he reflects 'What constant thought,
care and labour for her family that dove-like woman had borne
through the years, what work she had done for the village, which
respected and loved her'. And for Lucy, of course, the reader may
substitute the name Loetitia.

One might wish that Henry had indeed been content to bring his
Chronicle to a close with this novel, as he told Sue Caron (author of
A Glimpse of Ancient Sunlight) that he thought of doing. *Lucifer
Before Sunrise* ends on a note of calm and acquiescence as Phillip and

his youngest son, Jonny, pay a last visit to a beach near the farm before Phillip sets off to travel once more, alone, to Devon. Yet no doubt he felt that he wanted a more dramatic finale – and saw in the Lynmouth flood disaster of August, 1952, a climax that was at once impressive in itself, and symbolic. (It may be noted that the flood has slipped back in time to 1947: the book, beginning during the Nuremberg war trials, in other words in the late summer of 1946, ends only a twelve-month later.)

The title, *The Gale of the World,* is taken from the reported last words of General Mihailovitch before being shot: 'I and my works were caught in the gale of the world'. The setting is the northern border of Exmoor, and the villages of Lynton and Lynmouth. Phillip settles into what is described as a 'shepherd's cot' – virtually a revived version of Skirr Cottage, or indeed of Willie Maddison's Rat's Castle – lying somewhere on the north side of the Chains, the high ridge of Exmoor that runs east to west across the Somerset-Devon border, not far from one of the hut circles that are to be seen in several places in that part of the moor, and beside 'a little runner of the West Lyn'. In a position answering to this description there is a cottage, or small farm house, called Shallowford, as was the house at Filleigh, on the Fortescue estate, in which Henry lived during the Thirties. Possibly this was the place he had in mind as Phillip's refuge. However, there is another possibility: on the high ground of the Chains, near the source of the West Lyn in Ruckham Combe, ruins show where an actual shepherd's hut once stood.

Henry's admiration of Shelley seems to have been as keen in his fifties as it had been in his twenties, when he was writing *A Dream of Fair Women;* there is a good deal about the poet's association with Lynmouth in *The Gale of the World.* (Shelley and his first wife, the seventeen-year-old Harriet Westbrook, with Harriet's elder sister, stayed in Lynmouth for a few weeks of July and August 1812. They left hurriedly by sea, by way of Ilfracombe, when a servant of Shelley's was arrested in Barnstaple for distributing copies of a pamphlet the poet called 'A Declaration of Rights'. More romantically, Shelley had often rowed out from the little quay at Lynmouth at dusk to send off fire balloons bearing copies of his pamphlet, or set bottles, or waxed, sealed boxes, with little sails, afloat in the Bristol Channel.)

Phillip attends a seance at which a medium recites Francis Thompson's poem to Shelley while in a trance. The scene is one of several coloured by the supernatural, and a passage from another of

Henry's early literary mentors, Richard Jefferies, is quoted: the page
from *The Story of my Heart* in which the idea that no distinction
exists between natural and supernatural is expounded.

As elsewhere in the *Chronicle,* characters include several drawn
from life, among them Fred Riversmill (Sir Alfred Munnings,
whom Henry had known since his days in Norfolk, when Munnings
painted Old Hall Farm, and at whose cottage at Withypool he had
stayed briefly during the war) and Osgood and Rosalie Nilsson
(Negley Farson and his wife, who lived only a mile or two from
Henry in the Fifties.) Henry had suffered verbal savagings from
Farson, and his unflattering portrayal of his fellow writer and his
wife – who, by the time he was writing, had both died – shows how
deep was his resentment. Other characters emerge from earlier
novels – not only Laura Wissilcraft and Melissa Watt-Wilby from
The Phoenix Generation, A Solitary War and *Lucifer Before Sunrise,* but
Hugh ('Buster') Cloudesley who, in *The Gold Falcon,* was Manfred's
orphaned son. Even Corney, Manfred's alcoholic servant, reappears
as the landlord of a pub on Exmoor.

A cousin of Lucy's, Molly Bucentaur, has a daughter, Miranda,
who is in her last term at school before going up to Oxford, where
she is to read philosophy. Miranda, Laura and Melissa are all
attracted to Phillip. Laura, no longer as overtly neurotic as in *A
Solitary War,* is nevertheless deeply disturbed; she writes Phillip
effusive letters in which she refers to herself as 'your Ariel' and hails
him as 'my Prospero'. She is writing a novel, and also collaborating
with Buster Cloudesley on a biography of his father. Buster, nursing
a bizarre plan to rescue Hess from Spandau Prison using black
gliders, meanwhile frequently glides over Exmoor, taking off (with
some difficulty, one would suppose) from Porlock Marsh, using a
car engine to winch the machine into the air.

Gliding plays a considerable part in the story. Henry's second
son, John, a sergeant in the R.A.F., had won the British gliding
championship, and was a member of the British Team for the World
Gliding Championships on a number of occasions, in countries as
far apart as Argentina and Australia. For many years the team's
manager was Ann Welch, who had pursued an active career in
aviation from the time she first flew solo at Chivenor in 1934
(during the war she served in the Air Transport Auxiliary, whose
members carried out the often hazardous task of ferrying aircraft of
many different types from factories to R.A.F. stations). In *Happy to
Fly,* writing of the first post-war international gliding championship

in Poland, in 1958, she refers to 'John Williamson, son of my long-ago friend Henry'. At that event he was reserve pilot in charge of radios, but in later championships he was a full member of the team.

John was therefore ideally qualified to provide his father with the sort of technical information that always fascinated him, in order to make the gliding scenes authentic.

This is a novel of many deaths. Phillip's father, his Aunt Dora and his younger sister die; in the Lynmouth storm Buster and one of Laura's lovers die while gliding, and Miranda is among those drowned by the flooded river. It is also a novel in which the incest motif that has recurred in the *Chronicle* plays a grotesque final part. In *Donkey Boy,* a young girl employed by Hetty Maddison became pregnant by her own father; Tom Ching, the cause of Phillip's imprisonment for arson, committed incest with his sister, as did their father; Laura Wisselcraft's neurosis had its origin in incestuous attacks by her father; Richard Maddison's feelings for his daughter Mavis were overfond, though sternly repressed, and his unreasonable anger when her innocent friendship with a boy was misinterpreted led her to become neurotic and epileptic. In *The Gale,* Molly Bucentaur's big game shooting husband Peregrine returns after long absence and makes incestuous approaches to Miranda; jealous resentment leads him to knock Phillip down when he sees him with Miranda.

Melissa, a follower of a vaguely psychoanalytical cult called Diaphany, believes that Mavis – who now calls herself Elizabeth and has inherited Aunt Dora's cottage – must be reconciled with Phillip before he can break through the block preventing him from beginning the novels he plans. Antagonism between brother and sister has existed from early childhood, one facet of the permanent disharmony at 11, Hillside Road. Phillip as a child pushed Mavis into the fire, creating a guilt that has lived with him, and recurs at Lynmouth; Mavis, for her part, mocked Phillip's love of wild things, his easy tears and his calf love for Helena Rolls.

Not for the first time, Phillip contemplates suicide; he builds a pyre on the Chains, intending to sprinkle his father's ashes there, and shoot his dog and himself. In the event, he is struck by lightning, though not fatally; the dog is killed, and cremated on the pyre with Phillip's ancient Alvis Silver Eagle. (The cremating of the dog recalls the ending of *The Pathway,* after Willie Maddison's death.)

Phillip, with Laura, for whom the fire has acted as a beacon to
land her glider, go down to the flooded village in search of Lucy
and the children, who have been spending a camping holiday
nearby. All are safe. Lucy is still Phillip's wife: her petition for
divorce failed (did Henry find it impossible to impose upon his
other self the final admission of the break-up of his first marriage?)
Nevertheless it is with Melissa that Phillip, convalescent after
pneumonia, walks by the Taw-Torridge estuary quoting some of
Birkin/Mosley's vapid, orotund prose, concluding that 'All will be
achieved by the final order of the European'. He hopes 'to
complement Birkin's dream by writing my novels'. The form of the
Chronicle is thus circular: Phillip is about to write the sequence we
have just been reading.

The writing of this novel took Henry four years. He found it
hard going. Although some chapters were based to some extent on
personal experiences, and contained portraits of people he knew, it
is less autobiographical than the earlier volumes; he complained to
friends of his struggles in building up his story. Its completion was
a moment of triumph; he recorded the exact date and time that he
wrote the final sentence: 4.20 on a Sunday afternoon in February,
1968. He got up from his writing table, he said, crying out words of
grief and amazement while walking aimlessly about the rooms of his
cottage. In an article which appeared in the 'Daily Express' in the
following September, he spoke of feeling that the novel was 'the
very crown of a writing life of half a century'.

For all the over-subjectivity of its viewpoint, its unhappy political
bias and its central character's self-absorption and tendency to
self-pity, the *Chronicle,* encompassing three generations and a little
more than half a century, offers a remarkable recreation of aspects of
late-Victorian, Edwardian and Georgian life, the two wars and the
unstable inter-war period.

As a personal document it has its own special interest. If Henry
did indeed intend Phillip Maddison as a self-portrait, as he claimed,
it is one in which he did not spare himself, but sought out faults
with an eye that in an onlooker would appear pitiless. Again and
again Phillip disparages his own character and behaviour. As a boy
and a man he is thus ill at ease in the world, unable to accept, or
forgive, what he identifies as his own defects.

In *The Golden Virgin,* his mother recalls that her husband 'had
once spoken so happily of having a friend in his son'. And what a
son, Phillip reflects: 'selfish, cowardly, a liar, deceitful: better if he

had been killed'. He comes back to this in *The Gale of the World,* describing his boyhood self as 'a thief, a liar, a coward, and a mischief-maker on all planes'. Suffering from eye trouble, he decides that the cause is 'suppressed hysteria – a condition of self-frustration, self-denial; of cowardice. Yes, that was the cause of every disaster and non-fulfilment of his life'.

At the beginning of Part Four of *A Test to Destruction,* Henry sets a highly significant quotation from a diary written at Sebastopol in 1856 by a lieutenant of the 30th Foot named Augustus Williamson (is it possible that he was an ancestor? He would have been of the generation of Henry's grandfather): 'A man may bear a World's contempt when he bears that within that says he is worthy. When he contemns himself – there burns the Hell'. Throughout much of the latter part of the novel, Phillip's self-condemnation is fierce.

Moreover, both of Henry's other selves suffer at times from a sense of their own unreality. In *The Golden Virgin* Phillip laments that he has 'never been real even to himself. That was the terrifying truth . . . O, the damned silly idiocies of himself! Humiliations, silly lies which everyone saw through . . .' Similarly, Willie Maddison, speaking to Mary Ogilvie in *The Pathway,* and having described himself as 'a bird of passage. A peregrine falcon – or cuckoo who tries to fly like a hawk', decides finally that he is 'a phoenix – it has no real existence'. Willie, too, is self-critical; in *The Pathway* he says that he agrees 'with everything that everyone says about me, with this reservation: that I could put their case against me very much more clearly and concisely than they have done, and probably much less crudely'.

Such a degree of self-disparagement, if it in fact represented Henry's judgement on himself, might have led either to some kind of disabling neurosis or to a paralysis of his creative gift. Since it did neither, it would appear that a strong sustaining core of justified self-respect remained, fortified by his very creativity. Whatever his Rousseau-ish impulse to criticise his own behaviour throughout his writing life, he was confident of his value as a writer: much – though not all – of the best part of himself was indeed, in accordance with Dr Johnson's dictum, in his books.

CHAPTER SIXTEEN

The Last Years

The final pages of *The Gale of the World,* with their defiant reaffirmation of Mosleyite ideas, can give little pleasure to readers who do not share those ideas – yet there seems little doubt that for Henry, a lonely man seventy-two years of age when he wrote them (his second marriage was dissolved in 1968, although it had foundered by 1962), a stubborn adherence to the last of his heroes was a psychological necessity.

His huge project at last ended, after nineteen years, he felt a sense of both freedom and loss. He had nine more years to live and, despite the newspaper articles and other work already mentioned, little more to say. Now at last, perhaps, the élan vital he had said was lacking in 1948 – afterwards proceeding to prove triumphantly that it was not – was almost spent.

However, there remained one more idea for a short nature book, begun in 1955 at the suggestion of the then managing director of his publishers, Macdonald. At the time, Henry had finished *The Golden Virgin* and was at work on *Love and the Loveless,* but felt confident that he could break off to write the proposed book at the rate of a chapter a day during a holiday in Ireland. On the long journey north from Cork to Limavady to stay with his old friend Sir John Heygate, Henry eccentrically chose the driving seat of his (stationary) car as a writing desk, but lack of progress made him 'fractious, at times unbearable' to a 'silent wife and a whispering small boy' in the back seat. Even in the library at Bellarena the block remained, and the story was abandoned.

Sixteen years later, his mind freed by the completion of the *Chronicle,* Henry gradually took it up again and after a while found that 'by using the personal narrative method' he could at last carry forward the book, *The Scandaroon,* to completion. Published in 1972, it is virtually an expanded anecdote about some of the owners of racing pigeons in the Barnstaple of the early 1920s, although the publican, Sam, and his wife Zillah, bear a strong resemblance to Charlie Ovey, the landlord of the King's Arms in Georgeham, and his wife.

The 'personal narrative method' enabled Henry to reminisce once more about his Skirr Cottage days, and to introduce a boy, Peter Raleigh, the son of an admiral, to whom he said he was acting as tutor. The boy was in fact Patrick Foulds, the son of a composer. He is still alive. A retired army officer, he remembers Henry with respect and affection. For a few months during the summer of 1924, while his parents were abroad, Patrick lodged with Miss Gertrude Johnson at The Barn, Georgeham, and was nominally Henry's pupil. He recalls that as 'a small, very anxious child with spectacles and sticky-out ears', aged eight, he was alarmed by the prospect, but soon found that, although the three Rs had little part in his lessons, Henry threw wide the gates of his imagination – partly by giving him *Bevis* to read. S.P.B. Mais's depiction of the Henry Williamson figure, Brian Stucley, in *Orange Street,* as an unkind tutor has, in Patrick Foulds recollection, no foundation, although he admits that 'Henry roared at me occasionally, I suppose when I was being obtuse. But I was neither frightened nor subdued by his outbursts, which seemed like natural phenomena – volcanoes, earthquakes, etc. One marvelled, but kept clear!'

A project that occupied Henry's mind a good deal in the final years of his life was not writing, but the building of a house on the field at Oxford Cross. The idea of this house had been with him for a long time. Although it was designed as a dwelling, he hoped that it might be converted, after his death, into a Henry Williamson museum. It was as though he did not trust his books to be an adequate memorial – and certainly he did not trust the people of north Devon to honour him with one.

When he first applied for planning permission, it was refused. A year or two later, when it would have been granted, he complained that he could not afford the capital outlay. However, in 1973, with the help of Arthur Dennis, a builder in Braunton whom he had known for many years, he submitted plans once more and, in February, 1974, they were approved, and building began.

The house has a kitchen, dining room and lounge, four bedrooms and an attic room with an oriel window providing a magnificent view south over hills to the Taw-Torridge estuary and west to the Atlantic – one of those 'lighthouse windows' that had fascinated Henry since his stay in a high-up apartment in New York in 1930. The main room is a strange one, ceilinged on one side but rising above the stairway leading out of it to a gallery on the first floor from which the bedrooms open. Several wooden pillars, described in the plans as of yew, are incorporated in the room's design; they may be part of that load of yew wood of which Henry writes in *Goodbye West Country;* he transported it to Stiffkey, but may have brought some back. (Nevertheless in the house agent's brochure, when the house was for sale in 1982, it was said that they were thought to have come from a battleship of Nelson's time, which suggests a touch of romanticising on someone's part.)

During the period of house-building, although he visited his writing hut, Henry spent much of his time in his Ilfracombe cottage. At times he was intensely lonely. Throughout his adult life he had been in the habit of shouting aloud, when alone: as a young man, often with joy in the Devon countryside; later, increasingly, with exasperation or fury, especially on his Norfolk farm. Now he complained that he sometimes shouted in the misery of loneliness, so that passers-by or neighbours thought that he was quarrelling with some visitor. Music, and especially the music of Wagner, remained a solace; this too was shared with anyone within earshot, as he set his windows wide so that the sound poured out – by no means always appreciated, it may be supposed.

Companionship was to be found in local pubs. The then landlord of the George and Dragon, in Fore Street leading down to Ilfracombe harbour, remembers that on some days Henry could be a brilliant conversationalist, on others, sad and rambling. Another favourite place was the Royal Brittannia Hotel, on the harbourside, hardly a hundred yards from Henry's cottage. Above his usual chair in one corner of the bar there hung, for some ten years, a portrait of him by a local artist, Edward Ford, painted from life, although it is dated September, 1977, a month after Henry's death. An inscription reads:

'Henry Williamson
1895-1977
Author -Tarka the Otter, etc. Used to sit in this corner
and tell stories to his friends'.

On the painting itself is written – by Henry, according to Mr Ford – 'Henry Williamson Esq., happy at Combe, happy at Grebe'. (The painting was removed when the Royal Brittannia changed hands and is now in the Edwardian bar of the Collingwood Hotel, Ilfracombe.)

Combe is of course Ilfracombe. Grebe – apart from being the name of an attractive family of water-birds – was possibly a house in the area where Henry was made welcome.

A strange feature of this painting, and of another smaller one also painted by Edward Ford, is that it shows Henry with blue eyes. As a young man he had very dark brown hair and brown eyes, which at times could look broodingly dark. Although his eyes underwent the slight paling with age that is not uncommon, they remained at least hazel-brown, as colour photographs taken fairly late in his life (for instance, the one used on the jacket of the first edition of Daniel Farson's *Henry*) demonstrate. Yet it seems certain that Henry would have liked to have blue eyes, and also fair hair; it may have been a source of satisfaction to him that his always thick hair turned completely white as he grew older, and so came to resemble that silver-blonde colouring he admired. The three characters in his novels who in some way represent him – Willie and Phillip Maddison and Manfred Cloudesley – have blue eyes; Phillip's hair is brown, but at intervals in the *Chronicle* doting women refer to the blueness of his eyes. Manfred's love, Marlene, is a blue-eyed blonde, as are the girls for whom Phillip feels most deeply – the unattainable Helena Rolls of his boyhood, Lily Cornford with her 'large blue glistening eyes', Felicity Ancroft, Barley and Melissa. Phillip's eldest son Billy – in contrast to the brunet colouring of Henry's son Windles – has fair hair and 'dreamy blue eyes'. It seems that this obsession with blue eyes had its origin in very early childhood. In an article 'Out of the Prisoning Tower', which first appeared in the 'Spectator'and was included in an anthology, *John Bull's Schooldays,* in 1961, he speaks of having 'staring brown eyeballs, not blue like all proper boys, as my father told me at three years of age. His eyes were blue . . . mine took after my mother's'.

In May, 1965, Henry had presented a number of his manuscripts, including the original drafts of *Tarka,* to Exeter University. Ronald Duncan, one of the friends who went with him on this occasion, called it 'an ad hoc presentation' at which the Vice Chancellor arrived late and received the gift 'without adequate acknowledgement or grace'. (The Vice Chancellor, Sir James Cook, was a scientist, and admitted to knowing little of literature.) However, the ceremony was rather more elaborate than Duncan suggests: Ted Hughes, now Poet Laureate, E. W. Martin and Father Brocard Sewell made speeches, and the event was fairly well attended, the audience including a number of West Country Writers' Association members.

There is little doubt that Henry, then in his seventieth year, hoped that the University would mark his seventieth birthday by conferring on him an honorary degree. It chose not to do so; in fact Father Brocard Sewell has revealed that, despite the efforts of two successive Vice Chancellors, the Degree Committee refused such an award by majority decisions.

Now Henry's eightieth birthday was approaching – though there was a sad irony in the fact that, according to his own often repeated claim to have been a soldier of seventeen in 1914, it was only his seventy-ninth. However, by this time he was quite willing to acknowledge that he had been born in 1895. At last, surely, he would be the recipient of some honour. Writing to Father Brocard Sewell in 1974 he had said that he knew his peers; he quoted 'Masefield O.M.' as saying that he had written more classics than any man alive, an opinion in which 'Galsworthy O.M.' concurred. (In writing this he was looking back forty years: Galsworthy died in 1933.)

During the First World War, he had yearned for some award for bravery; receiving none, he had given Willie Maddison an M.C., showered decorations on Manfred Cloudesley, and later allowed Phillip Maddison to receive the D.S.O. In 1975, fictional compensations were no longer possible; his longing for a final recognition, not of courage, but of achievement, was intense.

Yet 1st December, 1975, came and went; there was no O.M., no honorary degree, no other honour, not so much as a *festschrift* from any fellow writers. Nevertheless the B.B.C., for whom he had so often broadcast, did not forget him. A television programme with the same title as that of 1968, 'No Man's Land' (and how appropriate that was – in one sense Henry had lived his entire life in a wild, strange-featured no man's land of his own imagination) was put out on B.B.C. 2 on his birthday, and in it he remembered yet once more the Christmas Truce of 1914 and his experiences in the First World War.

In addition, Daniel Farson, by writing an article, 'Recognising Henry Williamson', which appeared in the 'Daily Telegraph' colour supplement on 28th November, 1975, offered one section of the reading public a reminder that this writer, with his exceptional if uneven talent, had reached the age at which some recognition of merit might well have been conferred. The photograph taken to accompany the article is striking. It shows Henry in his writing hut, sitting in a straight-backed wooden chair beside the fireplace that was so important to him; he wears some kind of long garment that looks like a storeman's overall, though it may be a light raincoat. Behind him, windows pour leaf-filtered light over his writing table, scattered with notebooks and oddments. Overhead, bed-clothes sag down from his sleeping platform, although the corner of a divan on the floor may be seen. On an old chest of drawers is a bookcase; alongside it the rough plaster-work of the wall-panels is exposed.

Nothing could better illustrate his habitual indifference, when alone, to material possessions or comforts. (It is almost as if his standard of physical ease was set, for life, by the minimal amenities of an infantry officer's dug-out on the Western Front.) Here, at the end of his life, he is living much as in his early Skirr Cottage days, in frugality and solitude. If there is pathos in the picture, it does not lie in the apparent poverty of his surroundings, but in its portrayal of age and isolation, of a writer who no longer writes, who stares at the camera with stony distrust, a life-scarred, defiant old lion.

In his final twenty months of life little remained for him to do but talk to any friends or acquaintances who would listen – an Ancient Mariner, or Ancient Warrior, whose albatross was the First World War, hanging on him to the end. The bar of the Royal Britannia continued for a little while to be a haven where he could sit in his usual corner 'and tell stories to his friends', and Edward Ford's portrait provides proof that he was not altogether despondent, but could be 'happy at Combe' and happy also in whatever friendly house or terrain was known to him as Grebe.

The house on his hill-top field was completed before the end of 1975, but he did not live in it. Soon he grew forgetful and confused; one may wonder whether the disappointment of his eightieth birthday contributed to his deterioration. After admission to the Tyrell Cottage Hospital, Ilfracombe, it was evident that he needed the care of others. He was given it by the Alexian Brothers at their hospital, Twyford Abbey, at Park Royal in north London, where he died on 13th August, 1977. By a remarkable coincidence, it was on this day that David Cobham was directing, in his film of *Tarka the Otter,* the scene of Tarka's death.

For Henry Williamson, there was only one appropriate resting place. His body was brought back to Devon. On the day of his funeral, Georgeham church was full. Although many of the people he had portrayed in his village stories and sketches were dead, and although on visits during the war and afterwards he had felt himself ostracised by the villagers for his political views, a fair number attended the service, perhaps because some remembered the prankish, excitable, talkative young man who had made them laugh when they were children, both with him and behind his back, and others had heard tales of him from their parents.

His five sons were among the bearers who carried him to his grave beside the west door of the church. For this most restless of men, the inscription chosen for his headstone reads, with touching simplicity:

'Here rests Henry Williamson
1895-1977'

and his owl symbol. He lies just within the churchyard wall bordering the stream, a sparrow-flutter away from the two cottages in which he wrote the books that many readers still choose to regard as his best work and for which, even now, he is probably best known.

Afterword

During the Eighties the cottage in Ilfracombe, 4, Capstone Place, in which Henry Williamson spent so much time during his last years, became a gift shop named Tarka's Holt. A blue plaque attached to the outer wall recorded that it was 'The home of Henry Williamson, author of Tarka the Otter, 1895-1977'. In 1990 the gift shop transferred to No. 3, Capstone Place, and No. 4 was offered for sale as a private dwelling, described as a terraced stone-built cottage 'full of historical interest, rustic charm, and character', having 2/3 bedrooms, a study, sitting room and one other room referred to as 'spacious lounge/kit/diner'. Out of sight behind the cottage is a small garden. At the end of 1990 the property was still on the market.

Henry's field above Georgeham, with the new house in which he never lived, is a small-holding and craft pottery, and bears the name he always insisted on, Ox's Cross. There visitors may stay, and cream teas are offered. It is possible to walk down past the building Henry called his studio to his writing hut, its cladding renewed in recent years by the Henry Williamson Society. (At one time Henry spoke of leaving his field to the National Trust; in 1971 he opposed an application to establish a touring caravan site on land adjoining, and was reported to have made a settlement to his trustees leaving the property to the National Trust. Evidently he had second thoughts.)

Literary pilgrims visit the field, the Ilfracombe cottage and Skirr Cottage in Georgeham in fair numbers every year. Some no doubt also look at the house to which he moved soon after his marriage, and in which he wrote the greater part of *Tarka,* and certainly its final drafts, as well as *The Pathway, The Wet Flanders Plain* and many of the sketches and stories making up *The Village Book* and *The Labouring Life*. However, the fact that it is Skirr Cottage to which he always referred in his writing may prevent many from realising that Crowberry Cottage, as the Vale House of his day is now known, was of considerable importance in his early career.

North Devon is gradually beginning to commemorate Henry Williamson. South Molton has a Williamson Way, Georgeham has a Williamson Close. More importantly, the new library building in Barnstaple, opened officially in July, 1988, contains a Henry Williamson Room. His fictional otter is being called upon to name a number of things. Perhaps the most important is the Devon County Council's Tarka Project, designed, as one of its publications puts it, 'to use the Tarka the Otter story as a theme for a range of conservation, recreation and tourism initiatives'. It covers the magnificent valleys of the Taw and Torridge rivers and the country between them; it is intended that a walkers' trail shall eventually run from Lynton to Bideford and inland as far as Okehampton, thus linking Exmoor and Dartmoor. A project officer has been appointed, and is to be responsible for 'encouraging and co-ordinating initiatives under the Tarka theme, and in particular identifying ways to strengthen the distinctive character of Tarka Country by appropriate conservation measures such as improving otter habitats and creating ponds, providing advice and support, and fostering understanding and appreciation of the area'. It is to be hoped that conservation measures are not negated by the tourism generated, and the still largely untouched hinterland of Henry Williamson's Two Rivers does not undergo that destructive twentieth century blight known as development as the result of increased interest.

In addition, British Rail has named the branch line from Exeter to Barnstaple the Tarka Line. Yet another use of the name is to be found at the North Devon District Hospital, which has its internal Tarka Radio.

The above mentioned Henry Williamson Society was formed soon after his death; it has several hundred members and publishes a journal twice a year. Its declared aim is 'to encourage by all appropriate means, a wider readership and deeper understanding of the literary heritage left to us by the major twentieth century writer, Henry Williamson'. Many of Henry Williamson's books remain in print; new illustrated editions of *Salar, Tarka* and *The Story of a*

Norfolk Farm have been published, and the early volumes of *A Chronicle of Ancient Sunlight* have appeared in paperback. In fact, in the years since his death there has been no indication of any falling off of interest in his work.

It is therefore remarkable that such reference books as *Literature and Locality,* by John Freeman, *The Oxford Literary Guide to the British Isles,* edited by Dorothy Eagle and Hilary Cornell, and *Literary Britain, A Reader's Guide to Writers and Landmarks,* by Frank Morley, ignore him completely; no entry in these books records his association with either Devon or Norfolk. It was left to Bernard Price, in his *Creative Landscapes of Britain,* to include entries which explore Henry's west country and East Anglian years. It remains a puzzle that the editors of the other compilations named above could omit the name of a man who stands in the first rank of nature writers of the past hundred years; who had a knowledge of, and empathy with, the southern English countryside and its wild creatures, and a power to interpret them in clear, lively prose, that has not been surpassed in the twentieth century; and who completed two sequences of novels that, for all their idiosyncracies, are loving celebrations of a countryman's England in peace and war.

Notes

Chapter One

1. A full description of the event is provided by Brian Fullager in Henry Williamson Society Journal No. 10, October, 1984, under the title 'Lewisham 1984'.

Chapter Two

1. 'From *Dandelion Days*', by Fred Shepherd (H.W.S. Journal No. 6, October, 1982), gives some account of Henry Williamson's school and his later association with it. Colfe's was destroyed during an air raid in the winter of 1940/41, and was rebuilt in Horn Park Road, Lee, where it still flourishes, having become a public school.

Chapter Four

1. For an analysis of *The Incalculable Hour,* see essay with that title by J. W. Blench, (H.W.S. Journal No. 8, October, 1983).

Chapter Eight

1. See 'Henry Williamson, Broadcaster' by Valerie R. Belsey, H.W.S. Journal No. 8, October, 1983).

2. For information regarding the parents of William Leopold Williamson, who was born at Wood Street, Ryde, Isle of Wight, I am indebted to 'The Maddisons and the Turneys' by John Gillis, (H.W.S. Journal No. 2, October, 1980).

Chapter Eleven

1. See *A Breath of Country Air,* Part Two, Henry Williamson Society, 1991.

2. Ibid.

Chapter Thirteen

1. See 'The Silver Eagle' by Richard Williamson and Linda Pearce, (H.W.S. Journal No. 8, October, 1983).

2. Between the publication of her novel *Berg* in 1964, and her death by

drowning in 1973, at the age of only 32, Ann Quin published other novels, won a literary scholarship which took her to America, and travelled in the Mediterranean. An unhappy childhood left her prone to depressive breakdowns. Among his collected essays, *Like Black Swans* (Tabb House, Padstow, 1982), Father Brocard Sewell includes 'Ann Quin: In Memory', a study of this gifted but deeply troubled writer.

3. See *Frances Horovitz, Poet:* A Symposium, edited by Brocard Sewell. The Aylesford Press.

Chapter Fourteen

1. John Glanfield (H.W.S. Journal No. 5, May, 1982) has established that the Williamsons lived at 165 Ladywell Road for some years, and did not appear in the list of residents of Eastern Road until 1903.

   For a detailed description of No. 11 (now No. 21) Eastern Road, Brockley, see also 'Lindenheim' by John Glanfield: (H.W.S. Journal No. 5, May, 1982).

2. In his essay 'To the Fishponds and Back Again' (H.W.S. Journal No. 4, November 1981), John Gillis has identified many of the places which appear in the first three novels of *A Chronicle of Ancient Sunlight* under invented names.

3. For a detailed analysis of correspondence between Henry Williamson's fictional picture of the year 1917 on the Western Front as seen through the experiences of Phillip Maddison, and historical events, see 'The 286th Machine Gun Company' by Peter Cole, (H.W.S. Journal No. 18, October, 1988).

4. See letter from John Gillis, (H.W.S. Journal No. 8, October, 1983), and also 'Henry Williamson's Bedfordshire Roots' and 'A Gaultshire Guide' by Joan and Tom Skipper, (H.W.S. Journals Nos. 6 and 7, October 1982 and May, 1983).

5. In his essay 'Witness of the Great War'; included in *Henry Williamson: the Man, the Writings*.

Chapter Fifteen

1. It may be noted that the title *It Was the Nightingale* had already been used, in 1934, by Ford Madox Ford, author of the Tietjens tetralogy of novels concerning the First World War, which Henry reviewed in his long essay, 'Reality in War Literature'.

2. In *I'm on Starboard,* the story of the North Devon Yacht Club, compiled by Peggy Lines and published by the North Devon Yacht Club, Captain Jimmy Johnson recalls that Henry Williamson was frequently at the Club, and that 'It is hard to equate the smart gentleman in white tie at a Club Dance with the character in his autobiographical novel'. (sic) The book includes a photograph of Henry with two fellow guests at one such dance.

A Checklist of Henry Williamson's major writings

The Beautiful Years	Collins 1921
Revised edition	Faber 1929
The Lone Swallows	Collins 1922
Revised, illustrated edition	Putnam 1933
Dandelion Days	Collins 1922
Revised edition	Faber 1930
The Peregrine's Saga	Collins 1923
Revised, newly illusted edition	Putnam 1934
The Dream of Fair Women	Collins 1924
Revised edition, with a Valediction	Faber 1931
The Old Stag	Putnam 1926
Revised, illusted edition	Putnam 1933
Tarka the Otter	Privately printed, 100 copies, 1927
Another edition	Putnam, 1000 copies, 1927
Another edition	Putnam 1927
Revised edition	Putnam 1928
First illusted edition	Putnam 1932
The Pathway	Cape 1928
The Ackymals	Windsor Press, San Francisco, 225 copies, 1929
The Linhay on the Downs	Elkin Mathews, Woburn Books, 530 copies 1929
The Wet Flanders Plain	Beaumont Press, 320 copies/Faber 1929
The Patriot's Progress	Bles 1930
The Village Book	Cape 1930
The Wild Red Deer of Exmoor	Privately printed, 75 copies/Faber 1931
The Labouring Life	Cape 1932
The Gold Falcon [Anonymous]	Faber 1933
Revised edition [authorship acknowledged]	Faber 1947
On Foot in Devon	Maclehose 1933
The Star-born	Faber 1933
Revised, newly illustrated edition	Faber 1948
The Linhay on the Downs & other adventures	Cape 1934
Devon Holiday	Cape 1935
Salar the Salmon	Faber 1935
Illustrated edition	Faber 1936
Newly illustrated edition	Faber 1948
The Flax of Dream	Faber 1936
comprising a revised version of	
The Beautiful Years, Dandelion Days,	
The Dream of Fair Women and *The Pathway*	

Goodbye West Country	Putnam 1937
The Children of Shallowford	Faber 1939
Revised edition	Faber 1959
Newly illustrated edition	Macdonald & James 1978
As the Sun Shines [selected Prose]	Faber 1941
Genius of Friendship: T.E. Lawrence	Faber 1941
Another edition	Henry Williamson Society 1988
The Story of a Norfolk Farm	Faber 1941
The Sun in the Sands	Faber 1945
Life in a Devon Village	Faber 1945
(revised selections from *Labouring*	
Life, and *The Village Book)*	
Tales of a Devon Village	Faber 1945
(revised selections from *Labouring*	
Life, and *The Village Book)*	
The Phasian Bird	Faber 1948
Scribbling Lark	Faber 1949
The Dark Lantern	Macdonald 1951
Revised edition (paperback)	Panther Books 1962
[# *A Chronicle of Ancient Sunlight,* book one]	
Donkey Boy	Macdonald 1952
Revised edition (paperback)[# book two]	Panther Books 1962
Young Phillip Maddison	Macdonald 1953
Revised edition (paperback)[# book three]	Panther Books 1962
Tales of Moorland & Estuary	Macdonald 1953
How Dear is Life	Macdonald 1954
Revised edition (paperback)[# book four]	Panther Books 1963
A Fox Under my Cloak	Macdonald 1955
Revised edition (paperback)[# book five]	Panther Books 1963
The Golden Virgin	Macdonald 1957
Revised edition (paperback)[# book six]	Panther Books 1963
Love and the Loveless	Macdonald 1958
Revised edition (paperback)[# book seven]	Panther Books 1963
A Clear Water Stream	Faber 1958
Revised, illustrated edition	Macdonald & James 1975
A Test to Destruction	Macdonald 1960
Revised edition (paperback)[# book eight]	Panther Books 1964
The Henry Williamson Animal Saga	Macdonald 1960
(*Tarka, Salar* and nine early stories)	
The Innocent Moon	Macdonald 1961
Revised edition (paperback)[# book nine]	Panther Books 1965
In the Woods [a chapter of autobiography]	St Alberts Press
	(for The Aylesford Review)
	1961/1000 copies

It was the Nightingale	Macdonald 1962
Revised edition (paperback) [# book ten]	Panther Books 1965
The Power of the Dead	Macdonald 1963
Revised edition (paperback) [# books eleven]	Panther Books 1966
The Phoenix Generation	Macdonald 1965
Revised edition (paperback) [# book twelve]	Panther Books 1967
A Solitary War	Macdonald 1966
Revised edition (paperback) [# book thirteen]	Panther books 1969
Lucifer Before Sunrise [# book fourteen]	Macdonald 1967
The Gale of the World [# book fifteen]	Macdonald 1969
Collected Nature Stories	Macdonald 1970
(Tales of Moorland & Estuary with other selected early stories)	
The Scandaroon	Macdonald 1972

Occasional writings referred to in the text:

'Confessions of a Fake Merchant', included in *The Book of Fleet Street,* edited by T. Michael Pope, Cassell, 1930.

'Out of the Prisoning Tower', (reprinted from 'The Spectator') in *John Bull's Schooldays*, edited by Brian Inglis, Hutchinson, 1961.

'The Green Desert', Daily Telegraph, 18th April, 1969.

Published collections of occasional writings:

Days of Wonder: articles by Henry Williamson first published in the 'Daily Express' between 1966 and 1971. With an introduction by Richard Williamson. Illustrated by R. A. Richardson and D. Roberts. The Henry Williamson Society, 1987.

From a Country Hilltop, articles by Henry Williamson contributed to the Co-operative Society's monthly magazine, 'Home Magazine', between April, 1958, and January, 1964. The Henry Williamson Society, 1988.

A Breath of Country Air, Part One, articles by Henry Williamson conributed to the 'Evening Standard', February – December 1944. The Henry Williamson Society, 1990.

A Breath of Country Air, Part Two, is due to be published in 1991.

For Further Reading:

Henry Williamson, The Man, The Writings. With an introduction by Father Brocard Sewell. Tabb House, 1980.

Henry: A Portrait, by Daniel Farson. Michael Joseph, 1982.

A Glimpse of Ancient Sunlight by Sue Caron. Aylesford Press, 1986.

Entries concerning Henry Williamson in *Creative Landscapes of the British Isles* by Bernard Price. Ebury Press.

Two cassettes of recordings made by Henry Williamson for the B.B.C. are available from the Henry Williamson Society (Publications Manager, John Gregory, 14 Nether Grove, Longstanton, Cambridge, CB4 5EL). These are, Vol. I, 'I Remember', and Vol. II, 'The Hopeful Traveller'.

INDEX

The following abbreviations to distinguish characters and places in the novels of Henry Williamson, and also fictional names given to real people, are used in the index:

A